MW01129773

lonely planet KIDS

THE ROCKS BOOK

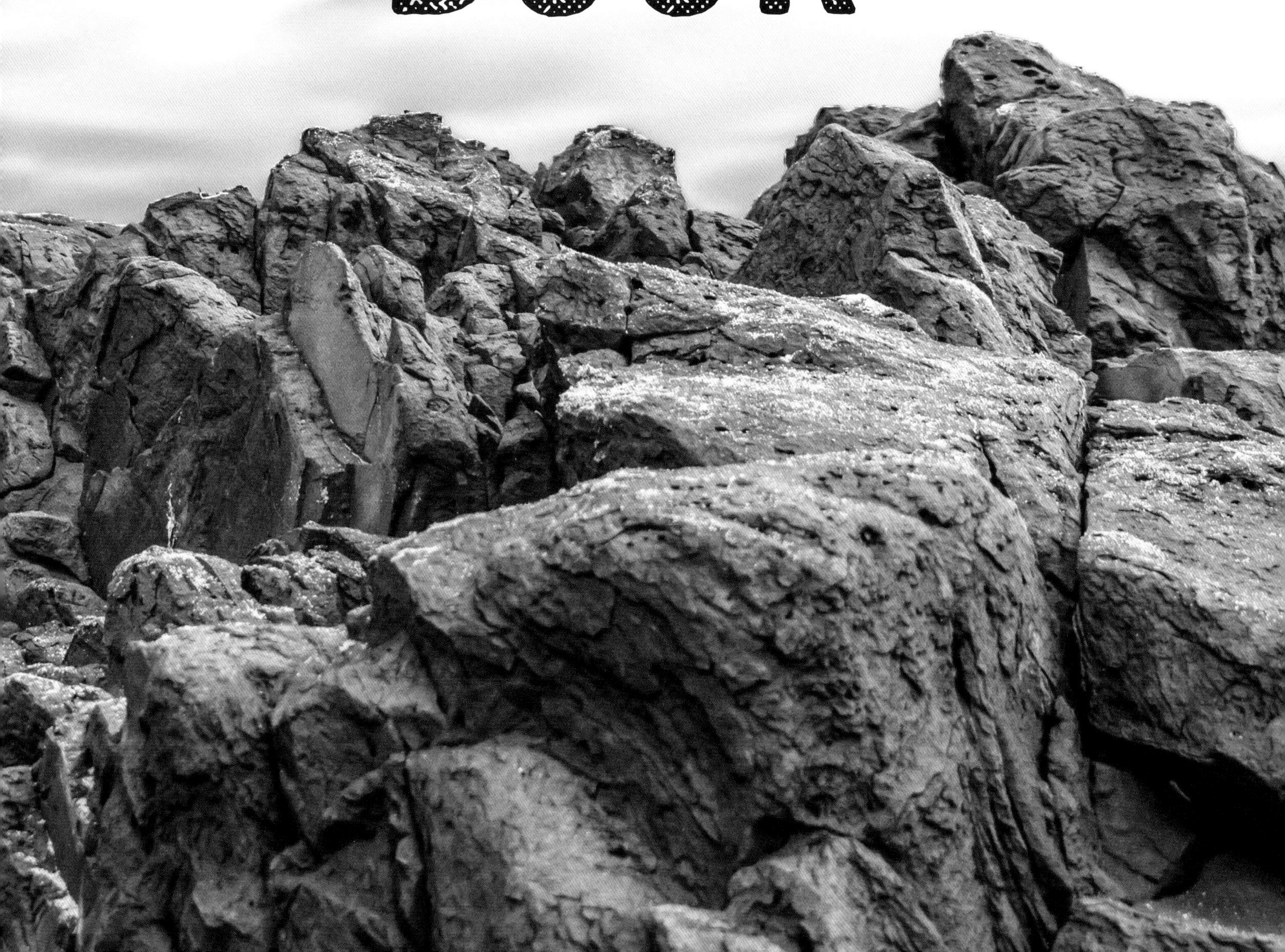

ACKNOWLEDGMENTS

Editorial and Design by Imago Group

Author: Nancy Dickmann
Illustrator: Daniel Limon @ Beehive Illustration
Consultant: Professor John Brodholt
Publishing Director: Piers Pickard
Publisher: Rebecca Hunt
Editorial Director: Joe Fullman
Editor: Katie Dicker
Art Director: Andy Mansfield
Designer: Dan Prescott, Couper Street Type Co.
Print Production: Nigel Longuet
Americanization: Kris Hirschmann

Published in October 2024 by Lonely Planet Global Ltd

CRN: 554153
ISBN: 978-1-83758-308-9
www.lonelyplanet.com/kids

Printed in Malaysia
10 9 8 7 6 5 4 3 2 1

STAY IN TOUCH
lonelyplanet.com/contact

Lonely Planet Office:
IRELAND
Digital Depot, Roe Lane (off Thomas St),
Digital Hub, Dublin 8, D08 TCV4

THE ROCKS BOOK

NANCY DICKMANN

Consultant
Professor John Brodholt

Illustrated by
Daniel Limon

CONTENTS

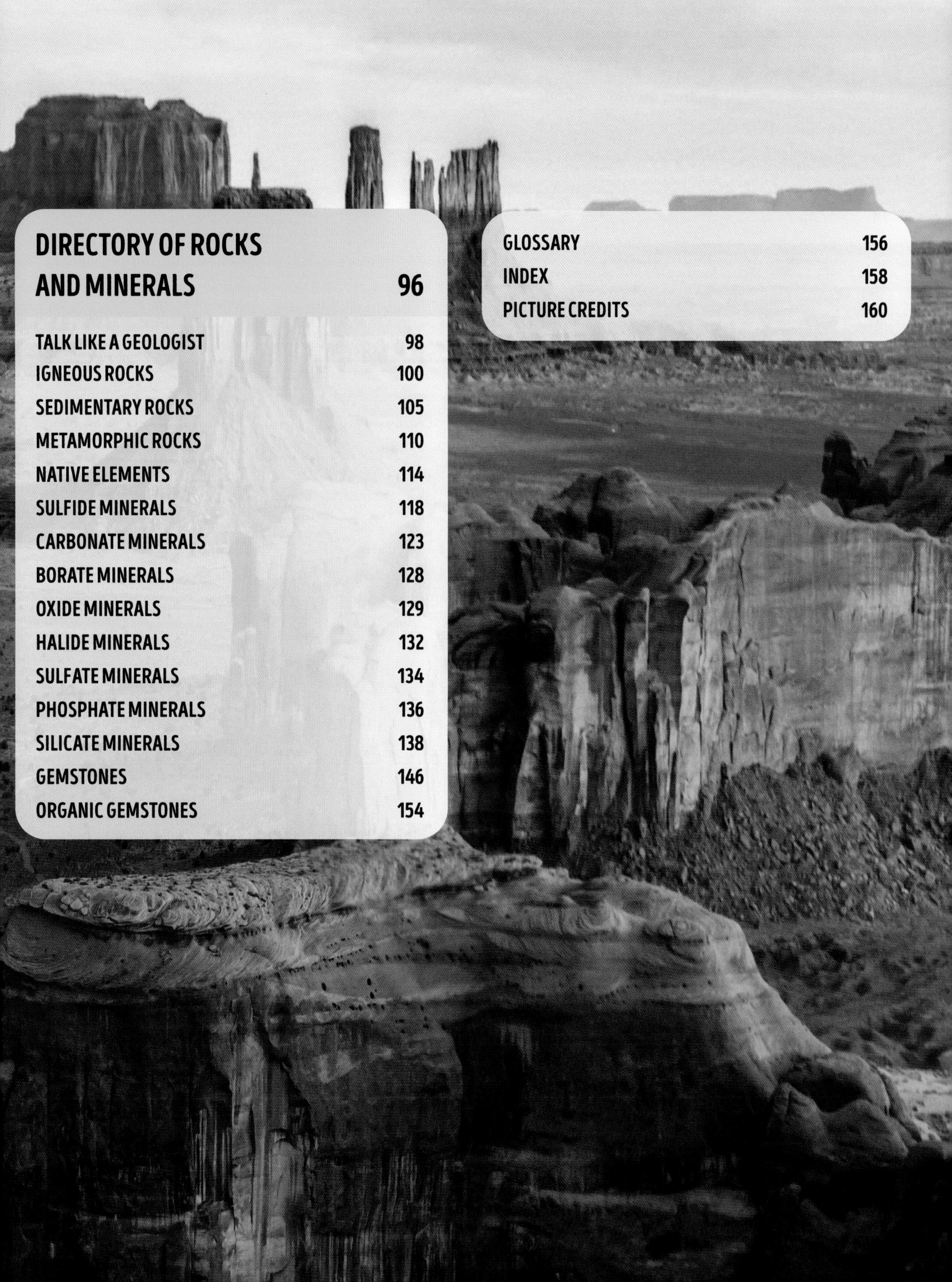

DIRECTORY OF ROCKS AND MINERALS 96

WHAT ARE ROCKS?

Have you ever really thought about the ground beneath your feet? It might be muddy, sandy, or pebbly. Even if you're standing on a paved surface, there are rocks and soil beneath it. These natural materials stretch all the way down to Earth's core.

A WORLD OF ROCKS

Pick up a handful of pebbles or gravel, and they probably all look pretty much the same. But Earth's rocks actually come in a huge range of different types. Some are sparkly and hard, while others are dull or soft. Rocks are a collection of minerals. On their own, some of these minerals can form beautiful colored crystals. Earth's wide variety of rocks and minerals is truly stunning!

The sand on a beach or in the desert is made up of tiny grains of rock! These grains have been ground down over thousands of years.

The coast is a great place to see rocks—from jagged cliffs and big boulders to smooth pebbles and grainy sand.

GEOLOGISTS

We know so much about Earth's rocks and minerals because of the work of geologists over the centuries. A geologist is a person who studies the materials that make up our planet. They may be out on location, chipping away at layers of rocks. Or they may work in a lab, analyzing rock samples and using computers. Geologists study how Earth has changed and what it looked like in the distant past.

Geologists study the distribution of rocks to see how our environment has changed. Laboratory tests also reveal more about the mineral content of rocks and properties that are useful to us in our daily lives.

OUR ROCKY PLANET

We live on a massive ball of rock that orbits a star called the Sun. Our planet is "only" about 4.5 billion years old, but if you want to trace the story of its rocks and minerals, you'll need to go much further back—all the way to the Big Bang, about 13.8 billion years ago.

Earth is one of four rocky planets that orbit the Sun in the inner Solar System. Earth is the only planet with liquid water oceans on its rocky surface, giving it a blue appearance from space. This water helps it to support life.

FROM PARTICLES TO STARS

Before the Big Bang, all space, time, and energy was contained within a single point called a singularity. Then, all of a sudden, it expanded rapidly. Tiny particles spread out and began joining together, eventually forming atoms of hydrogen and helium. They came together in huge clouds of gas, where gravity pulled atoms into their centers to create the first stars. Inside the stars, atoms fused together to form heavier elements such as oxygen, carbon, and iron.

New stars are forming all the time in huge clouds of gas and dust called nebulae. This image shows the Eagle Nebula.

PLANETS FORM

Our Sun formed about 4.6 billion years ago from a rotating cloud of dust and gas. This cloud was made up of the remains of older stars. It formed a disk shape, and the densest part—at the center—became the Sun. The rest of the material began clumping together into small rocky particles. Gravity pulled the bigger clumps together, and they eventually grew into the planets—including Earth.

SEPARATING OUT

The bigger Earth grew, the greater its gravity, and the hotter it got on the inside. Its rocks began to melt and separate out. Denser elements, such as iron, sank toward the center. Less dense elements bonded with other elements, such as oxygen, and rose to the surface to form the minerals that make up the rocks in Earth's crust. This includes many oxides and silicates—compounds of oxygen and silicon. Earth has rocks of all ages on its surface. The movement of Earth's tectonic plates (see page 12) causes some rocks to be recycled. But in a few particular places, such as northwest Canada, you can still see rocks that date from Earth's ancient crust.

This sample of a rock called Acasta gneiss, from Canada, is among the oldest known exposed rocks on our planet, at over 4.2 billion years old.

EARTH'S LAYERS

Did you know that our planet is not the same all the way through? Despite what you read in science fiction books, you can't actually tunnel to the center of Earth without being crushed by pressure and vaporized by heat. But if you could, you'd go on a journey through four very different layers.

Earth is surrounded by a magnetic field that is produced in the outer core. When charged particles from the Sun interact with it, they create the shimmering colored lights in the sky, called auroras. These are sometimes visible as wavy bands of light in the sky, like the ones seen here in Norway.

CORE

The core is the densest part of Earth. It has two parts—a solid inner core which is a ball about 1,500 miles (2,400 km) across, and a surrounding liquid outer core about 1,400 miles (2,250 km) thick. Both are made mainly of iron and nickel and are extremely hot, reaching temperatures of over 9,000 °F (5,000 °C). The movement of the molten metal in the outer core produces Earth's magnetic field, which protects us from harmful radiation from the Sun.

MANTLE

By volume, the mantle is Earth's biggest layer. It's about 1,800 miles (2,880 km) thick and made up of dense rock that is rich in iron and magnesium. You often hear the mantle's rocks described as molten, but they're not runny like the lava that erupts out of a volcano. Instead, they're solid but can move slowly like a very, very thick paste. The mantle gets cooler as you move upward from the lower regions, but even near the crust it's still about 1,300 °F (700 °C). In a few places, rock that should be part of the mantle under the oceans gets pushed to the surface of the land and exposed. The Lizard Peninsula in Cornwall, England, is one example (left).

INGE LEHMANN (1888–1993)

We owe the discovery that Earth's core has two layers to the Danish scientist Inge Lehmann. She trained as a mathematician before switching to seismology—the study of earthquakes and how they travel through Earth's rocks. She set up stations to measure seismic waves, and she used the data they produced to discover that the core is made up of two separate parts.

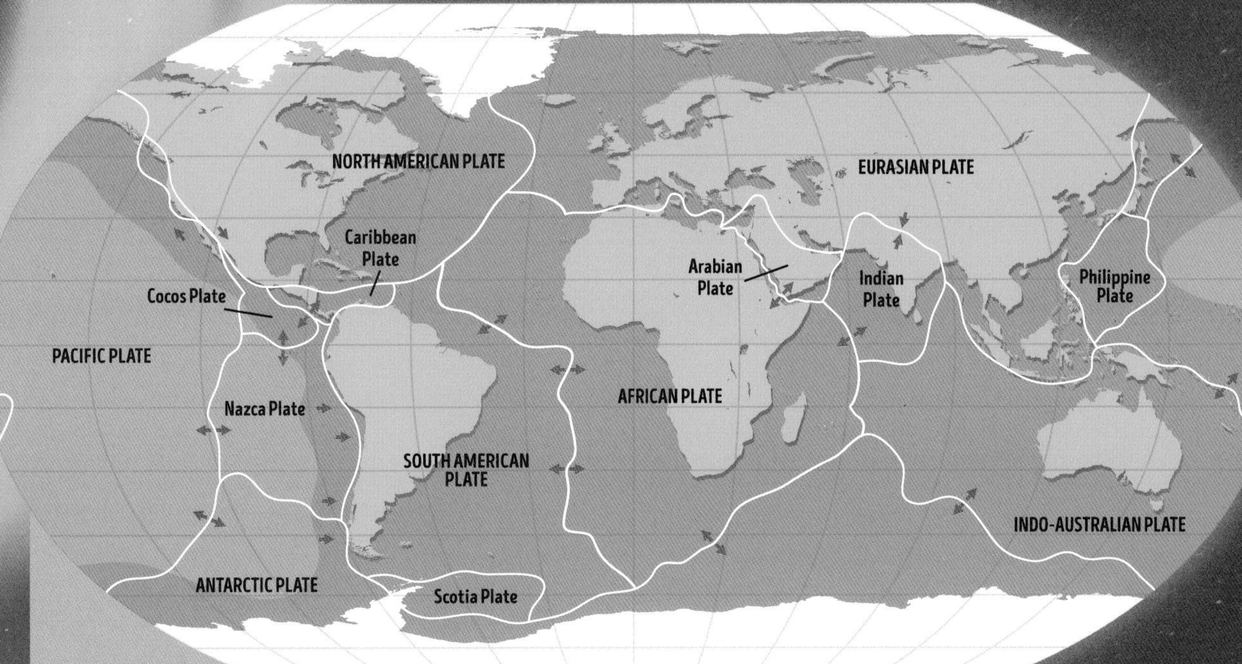

Seven major tectonic plates cover nearly 95 percent of Earth's surface. They are labeled here in capitals.

CRUST

The top layer is the crust, which forms a hard outer layer like the shell of an egg. Some of its rocks are dense and rich in iron and magnesium, while others are lighter and made mainly of silicon and aluminum. Earth's crust is not a single piece of rock. Instead, it's broken up into more than a dozen pieces, which are called tectonic plates. Some of these plates include the continents we live on. Others, which are thinner, form the ocean floor. Some plates include a bit of both!

CRUST OR LITHOSPHERE?

You can tell where the crust ends and the mantle begins by looking at the chemical composition of the rocks. The rocks of the crust are rich in feldspar and quartz minerals (see page 26), while mantle rocks have lots of iron and magnesium and are made up of minerals such as olivine (see page 138). The boundary between the crust and the mantle is called the Mohorovičić discontinuity (or "Moho" for short), after Andrija Mohorovičić, the Croatian geologist who discovered it. But geologists often divide the two layers in a different way: by looking at how they move. They talk about the lithosphere, which is made up of the crust and the upper layer of the mantle. These move as a single unit on top of the asthenosphere, which is the rest of the mantle.

SHIFTING PLATES

The hard rocks of Earth's tectonic plates (see page 11) sit on top of a layer of hotter, softer rock called the mantle. They move around incredibly slowly—roughly 2 in (5 cm) per year—about the speed your fingernails grow! Some plate edges move toward each other, while others move away. Although this movement is slow, it can cause very noticeable changes to the landscape. Many mountain ranges, such as the Himalayas in Asia, formed when two plates collided.

SINKING UNDER

When an oceanic plate meets a continental plate (see page 11), the oceanic plate sinks. The continental plate is thicker but less dense, so the edge of the oceanic plate is forced to sink below it. This forms what's called a subduction zone. As it sinks, the rock of the oceanic plate heats up so much that it begins to release fluids. This causes the mantle rock above it to melt and form magma—which sometimes erupts to the surface and cools to form new rock. This process is Earth's rock recycling system!

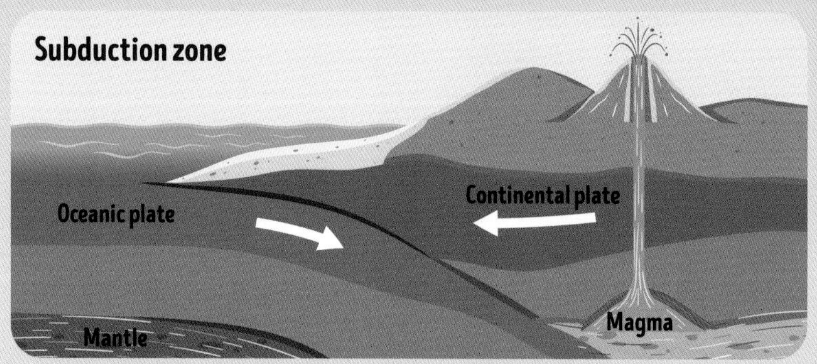

PULLING AND SLIDING

When two plates push toward each other, it's called a convergent boundary. In places where they pull apart, it's called a divergent boundary—along this kind of boundary, the land splits and magma can bubble up. Plates can also meet in what is known as a transform boundary, where they slide horizontally past each other instead of pushing or pulling. The plates don't just glide past each other. They can get stuck, which can cause earthquakes when they eventually release and move.

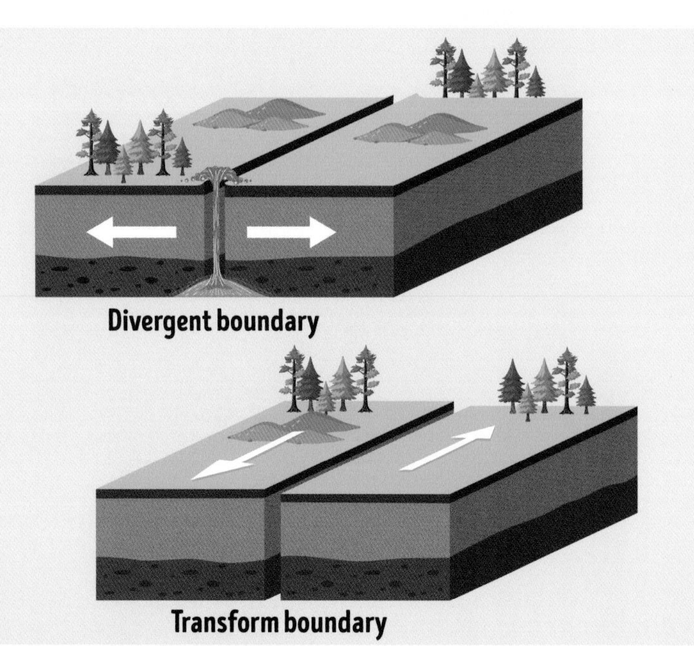

The mountains of the Himalayas, including Mount Everest (center), began to form about 50 million years ago. As tectonic plates slowly collided over millions of years, they forced the rocks on their edges to crumple and fold upward.

THE RING OF FIRE

The movement of tectonic plates can cause volcanoes and earthquakes. These phenomena are most common in places where two plates push together or split apart. The huge horseshoe-shaped area that forms the edge of the Pacific Plate is often called the "Ring of Fire," owing to the large number of volcanoes that form there. Around 90 percent of the world's earthquakes also take place in this region.

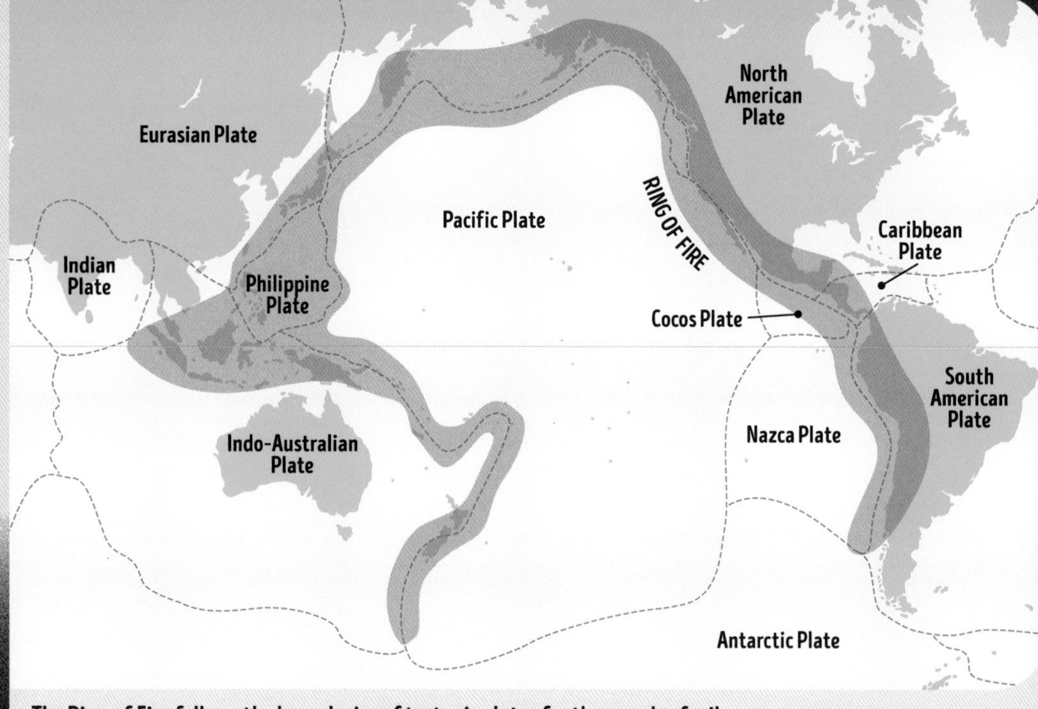

The Ring of Fire follows the boundaries of tectonic plates for thousands of miles.

Eurasia

North America

PANGAEA

South America

Africa

India

Antarctica

Australia

ALFRED WEGENER (1880–1930)

The theory of plate tectonics was first developed by the German geologist Alfred Wegener in 1912. After noticing that the continents seemed to fit together like jigsaw pieces, he analyzed rocks and fossils in different continents, looking for similarities that would show they were once connected. However, his theory wasn't widely accepted until the 1960s, decades after his death.

ANCIENT EARTH

Earth's tectonic plates have had billions of years to move around. Long ago, the arrangement of continents looked very different! Earth's landmasses have come together and then split apart. Around the time that dinosaurs first appeared, about 230 million years ago, all the world's land was part of a "supercontinent" called Pangaea. If you look at a map, the coast of South America looks like it would fit very neatly into Africa's coast. And in fact, the two continents were once connected!

IGNEOUS ROCKS

The majority of rocks in the upper part of Earth's crust are igneous. These are rocks that form when magma cools underground or when lava cools on Earth's surface. They're not always easy to spot. That's because most of them are hidden from view—either covered by layers of other types of rock, or deep below the waters of the oceans. Geologists have discovered hundreds of different types of igneous rocks.

This lava has cooled rapidly in air to form a thick, black crust. When magma comes to Earth's surface, we call it lava. Magma can cool underground but lava cools more quickly when it comes into contact with air or ocean water.

HOT ROCKS

What makes a rock igneous all depends on how it forms. And the clue is in the name! The English word "igneous" comes from a Latin word meaning "fiery" —and igneous rocks are forged in fire. Magma is an underground mixture of hot, liquid rock and soft chunks of slightly cooler semi-solid rock containing dissolved gases and many different minerals. When it cools, it crystallizes and hardens to form igneous rock.

Pumice is an igneous rock that's hurled from exploding volcanoes and is packed with holes formed by bubbles of trapped gas.

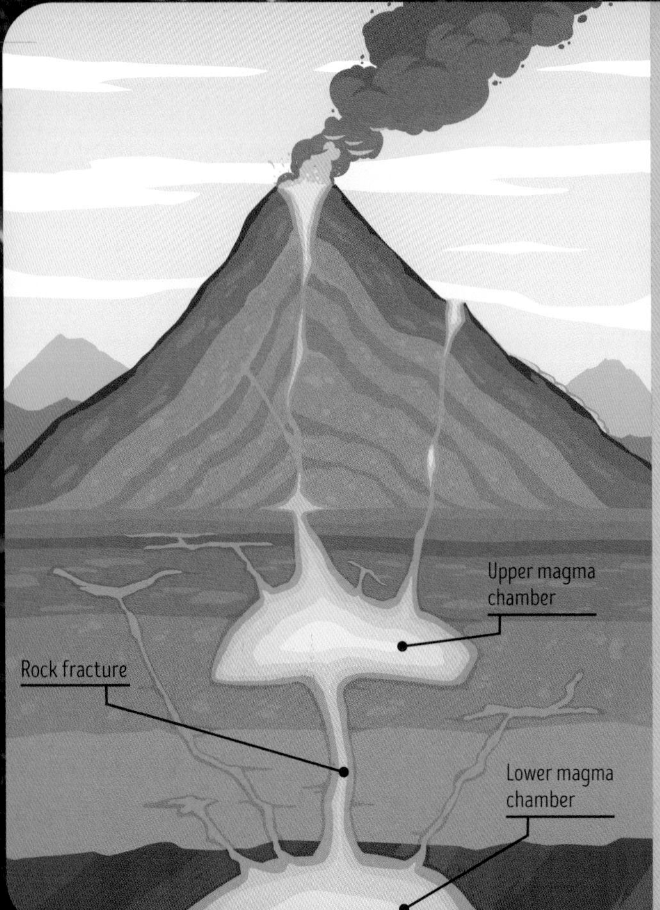

UNDER PRESSURE

It's incredibly hot in Earth's mantle, but most of its rocks stay solid. This is thanks to the immense pressure of the layers above pressing down and stopping the rocks from melting. However, there are some places, such as beneath mid-ocean ridges or hotspots, where the hot mantle can rise up and melt into magma. This molten rock is lighter than the solid rock, so it keeps rising, sometimes creating cracks or fractures in the rock. If it reaches a point where it can't rise any farther, it forms a pocket or "magma chamber" and this can happen in a few places throughout the rock. Many geologists now believe magma chambers are filled with a crystalline "mush," rather than completely liquid rock.

BREAKING THROUGH

A lot of the molten rock deep underground never makes it all the way to the surface. It eventually cools and hardens into solid rock, staying right where it is. These igneous rocks are described as "intrusive," although some may eventually be pushed up to the surface and exposed for us to see. Some igneous rocks form from magma that bursts through cracks in the crust during volcanic eruptions. Once exposed to air, they cool to form what we call "extrusive" igneous rocks.

An eruption from Fagradalsfjall, one of Iceland's active volcanoes. With each eruption, the lava cools to form igneous rock.

MEET THE FAMILY

Depending on how they formed, igneous rocks can look very different from each other. There is hard, sparkly granite (see page 101), which you might see in someone's kitchen countertops. Perhaps you've scrubbed dead skin away using pieces of light pumice (see page 103). You may even have seen arrowheads or other objects made from black, glassy obsidian (see page 102). Although these rocks look very different, they all formed from cooled magma or lava.

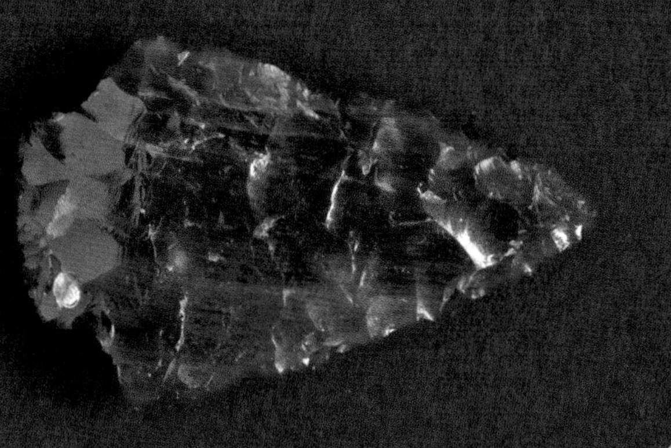

Early civilizations used obsidian rock to create blades and arrowheads. Obsidian is hard and brittle. It fractures to leave a sharp edge.

CHARLES DARWIN (1809–1882)

Although he is more famous for studying animals, Charles Darwin was also interested in geology. On the five-year expedition where he developed his theory of evolution, he collected samples of different types of igneous rocks. By looking at their properties, such as the density of their crystals, he theorized that any variation was caused by differences in how molten rock cooled to form the rocks.

SEDIMENTARY ROCKS

Earth's surface is constantly changing. Rocks crumble and wear away, and living things die and decompose. These processes lead to the formation of sedimentary rocks, which are found everywhere on Earth—from deserts and mountains to the bottom of the ocean. They form a thin layer at the surface, over thicker layers of igneous and metamorphic rocks.

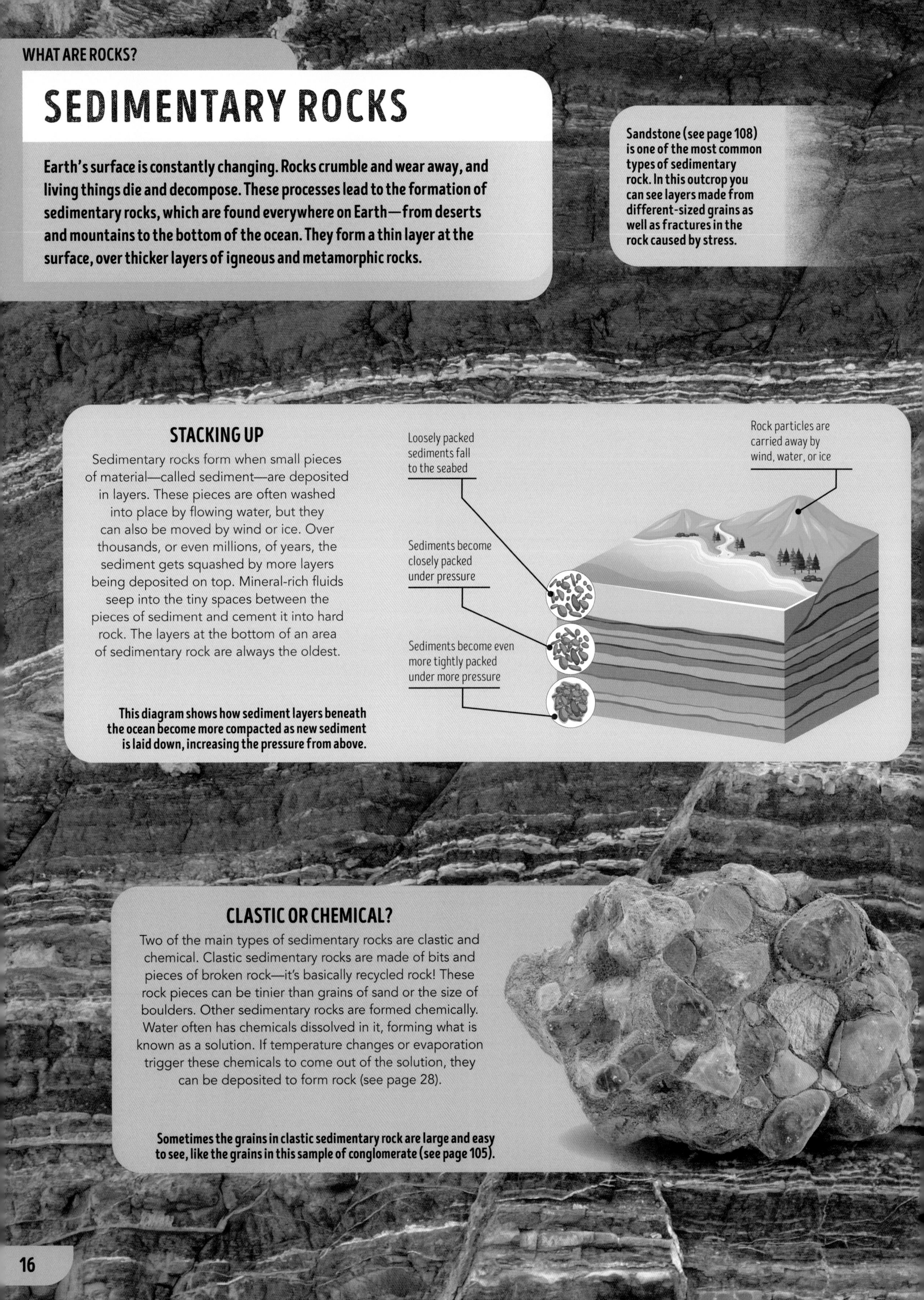

Sandstone (see page 108) is one of the most common types of sedimentary rock. In this outcrop you can see layers made from different-sized grains as well as fractures in the rock caused by stress.

STACKING UP

Sedimentary rocks form when small pieces of material—called sediment—are deposited in layers. These pieces are often washed into place by flowing water, but they can also be moved by wind or ice. Over thousands, or even millions, of years, the sediment gets squashed by more layers being deposited on top. Mineral-rich fluids seep into the tiny spaces between the pieces of sediment and cement it into hard rock. The layers at the bottom of an area of sedimentary rock are always the oldest.

This diagram shows how sediment layers beneath the ocean become more compacted as new sediment is laid down, increasing the pressure from above.

CLASTIC OR CHEMICAL?

Two of the main types of sedimentary rocks are clastic and chemical. Clastic sedimentary rocks are made of bits and pieces of broken rock—it's basically recycled rock! These rock pieces can be tinier than grains of sand or the size of boulders. Other sedimentary rocks are formed chemically. Water often has chemicals dissolved in it, forming what is known as a solution. If temperature changes or evaporation trigger these chemicals to come out of the solution, they can be deposited to form rock (see page 28).

Sometimes the grains in clastic sedimentary rock are large and easy to see, like the grains in this sample of conglomerate (see page 105).

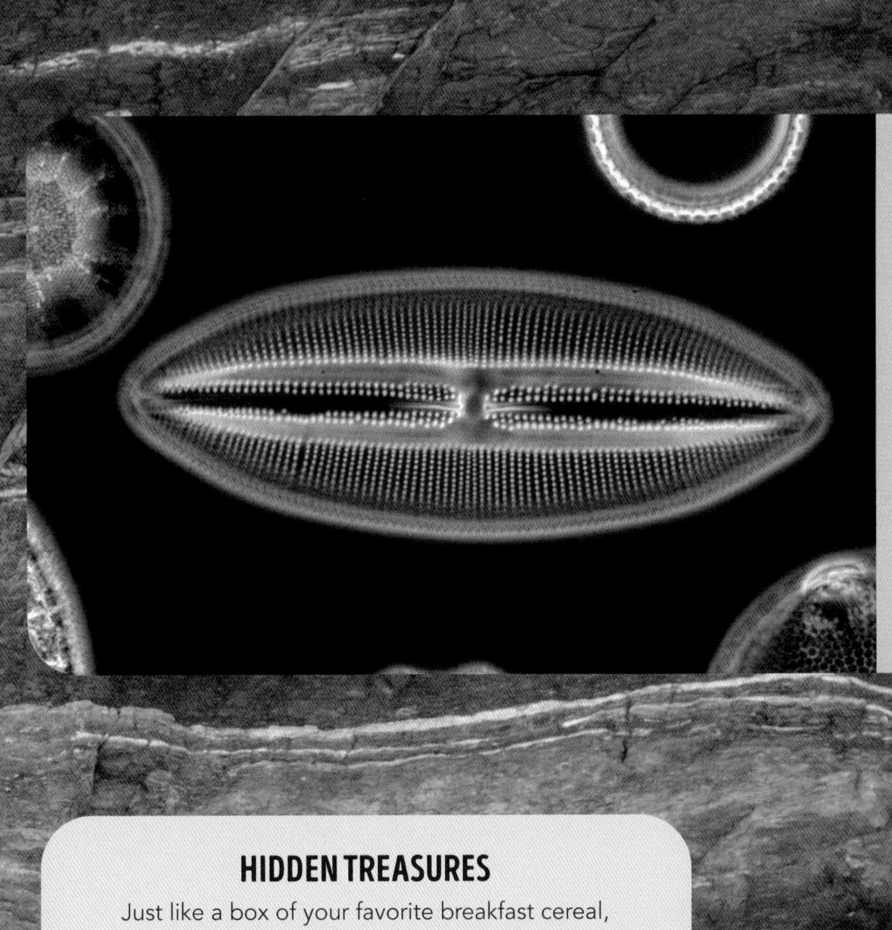

FORMED FROM LIFE

Some sedimentary rocks have been formed from the remnants of living things. When they died, their remains were laid down, compacted, and turned into rock, in a similar way to how clastic sedimentary rocks form. For example, the sedimentary rock coal (see page 106) is made from dead trees. Most types of limestone (see page 107) are formed from the remains of sea creatures such as corals, which produce outer skeletons rich in calcium carbonate.

Microscopic algae, such as this one, have outer skeletons of silica. Their remains can form a hard stone known as chert.

HIDDEN TREASURES

Just like a box of your favorite breakfast cereal, sedimentary rocks often have a prize hidden inside—fossils! It's easy for dead plants or animals to get washed away and buried among the layers of sediment. Above ground, oxygen helps to make their bodies rot and break down. But once they're covered, they're no longer exposed to oxygen, so their bones and shells are preserved. Very occasionally, the soft body parts might also be preserved such as in the famous Burgess Shale area of Canada (see page 41). Eventually minerals replace the once-living material, leaving a rock copy of the animal or plant as a fossil.

This Sinosauropteryx fossil shows the detail of some feathers. As body parts decomposed, minerals filled the gaps left behind.

STRIPES AND BANDS

You can often see stripes or bands of different colors in sedimentary rock. Even if the color is all the same, you are likely to see different layers. This is because of the way the rocks formed, as layers of sediment were laid down and gradually stacked up. Different minerals can give each band a different color. It's a little like the way that tree trunks have rings, showing each year's layer of new growth.

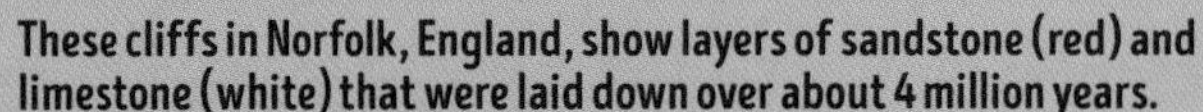

These cliffs in Norfolk, England, show layers of sandstone (red) and limestone (white) that were laid down over about 4 million years.

METAMORPHIC ROCKS

Pick up a rock—it looks and feels pretty solid, doesn't it? Most rocks are hard and tough. They last a long time. But did you know that rocks can change? There are incredibly powerful natural forces, such as heat and pressure, within Earth. And over time, these can change one type of rock into another. These changed rocks are known as metamorphic rocks.

SQUEEZING DOWN

Many metamorphic rocks form when other types of rock—either igneous or sedimentary—are put under pressure. Some form deep within Earth, where the sheer weight of the rock above creates huge amounts of pressure. Others form when two or more tectonic plates push together with immense force. This pressure is so strong that it actually rearranges the atoms inside the rocks, pushing them closer together and causing new minerals to form. Some rocks that form at great depths but are later pushed to Earth's surface may also "metamorphose" as their minerals change and react to the lower pressure at Earth's surface.

Many mountain ranges, like Europe's Alps, have metamorphic rocks at their core. It takes great pressure to push up a mountain—enough to change the rock itself!

FEEL THE HEAT

Heat can also make existing rocks turn into metamorphic rocks. If they are heated up enough to become fully molten, they form new igneous rocks. Rocks go through metamorphism when they heat up just enough for their structure to change, but not enough to melt. This often happens in places where magma pushes its way into existing rock, deep underground. The areas of rock nearest the magma pocket heat up, so the atoms rearrange themselves or the different minerals might react with each other. This can cause limestone to metamorphose into marble, for example.

When a magma chamber comes into close contact with sedimentary rocks, a small area of those sedimentary rocks will be heated enough to change.

Shale
Limestone
Shale
Limestone
Sandstone
Shale
Magma
Marble
Quartzite
Hornfels

SAME, BUT DIFFERENT

A rock that has gone through metamorphism turns into a new type of rock. It might be a different texture or color, and its crystals might change shape. In fact, that's how these rocks get their name—"metamorphic" comes from Greek words meaning "to change form." We use the closely related word metamorphosis for the process by which living things change form—for example, a caterpillar changing into a butterfly.

Sandstone

Quartzite

When sandstone goes through metamorphism, it can become a different type of rock called quartzite. These rocks have a completely different look and feel.

The bands of color in this schist formed under great pressure. They look like the bands of color in sedimentary rock but they formed in a different way. We call this effect foliation.

FOLIATION

All the pressing and squeezing needed to form metamorphic rock can leave a mark. Some types of metamorphic rock have bands or lines running through them, like a length of ribbon that's been bunched up. This is called foliation, and it happens when pressure squeezes the minerals in rock so much that they become aligned. The bands of foliation show the direction of the pressure that was applied.

HOW WE USE IT

LAPIS LAZULI

The majority of rocks are dull in color, so the bright blue of lapis lazuli really stands out! This beautiful metamorphic rock forms when limestone or marble are changed by heat. Lapis lazuli has been mined in Afghanistan for at least 9,000 years, and people carve and polish it to make jewelry. It also used to be ground into a powder to make a pigment called ultramarine. Painters loved this deep-blue pigment, but it was extremely expensive.

When Vermeer painted *Girl With a Pearl Earring* in 1665, he used ultramarine for the girl's deep-blue headscarf.

THE ROCK CYCLE

Earth's rocks are constantly changing. Old rocks break down and new rocks form. Existing rocks are changed into new types. It might take millions of years, but these processes are a way for our planet to recycle its rock. It's all part of a natural cycle—the rock cycle!

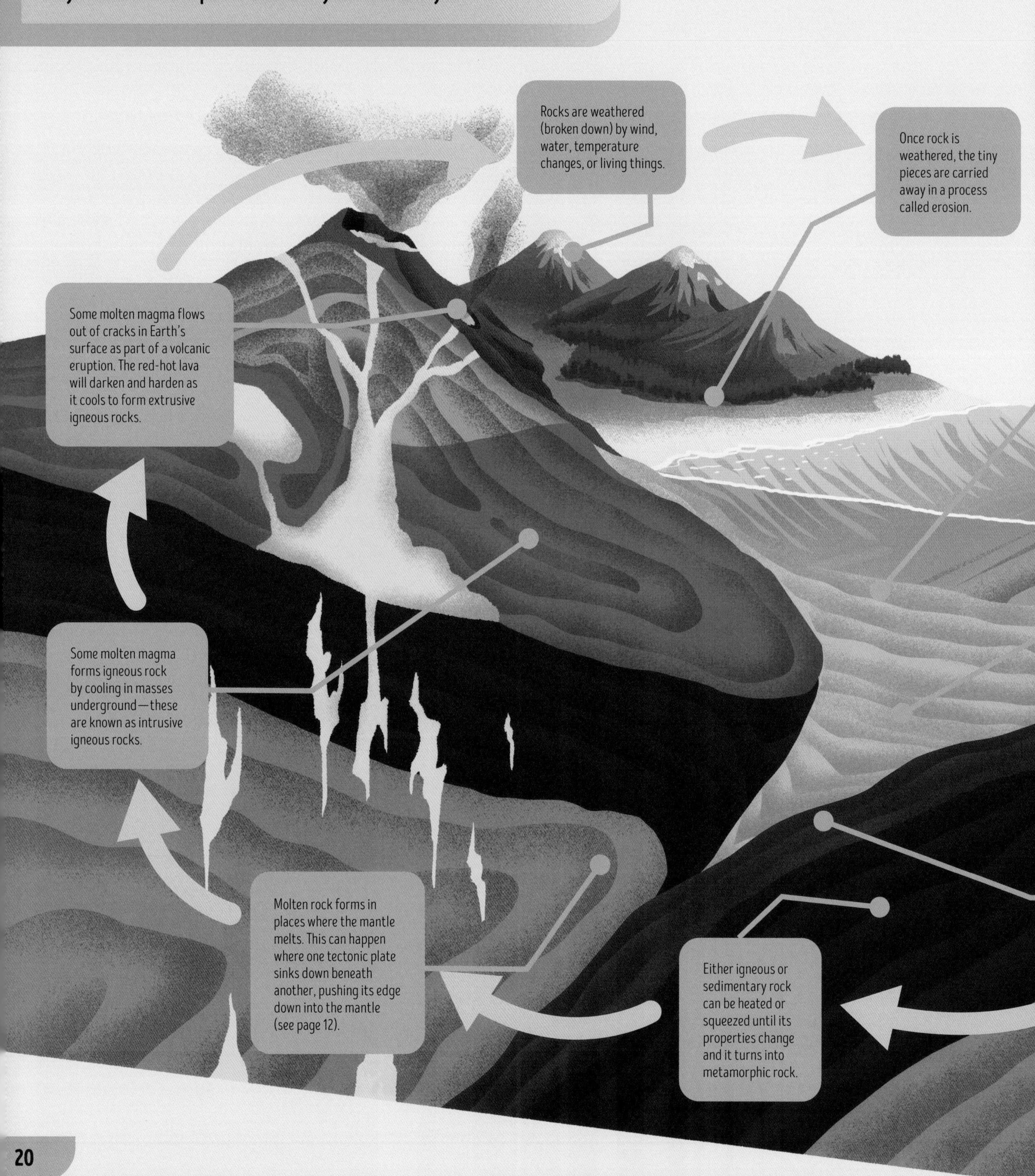

BREAKING DOWN, WASHING AWAY

No kind of rock will last forever! Igneous, sedimentary, and metamorphic rocks can all be broken down in a process called weathering. Weathering can be caused by wind, flowing water, or changes in temperature. It can also be caused by growing plants or the actions of animals. Even chemicals in rain can dissolve rock. The pieces that break off can be recycled into new rock through the processes of the rock cycle.

Over many years, fast-flowing flood waters carved these soft sedimentary rocks into beautiful curves at Antelope Canyon, Arizona.

The tiny pieces of sediment produced by weathering are deposited in layers.

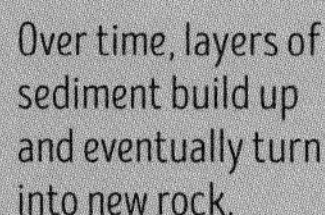

Over time, layers of sediment build up and eventually turn into new rock.

New rock can be pushed around by the actions of tectonic plates. It can be pushed upward, or forced farther down into the crust.

AN ENDLESS CYCLE

There is no start or end to the rock cycle—it's an endless loop that plays out over millions or even billions of years. At its heart, it's all powered by the heat deep within Earth, and modified by the actions of water, wind, gravity, and living things. Earth is what scientists call "geologically active." There is evidence that other rocky planets, such as Venus and Mars, have gone through similar changes.

Jupiter's moon Io is extremely geologically active, with hundreds of volcanoes. Its surface is streaked with red, yellow, black, white, and green lava.

JAMES HUTTON (1726–1797)

One of the first people to propose the idea of the rock cycle was James Hutton, a Scottish scientist often called the "father of modern geology." He lived at a time when many people thought Earth's oldest rocks were only about 6,000 years old, based on dates in the Bible. But Hutton knew that soil and rock could both be eroded, and that some rocks had once been molten, or had been pushed up to the surface by natural forces. He put all his observations together into a theory of a cycle that, he said, showed "no vestige of a beginning, no prospect of an end."

ROCKS, MINERALS, ELEMENTS AND, ORES

When reading about Earth's geology, you'll hear a lot of different terms, such as "mineral" or "ore." But what do they all mean, and what's the difference between, for example, an element and a chemical? And why does it have to be so complicated, anyway? Aren't rocks just rocks...?

Iron ore is extracted from the rocks in this mine in India. The ore is then processed to release the chemical element, iron.

ROCKS

Everyone knows what a rock is, right? It's a hard, solid lump of stone. A rock can be small, like a pebble, or big like a boulder. But "rock" is a very generic term—lots of different things can be called "rock." Simply put, a rock is a natural object, formed by nature instead of by humans. Most rocks are a mix of two or more different minerals. They can also include organic material from the remains of living things.

Coquina is a type of sedimentary rock made from the shells of sea creatures that have been squashed together.

MINERALS

The requirements for being a rock are pretty loose, but the requirements for being classed as a mineral are a lot stricter. A mineral is a solid, naturally occurring substance that is not made of anything that was once living. Many minerals contain a mix of two or more chemical elements. The atoms that make up these elements must be arranged in a pattern. This pattern repeats over and over to form three-dimensional crystals. The examples of the mineral quartz (see page 144) shown below look different because they contain impurities, but they have the same proportion of elements—one silicon atom to two oxygen atoms.

Amethyst

Smoky quartz

Clear quartz

Rose quartz

ELEMENTS

All minerals and rocks are made up of the 94 elements that exist naturally on Earth. An element is a substance that cannot be easily broken down into a simpler substance by chemical means. For example, salt is made up of the elements sodium and chlorine, calcite is made of three elements (carbon, calcium, and oxygen), while tourmaline minerals are made of more than eight elements. Some elements can form minerals on their own, without bonding to other elements. We call these "native elements."

Sulfur (see page 117) is a chemical element that is often found as a mineral in its native form.

ORES

Often the minerals or elements that we want to use are locked up in rocks, where they are mixed with other materials. These rocks are called "ores," and you'll usually see them described as an ore of a specific material. For example, calling a rock an "iron ore" just means that there's iron inside it that can be extracted to use. Over the years, scientists have developed processes for extracting different metals from their ores.

Ores are heated in a blast furnace to release the valuable mineral they contain. This is known as smelting.

THEOPHRASTUS (372–287 BCE)

Theophrastus was an ancient Greek philosopher who studied under Aristotle. After his teacher retired, Theophrastus took over running the school he had founded. He often wrote about the natural world, especially plants, and he wrote a short work called "On Stones." In it, he described many different rocks, looking at their origins and uses. He also tried to organize them into groups based on their properties. It was one of the first works of its kind, and it was used as a source by later scholars.

MINERAL FAMILIES

There are thousands of different minerals found on Earth. Some are made up of just one chemical element, but the vast majority are compounds formed of two or more elements. Geologists divide minerals into different categories or families, based on the elements that they contain. Let's look at the most common mineral families. There are plenty of others, including phosphates, arsenates and vanadates, but they're much rarer.

The periodic table lists Earth's chemical elements (see page 23). It cleverly organizes elements into groups that have similar chemical properties, and separates out metals, semi-metals and non-metals.

SULFUR-BASED MINERALS

Minerals that contain sulfur are placed into one of three main groups: as sulfide minerals, sulfate minerals and as sulfur itself. In sulfide minerals, sulfur is combined with one or more metals. They are often soft but fairly dense, and many have a metallic luster. Crystals of sulfate minerals, on the other hand, have a sulfur atom bonded to four oxygen atoms. These minerals are rarer than sulfides. Sulfur can also be found in its native form, as a single element.

Sulfide minerals include ores of important metals, such as the copper used in wiring. This sulfide ore contains copper and nickel.

OXIDES

Oxide minerals contain oxygen—the name is probably a bit of a giveaway! These minerals have a structure of closely packed oxygen atoms. In a simple oxide, atoms of one type of metal or semi-metal fill the spaces in between. A multiple oxide can contain several different metals or semi-metals.

Rubies are a simple oxide made up of aluminium and oxygen, colored red by tiny amounts of chromium.

HYDROXIDES

Hydroxide minerals form when a metallic element combines with a hydroxyl—an oxygen atom and a hydrogen atom joined together in a way that bonds easily with other substances. These minerals often form when water weathers other elements, so they are frequently found in places like mountain ranges.

Bauxite is a hydroxide that is the main ore of aluminium, the metal used to make these drinks cans.

HALIDES

A halide mineral is one in which a halogen, such as chlorine or fluorine, bonds with a metal. A halogen is a non-metal element that bonds easily with other elements. More complex halides may have aluminium bonded to a halogen, which then bonds with a third element.

The salt we use on our food is a simple halide mineral made of sodium bonded to chlorine. The sodium in salt is a very soft silvery-white metal!

CARBONATES

The structure of a carbonate mineral is based on an arrangement of atoms called a carbonate. In this, an atom of carbon is bonded to three oxygen atoms arranged in an equilateral triangle. This can then join with atoms of a different element to form carbonate minerals. For example, adding calcium to a carbonate forms calcium carbonate—better known as chalk!

SILICATES

Silicates are minerals that contain both silicon and oxygen. In many minerals, one atom of silicon bonds with four oxygen atoms to form a tetrahedron (triangular-sided pyramid) shape. This group includes some of the most common minerals, such as quartz and feldspar (see page 26). It's subdivided into smaller groups based on the patterns formed by the way the tetrahedrons join together.

Silicate minerals make up more than 90 per cent of Earth's crust and mantle! This quartz outcrop is located in Australia.

BORATES

Borate is a compound of boron and oxygen, just as carbonate is a compound of carbon and oxygen. When borate bonds with one or more metals, it makes borate minerals. Volcanic activity often releases solutions rich in borate, and if these flow into a closed basin (a low-lying area that water flows into but not out of), the water can evaporate, leaving the borate behind. Most borate minerals are rare.

Borate deposits are more common in deserts, where there is little water, like this old borax mine in Death Valley, USA.

THE USUAL SUSPECTS

Many of the thousands of minerals found on Earth are very rare, and are found only in small amounts in a few locations. Others are much more common. In fact, about 95 per cent of Earth's crust is made up of just ten different minerals! Here are a few of the minerals that you're most likely to find.

Granite makes up most of the upper continental crust. It is rich in minerals in the feldspar and mica groups, as well as quartz.

FELSIC OR MAFIC?

Geologists divide igneous rocks into two main groups, depending on the elements they contain: felsic rocks and mafic rocks. Felsic rocks, such as granite, tend to be made up of lighter elements like silicon, oxygen and aluminium. Mafic rocks, such as basalt, are rich in magnesium and iron. Both types of rock can undergo metamorphism, or be weathered and turn into sedimentary rock.

Felsic minerals, such as quartz (left), tend to be lighter in color than mafic minerals, such as pyroxene (right).

TOP FELSIC MINERALS

A group of minerals known as feldspars make up the biggest group, forming about half of Earth's crust. These minerals are mainly made of silica (a compound of silicon and oxygen) and aluminium. Coming in second is quartz, a felsic mineral made up mainly of pure silica and a common component of sand. A smaller group of minerals known as micas include other elements such as potassium, lithium and hydrogen.

Minerals in the mica group often peel into thin sheets.

TOP MAFIC MINERALS

A group of mafic minerals called pyroxenes make up about 10 per cent of Earth's crust. These minerals often contain sodium, calcium and aluminium, alongside iron and magnesium. Amphiboles are closely related mafic minerals that also contain hydrogen and oxygen. A third type, the olivines, are even richer in iron and magnesium.

Olivines are the main mineral found in the upper mantle, but they're also sometimes found at the surface.

UNDER OUR FEET

Earth's crust is just a thin outer layer, making up only 1 per cent of our planet's total volume. The mantle is the biggest layer by far, making up 84 per cent of the planet. And it's a mantle mineral called bridgmanite that takes the crown as the most abundant mineral on Earth—it makes up about 40 per cent of Earth's volume but it's found too deep for us to see! It's only stable at the high temperatures and pressure found in the mantle, although scientists have found samples of it in a meteorite.

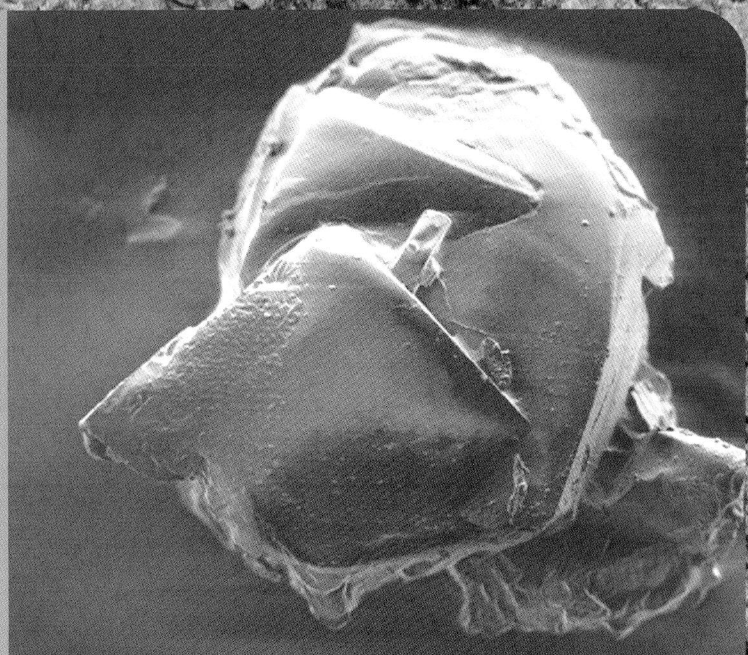

This bridgmanite sample was made in a lab at pressures similar to those found 700 km (435 miles) underground. The crystal is the width of a human hair.

HOW WE USE IT

QUARTZ

Quartz has many uses, but one of them relies on a unique property, called piezoelectricity. Squeezing a quartz crystal produces an electric charge and the effect also works in reverse—applying an electric current to a quartz crystal will make it squeeze and vibrate. Because it vibrates at a constant rate, this vibration can be used to turn the gears in a watch or clock.

In a quartz clock, the quartz crystal oscillator (top left) and rotor (left) move the gears for the second, minute and hour hands.

CRYSTALS

You've probably seen crystals in gift shops—they're often brightly colored and sometimes see-through, with interesting geometric shapes. But did you know that most minerals are crystals at heart? A material is crystalline if it's solid and made up of a repeating three-dimensional pattern.

Quartz crystals are made from atoms of oxygen and silicon that have joined together as tetrahedrons (triangular-sided pyramids) which stack together to make crystals.

ATOMIC STRUCTURE

Atoms and molecules make up everything in the universe, but they are much too small to see clearly. However, the way they join together decides what a crystal's shape will be, and that's something that we *can* see! Atoms join together to form building blocks called 'unit cells'. The shape of the unit cell is reproduced over and over to form a lattice, and this gives a crystal its structure. Crystallography is the science of working out a crystal's atomic structure.

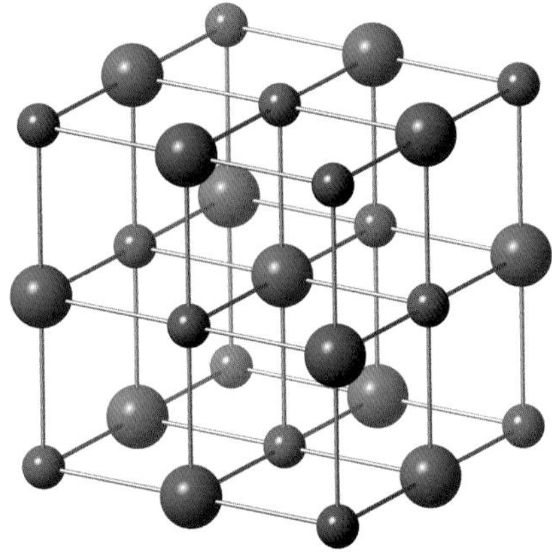

Crystals of sodium chloride (salt) have a regular cubic structure. Sodium atoms (blue) alternate with chloride atoms (green) in a 3D pattern.

ROSALIND FRANKLIN (1920–1958)

Rosalind Franklin was a British crystallographer who is best remembered today for her work in discovering the structure of the DNA molecule. However, she also made discoveries about the atomic structures of coal and graphite. Franklin used a technique called X-ray diffraction, which involves sending a beam of X-rays into a crystal. Watching how the X-rays scatter gives clues to the crystal's atomic structure.

HOW CRYSTALS FORM

Crystals can only form when the conditions are right. Some crystals form when hot magma underground cools down—a little like water freezing into ice. Other crystals form when a molecule of a substance dissolved in water bumps into something solid, such as a speck of dust or a bit of rock. Soon, other similar molecules begin to stick to it, and eventually they form crystals. Crystals can also form when the balance of ingredients in a solution changes, so there is more solute (dissolved solid) than solvent (the liquid). This happens when sea water evaporates on a sunny day, leaving salt crystals behind in a process known as 'precipitation'.

You can grow crystals at home with a chemistry kit, by letting special mineral-rich solutions evaporate. It will take a few days in a warm, dry environment.

CRYSTAL SYSTEMS

Crystals form in shapes with flat faces called facets, and, in most minerals, these faces are too small to see without a microscope. However, some individual crystals grow large enough that we can see their shape clearly. Geologists divide crystals into six different systems, based on their shape: cubic, tetragonal, orthorhombic, hexagonal, monoclinic and triclinic. A cubic crystal is shaped like a dice. A tetragonal crystal is like a cube that's stretched or shrunk in one direction, while orthorhombic crystals are stretched or shrunk in two directions, like the shape of a book. Hexagonal crystals have six sides arranged in a hexagon. A monoclinic crystal looks like a prism formed from a parallelogram, while a triclinic crystal is the most complicated, like a three-dimensional rhombus.

Pyrite crystals have a clear cubic shape. They form an almost perfect cube which looks man-made, but is completely natural.

CRYSTAL HABITS

When a geologist describes a crystal's habit, they're not talking about its daily routines! Instead, it's the tendency for crystals to grow into particular shapes. These shapes depend on the mineral's atomic structure, but the conditions of the environment in which the crystal grows will also affect its habit. Here are some common crystal habits.

NAME	SHAPE
bladed	long and flattened, like knife blades
botryoidal	connected round lumps like a bunch of grapes
concentric	formed in layers like an onion
dendritic	slender, plant-like branches
fibrous	long, thin strands
lamellar	flat, plate-like layers
lenticular	lens shapes, like lentils
massive	forming a solid mass where individual crystals can't be seen
radiating	radiating out from a center, like a spiral

GEODES

Sometimes, crystals form in hollow rocks, forming structures called geodes. Geodes can begin to form as air bubbles in igneous rock, or dissolved spaces in sedimentary rock. Dissolved minerals can seep into these spaces and, over millions of years, gradually form crystals.

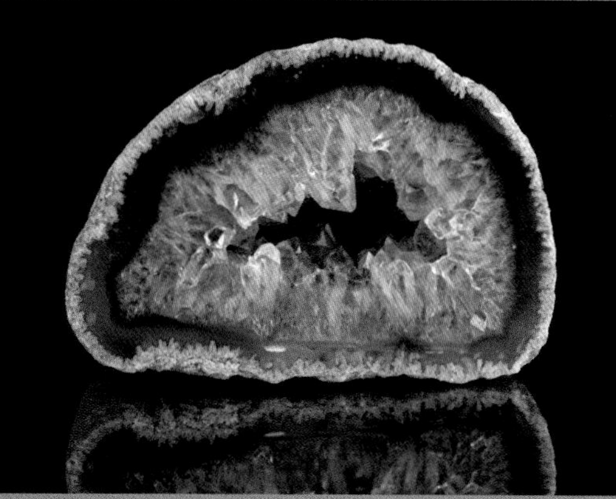

Quartz crystals have formed a stunning feature in the hollow space of this rock.

GEMSTONES

How would you describe a gemstone? You might say that gems are beautiful and sparkly, or colorful and expensive. But in fact, there is no geological definition for a gemstone. Most of them are just minerals that are prized for their beauty and durability. Gemstones are also rare, which makes them special. No wonder we put them in jewellery and royal crowns!

Cut gemstones are highly prized for their color, sparkle and rarity.

CRYSTALS AND AGGREGATE GEMSTONES

Many gemstones are large crystals of a particular mineral. For example, diamond is pure carbon, sapphire and ruby are versions of the mineral corundum, and emerald and aquamarine are versions of the mineral beryl. These gemstones are often translucent, with flat faces. Other gems, such as jasper or jadeite (see page 149), are described as aggregates. They are opaque and don't look like crystals—that's because they're made up of huge numbers of microscopic crystals.

Even before it is cut, you can often see the crystal shape of a red ruby (corundum, left), while other gems such as jadeite (right) are opaque.

ORGANIC GEMSTONES

There are some materials we call gemstones that aren't minerals at all! These gems are natural materials made by living things—for example, pearls form inside oysters and other shellfish. Amber is tree sap that has been fossilized, and shiny black jet is fossilized wood. These organic materials (see pages 154–155) are just as beautiful as other gemstones, but they are not minerals.

Oysters form pearls to protect their soft, delicate bodies from grit. This man is extracting a pearl from an oyster shell to be used for decoration or jewellery.

LOOKING THEIR BEST

An uncut diamond (shown right) looks like an ordinary glassy pebble. Other gem minerals come out of the ground looking bumpy and rough. To make gems look their best, we cut them into shape and polish them. This lets their color and texture shine through. Crystal gemstones such as emeralds (below) are cut into shapes with many flat faces and set into rings or other jewellery. The faces make them sparkle and shine when light hits them.

HOW WE USE IT

CUTTING DIAMONDS

Diamond is the hardest mineral, so how do we cut it into shapes? It turns out that, although diamond is hard, the way that its atoms are arranged makes it brittle in certain places. Diamond cutters can split a diamond by hitting it sharply at a particular angle. Diamonds are also used to cut themselves! Cutters may use a laser or a rotating saw with diamonds in its blade. To make small, delicate faces, they use diamond-tipped tools.

Diamond cutters use their tools to turn an unshaped lump of diamond (left) into a sparkling gemstone (right).

HEALING POWERS?

Over the centuries, many people have believed that gemstones have special powers. They claimed these stones could protect against evil spirits or heal the body. Wearing a gem such as amethyst or moonstone was thought to cure physical ailments or illness. Today, many people still believe that some crystals, such as quartz, give off healing energy in the form of vibrations. So far, there is no scientific research that backs up these claims.

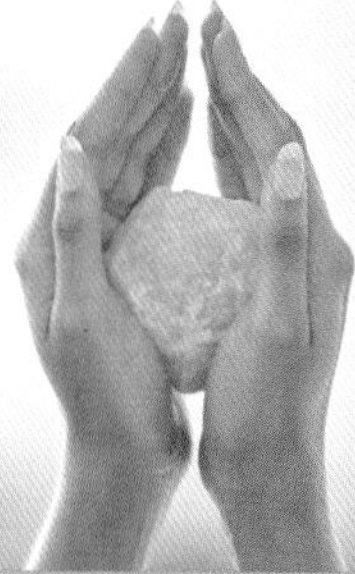

Some people believe that pink-colored rose quartz can replace negative energies with positive energy.

ROCK FORMATIONS

Once a rock is formed, that's not the end of its story! Rocks change over time through tectonic movements, weathering and erosion. Over millions of years, these forces have shaped the rocks on Earth's surface—sometimes into unusual shapes. These rock formations have created some of our most stunning landscapes!

The sedimentary rocks of Antelope Canyon, Arizona, USA, were carved into these shapes by fast-flowing floodwater during the wet season. The water also carried sand which scoured the landscape.

MOUNTAINS AND VOLCANOES

There are mountains all over the world, towering over the surrounding land. Many of these mountains formed when two tectonic plates collided (see page 12), forcing the land upward in folds. Other mountains formed as volcanoes, gradually growing each time more lava erupted. Once a mountain has formed, it can still be shaped—for example, when glaciers grind the summit into a pyramid-shaped peak or following a volcanic eruption, as happened to Mount St Helens, USA, in 1980.

Mount St Helens pictured after the eruption that lowered its summit by over 400 m (1,300 ft).

MESAS, BUTTES AND HOODOOS

A mesa is a mountain or hill with a flat top, like a table (*mesa* is the Spanish word for 'table'). It usually forms when erosion washes away soft sedimentary rock beneath hard rock, leaving a cliff with the hard rock ('caprock') forming the top of the mesa. With persistent erosion, the soft rock eventually undercuts the hard rock, and part of the 'table top' breaks off. Mesas are usually wider than they are tall. Buttes are similar to mesas but are taller than they are wide. In some places, erosion reduces the rock to tall, narrow spires that might be carved into eerie shapes. These are called hoodoos.

Bryce Canyon, in the southwestern United States, is filled with hoodoos up to 60 m (200 ft) high.

CANYONS AND GORGES

As rivers flow, their waters dig into the land beneath them and wash it away. Over long periods of time, rivers can carve canyons deep into the rock, revealing its different layers. Canyons can also be formed by tectonic activity, when plates shift and push up an area of rock. Other canyons form as a rift between two mountain peaks, and a river might then carve it out even deeper. A gorge is like a canyon, but is usually a smaller formation that is steeper and narrower.

Samaria Gorge in Crete, Greece, was carved by a river between two mountains. At its narrowest, it is just 3 m (10 ft) wide.

INSELBERGS AND TORS

Mountains usually form in ranges, but sometimes you'll find an isolated mountain, knob or ridge that rises up from an otherwise flat landscape. These are known as inselbergs or monadnocks. They usually form when a body of hard rock such as granite is left behind after the softer rocks surrounding it wear away. A tor is a similar but smaller feature where weathering has caused cracks that separate the rock into smaller boulders.

In some parts of Africa, tors are often known as kopjes, a Dutch word meaning 'little head'. This kopje is located in Tanzania.

CAVES

Caves form in rocks that dissolve easily in water, such as limestone or dolomite. When rain falls and then seeps into the ground, it picks up carbon dioxide, which turns it into an acid. This acid is strong enough to eat away at limestone below ground, leaving hollow caves. When more water seeps in, carrying dissolved calcium carbonate, it can form new rock in bizarre-looking formations such as stalactites and stalagmites.

Impressive stalactites hang from the ceiling of this cave in Ebensee, Austria, where water has evaporated, leaving calcium carbonate behind.

ROCKS FROM SPACE

Earth's rocks and minerals come in an amazing variety, but there is one type of rock that is truly out of this world! Meteorites are rocks that crashed into Earth from space. They often have a different mineral composition from Earth rocks, so scientists love to study them.

A meteoroid travels at high speed. The frictional force as it enters Earth's atmosphere causes it to burn up. We call this fireball streaking across the sky a meteor or shooting star.

WHAT'S IN A NAME?

Before they reach Earth, meteorites are called meteoroids. Most are small to begin with and burn up completely when they enter Earth's atmosphere. A few survive the trip and land on the ground as meteorites. The vast majority are broken-off pieces of larger asteroids, but a few are pieces of Mars or the Moon that were sent flying through space to land on Earth.

In 2013, a 9-m (30-ft) wide meteor traveling at 65,000 kph (40,000 mph) was seen above the skies of Chelyabinsk, Russia.

METEORITE MATERIAL

Asteroids are the pieces of rocky rubble that were left over when the Solar System formed. The oldest ones are mainly made of silicate minerals (see page 25), while others have varying amounts of nickel and iron. Most meteorites have similar properties and fall into one of three groups: iron meteorites, made almost completely from metal; stony meteorites, which are mainly silicate minerals; and stony-iron meteorites, a mix of the two.

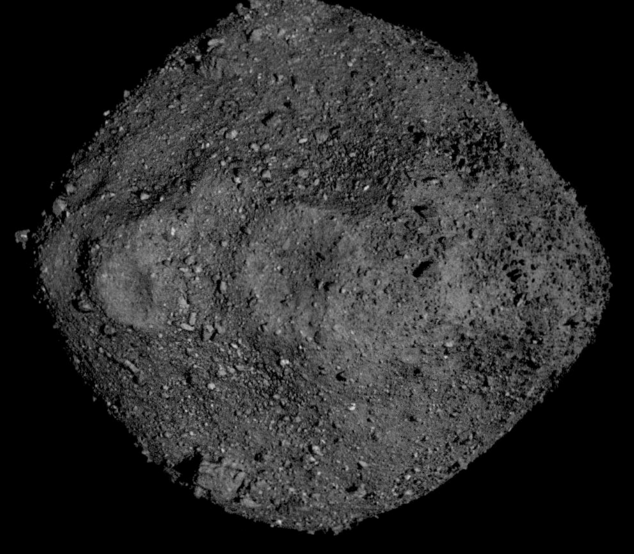

In 2023, a US spacecraft returned a sample of rocks from the distant asteroid Bennu (above) to Earth, for scientists to study.

FINDING METEORITES

Most meteoroids break up as they fall through the atmosphere, and the meteorites that do land are often small and hard to find. They're easier to spot in places like Antarctica, where they stand out from the surroundings. Meteorites can be hard to tell apart from Earth rocks at first glance, but there are some telltale clues. A meteorite will be dense and fairly heavy for its size, and they often have an irregular shape with fingerprint-like pits in the surface. Many are magnetic.

This meteorite was found on the ground in Chile's Atacama Desert.

THE BIGGER THEY ARE...

Meteorites are traveling fast when they hit the ground—fast enough for larger rocks to leave a crater in the ground. And the bigger they are, the bigger the crater! Over its long history, Earth has been hit by multiple large rocks, including the asteroid that helped wipe out the dinosaurs about 66 million years ago. These craters erode over time, but some are still visible on Earth's surface today.

This crater in Arizona, USA, was formed about 50,000 years ago when an asteroid 46 m (150 ft) across slammed into the ground.

EMAN GHONEIM (1968–)

Eman Ghoneim is an Egyptian geographer who specializes in using high-tech remote sensing tools to study Earth's landforms. She mainly searches for underground water and areas of flood risk, but in 2006 she and her colleagues used views from space to discover what might be the remains of an enormous impact crater in the Sahara Desert. Its sheer size—31 km (20 miles) across—makes it hard to spot except from space, especially considering that it has been eroded by water and wind.

IS IT A MINERAL?

Plants and animals are living things, and minerals are not. When you put it like that, it feels very cut and dried, but sometimes nature can be confusing. There are some materials that are hard and look very much like minerals but are something else entirely. They had their origin in living things, and that disqualifies them from being minerals.

ORGANIC AND INORGANIC

Scientists often divide materials and substances into two categories: organic (coming from or relating to living things) and inorganic (not relating to living things). All organic substances contain carbon, and so do some inorganic substances. By definition, minerals are inorganic. It can be confusing because sometimes we use organic materials, such as amber, jet, or pearls, in a similar way to minerals. But these materials have a living origin. Some organic substances, such as jet and coal, are often referred to as organic rocks.

MADE FROM NATURE

Some organic substances come from prehistoric plants. Amber (see page 154), for example, is fossilized resin, a liquid produced by trees. It oozed out of their trunks millions of years ago. Copal is a similar substance, and both are often carved into beads or figurines. Shiny black jet is also derived from plants—it's an early stage in the formation of coal. All of these substances look like minerals or crystals, but they are not.

Some specimens of amber have insects inside. They were trapped in the sticky tree resin and fossilized along with it.

HOW WE USE IT

CARVING JET

Humans have been carving jet (see page 154) since prehistoric times. It's soft enough to carve easily, and it polishes to a glossy black sheen. There are large deposits of jet in Whitby, England, and it was widely traded—historians have found items made from Whitby jet in Scandinavia and mainland Europe. When her husband died in 1861, Britain's Queen Victoria wore black mourning clothes along with black jet jewelry, starting a trend that many other people followed.

This early Bronze Age necklace from Britain, carved from jet, is about 4,000 years old.

Coal and diamond both contain the element carbon. Diamond (see page 146) is inorganic. It's a mineral that is made from pure carbon. Coal (see page 106) is organic. This sedimentary rock formed from the remains of ancient plants and is mostly carbon.

PETRIFIED PLANTS

Some parts of the world have petrified forests—there is a spectacular one in Arizona (see page 52). These are not forests of standing leafy trees, but rather places where toppled trunks made of stone lie on the ground. They are the remains of prehistoric trees, but they have become minerals! After they died, they were buried, and mineral-rich fluids seeped in. Over time, all of the trees' organic matter was replaced with minerals such as calcite or pyrite.

You can still see the rings and grain of the original wood in this petrified wood fossil found in Arizona.

ANIMAL ORIGINS

Some organic substances form from animals rather than plants. Pearls (see page 155), for example, are produced by oysters and other shellfish. Their soft bodies secrete a substance to protect them from any grit that gets inside the shell. Layers build up to form pearls. Coral (right, and page 155) is another organic material, formed from the skeletons of corals that live in shallow oceans. It can form a hard mass that is often pinkish-orange and can be carved into beads and jewelry.

The insides of some shells are covered in nacre, the same material that forms pearls. The nacre inside this abalone shell (left) gives it a colorful iridescent shimmer.

FOSSILS

Earth has a long history, and during that time many different creatures have roamed the land and swum in the seas. Many of these animals—and plants too—became extinct thousands, or even millions, of years ago, and new species evolved to fill the gap. However, we can still learn about these extinct species by studying their fossils.

BONE OR ROCK?

A fossil is a remnant of an organism preserved in rock. Many fossils, such as the dinosaur skeletons you see in museums, look like bones. That is what they were once, but not any more! All the organic material in the original remains has been replaced by minerals. The minerals keep the shape of the original body part, and they can show incredible detail.

This fossil of *Archaeopteryx*, a birdlike dinosaur that lived in Europe 150 million years ago, shows the creatures' wings, legs, and tail.

Archaeologists excavate fossilized dinosaur bones and the reconstructed skeletons (or replicas) are often displayed in museums, so we can see for ourselves what these prehistoric creatures looked like.

MARY ANNING (1799–1847)

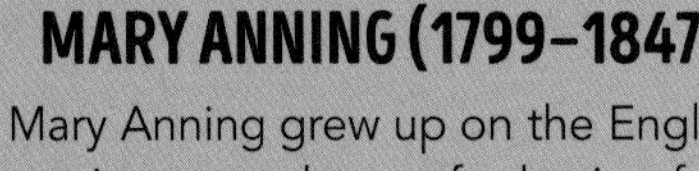

Mary Anning grew up on the English coast in an area known for having fossils in its cliffs. From a young age, she helped her father find fossils to sell to collectors, and she became a skilled fossil hunter herself. Anning discovered fossils of large marine reptiles, such as *Ichthyosaurus* and *Plesiosaurus*, and wrote scientific papers about them. She is also the inspiration for the tongue-twister "She sells seashells by the seashore"!

TRACE FOSSILS

Fossils of animal parts, such as bones and teeth, are called body fossils. Trace fossils are different. They don't show the body of an animal or plant—instead they show traces that the living thing left behind. Fossilized footprints are a good example, as are fossils of burrows and worm tracks, and the imprints of prehistoric leaves and palm fronds.

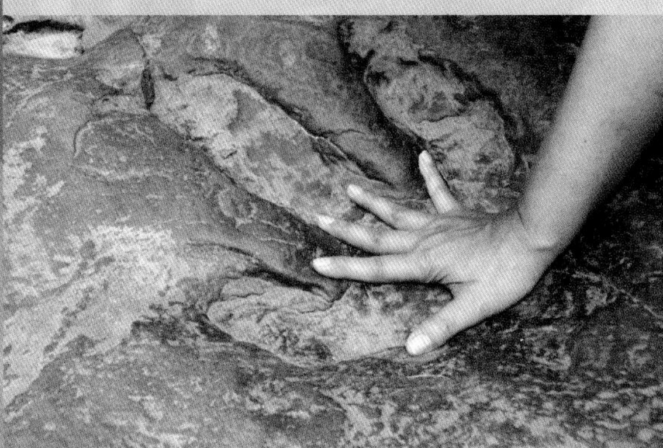

Fossilized dinosaur footprints, like this one from Thailand, teach us about how different dinosaurs walked and ran.

LARGE AND SMALL

Some dinosaurs were enormous, and paleontologists (see page 43) often find fossils of their bones. However, much smaller organisms can be fossilized too. Scientists have found fossils of single-celled prehistoric organisms such as diatoms and radiolaria, and even tiny grains of fossilized pollen. These super-small fossils are clues that help us learn more about what the climate and environment were like millions of years ago.

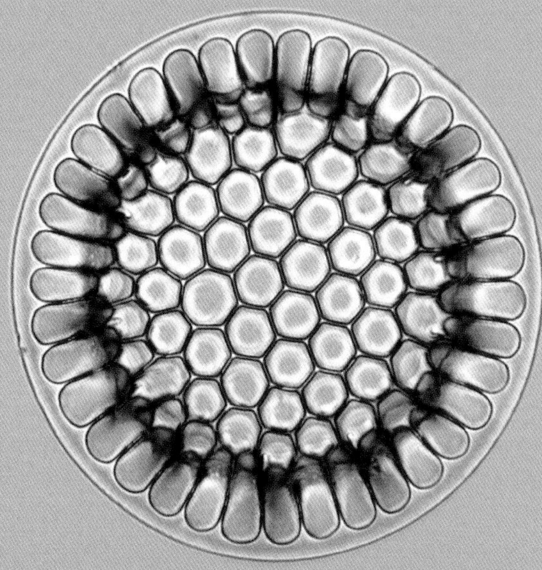

Tiny fossils, like this 40-million-year-old algae, are greatly magnified by a scanning electron microscope to be studied.

FOSSIL FUELS

You often hear about "fossil fuels" in news about the climate. They are called fossil fuels because they formed from the remains of prehistoric plants and animals that were buried millions of years ago. This term refers to coal, oil, and natural gas. We burn these materials as fuels in vehicles and power plants—activities that release carbon dioxide and contribute to climate change.

An oil rig off the coast of California. We drill down to extract fossil fuels buried deep in Earth's crust.

HOW FOSSILS FORM

Countless billions of plants and animals have lived and died on Earth, but only the lucky few get turned into fossils—and even fewer get dug up and discovered! For a living thing to become a fossil, the conditions must be just right. Otherwise they'll decompose, with their bodies broken down into different substances and lost forever.

These fossilized prehistoric ferns have preserved the minute detail of the stems and leaves to show us what these ancient plants looked like.

DYING IN THE RIGHT PLACE

It doesn't take long for a dead body to rot away. The soft tissues, such as skin and muscles, will go first, leaving harder parts such as bones and beaks behind. Even those will eventually decompose. But if the remains are covered over quickly, blocking the oxygen needed for decomposition, they can last long enough to be fossilized. For land plants and animals, this often happens near lakes or rivers, where a flood can cover their remains in mud or silt.

Most dinosaur fossils are of animals that lived near water, like these *Triceratops* would have done, 66 million years ago in North America.

FOSSILIZATION

Once an animal skeleton or plant is buried, mineral-rich water begins to seep in. Over time, these minerals gradually replace the organic materials in the remains. They form mineral crystals within spaces in the bones. At the same time, more and more layers of sediment are piling up on top. The pressure this creates together with reactions with fluids, hardens the material below, forming sedimentary rock. The fossil is trapped within the layers of rock. Depending on conditions, it takes at least 10,000 years for fossils to form, and even longer for them to be discovered!

This diagram shows how, over time, dinosaur bones became buried between layers of rock and soil, sinking deeper below ground.

COMING TO THE SURFACE

Many fossils stay buried forever, never to be found, especially those that formed beneath the ocean floor. However, sometimes tectonic plate movements can push areas of rock up to the surface. Rock can also be pushed up when new igneous rock forms below it, or when heavy ice sheets melt. Once rocks are near the surface, they will weather and erode over time, which may expose any fossils hidden inside.

Fossils of complete skeletons, such as this *Seymouria*, are rare and excavating them from the surrounding rock is delicate work.

FINDING FOSSILS

Dinosaur fossils may be the most famous, but the vast majority of fossils that scientists find are from animals that lived in the sea, such as shellfish and sharks. This is because the ocean floor is covered in sand and other sediments, so bodies can be covered over quickly. These fossils often wash up onto beaches. Another good place to look for fossils is recently exposed outcrops. But stick to sedimentary rock—fossils in igneous or metamorphic rocks are extremely rare!

This fossil shows the curved shell of an extinct tentacled sea creature called an ammonite that lived about 200–66 million years ago.

SOFT REMAINS

Very occasionally, the soft body parts of a prehistoric creature can be preserved, such as in the Burgess Shale area of Canada. Found high in the Rocky Mountains, this area has preserved some of Earth's oldest marine life, dating from over 500 million years ago. It is believed that these creatures were buried in an underwater avalanche of fine mud that quickly preserved the structure of their body parts.

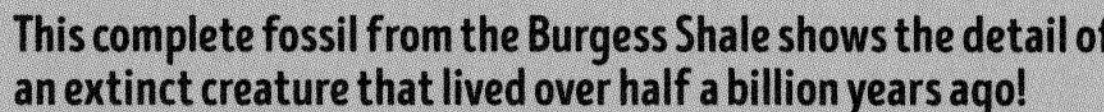

This complete fossil from the Burgess Shale shows the detail of an extinct creature that lived over half a billion years ago!

ROCK DETECTIVES

Anyone can look at rocks and pick them up. But it takes a geologist to really understand their properties and how they formed. Geologists are scientists who study the materials that make up Earth. They also research the processes that have changed our planet over millions of years. They investigate our past, using rocks as clues—they're rock detectives!

A geologist monitors an eruptive vent at the top of Mount Etna in Sicily, Italy. Studies like this help us to predict future eruptions and what their impact might be.

IN THE FIELD

Geologists often work in the field, where they measure and map landscapes and collect samples. They might use simple tools such as hammers, picks, magnifiers, and rock-testing kits. Many geologists also use more complicated equipment, such as drills to dig down and take samples of rocks deep underground, or ground-penetrating radar that can "see" structures below the surface, without the need to dig.

This geologist is working in the remote outback of Australia, examining an outcrop of iron-rich rock.

SU SONG (1020–1101)

Su Song was a Chinese government official with a keen interest in science. He studied the movement of the stars and built a complicated early clock. Su Song was also interested in the natural world, and with a team of scholars he wrote a book about the use of minerals, plants, and animals in medicine. He studied ores and crystals and wrote descriptions of many different minerals, such as realgar (see page 121).

WE NEED GEOLOGISTS!

The work of geologists is incredibly useful—it's much more than just cataloging pretty rocks! We rely on geologists to keep people safe by monitoring volcanoes, measuring earthquakes, and tracking fault lines. They help find underground deposits of useful minerals for mining, along with oil and gas. Geologists also study the soil and areas of underground water, and help us to manage these important resources.

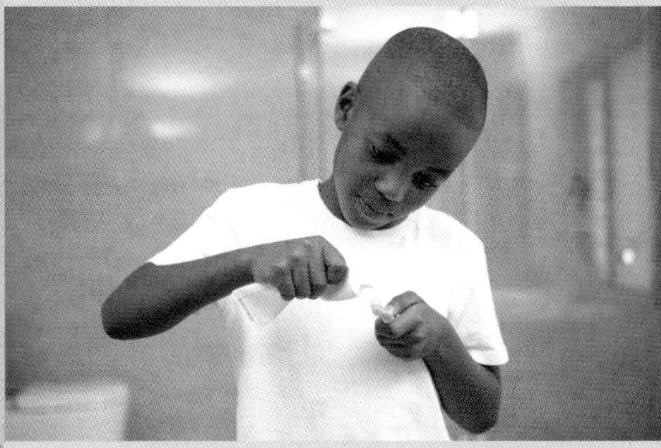

Geologists find useful minerals, such as fluorite. This produces the fluoride added to toothpaste to help strengthen teeth.

IN THE LABORATORY

Collecting samples is just the first step. Many geologists learn more about them by working in laboratories, using microscopes and chemical methods to study rock and mineral samples. They also use tools for testing the strength of different rocks. Geologists make use of computers and specialist software to create detailed maps of Earth's structure. They also create digital models to show how processes such as earthquakes and mountain forming work.

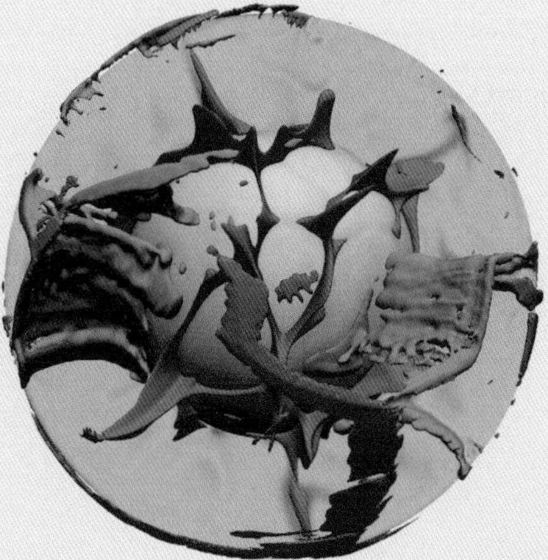

This computer simulation shows the movement of cold, dense rocks sinking into the mantle (blue) and hot, low density rocks rising from the core (red).

PALEONTOLOGY

Paleontology is similar to geology, but these scientists study the remains of prehistoric living things, mainly fossils. Because fossils are usually embedded in rock, and are mainly made up of minerals, paleontologists use many of the same tools and techniques as geologists do. They carefully extract fossils from rock and take them back to the laboratory to study, helping us learn more about ancient life on Earth.

QUARRYING, MINING, AND SMELTING

High-quality marble has been extracted from the quarries of Carrara in northern Italy since Roman times.

Rocks and minerals are important resources—we use them every day. Once geologists have found a deposit of useful rocks or minerals in Earth's crust, we need to extract them and convert them to a form that we can use. Different processes have been developed over the centuries that allow us to make use of Earth's most valuable resources.

QUARRYING

A quarry is a place where people dig down into the ground to remove rocks and minerals, from crushed sand to large blocks of stone. People have been quarrying rock for thousands of years, and archaeologists have found quarries used by the ancient Egyptians, Romans, and Chinese. Once gunpowder was invented in the 9th century, people used it to blast the rock. Now modern saws, drills, and cranes allow quarriers to extract even bigger blocks.

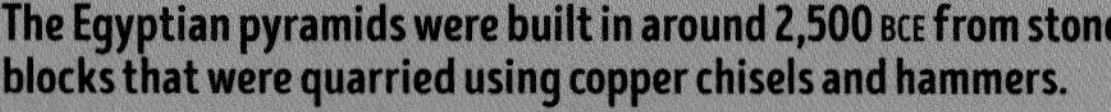

The Egyptian pyramids were built in around 2,500 BCE from stone blocks that were quarried using copper chisels and hammers.

MINING

Quarrying takes rocks from the surface, but to find some minerals you need to go deep underground. Miners tunnel into the earth, looking for valuable resources such as coal, diamonds, gold, or ores. They dig with machines and hand tools, following layers or veins of useful minerals within the rock. Mines often have railways or lifts to carry materials to the surface. Even with modern equipment, mining is dangerous work.

A miner uses a head torch to examine the rockface of a coal mine in Pennsylvania.

DREDGING

Sometimes the rocks you want are not underground, but underwater! Dredging is the process of retrieving material from the ocean floor, or from river beds or lake beds. Sometimes people dredge these areas to modify the water flow, build dams and harbors, or clear space for ships. But dredging is also a way of gathering sand, gravel, or mineral deposits. Unfortunately, dredging can disturb marine ecosystems and harm the plants and animals that live there.

This dredging ship sucks up material like a vacuum. Excess water flows through an overflow pipe back into the sea.

SMELTING

Once ore is mined, we still need to extract the valuable minerals and elements locked up inside it. The process of extracting metals from ore is called smelting, and it involves heating the ore by enough to melt the metal within. Ancient people learned to smelt copper around 7,000 years ago, followed by tin, lead, silver, and iron. Today we use modern equipment and chemical reactions to smelt and refine a wide range of metals.

Ores are smelted at temperatures of up to 2,500 °F (1,370 °C) in this iron and steel factory.

KARL JOSEF BAYER (1847–1904)

Aluminum is strong but lightweight, making it incredibly useful. There is plenty of it in Earth's crust, but it was so hard to extract from its ore that for a time it was more expensive than gold! Then, in 1888, the Austrian chemist Karl Josef Bayer patented an efficient process for producing aluminum oxide from the ore bauxite. Around the same time, two other chemists—Hall and Héroult—developed a way to extract pure aluminum from aluminum oxide.

HOW WE USE ROCKS

You may not realize it, but you use rocks and minerals every day. From the graphite "lead" in your pencil to the clay used to make the plates and bowls you eat from, rocks and minerals are everywhere! Throughout human history we have come up with better and more efficient ways to use rocks and minerals, and these materials continue to play an important part in our daily lives.

A selection of clay pots from Pakistan. The clay we use to make pots, vases, and crockery is formed by the chemical weathering of rocks containing feldspar.

BUILDINGS

Stone is a great building material for homes and other buildings. It's strong and hard-wearing, and has been used for many thousands of years. As well as the large stones used in walls, crushed stone can be used to make concrete, and sand can be melted to make glass for windows. Minerals such as gypsum are used in plaster and plasterboard, and kitchen worktops are often made of hard stones such as granite.

Stone is extremely durable. King's College Chapel in Cambridge, UK, was completed in 1515 and still stands today.

METALS

The metals that we extract from rocky ores have a huge variety of uses, from forming the outer bodies of vehicles to the interior structures of skyscrapers. Inside buildings, metal pipes carry water and gas, and copper wiring carries electricity. We pay for things with metal coins and eat our food with metal cutlery. Metals are also important components in electronic devices such as computers and smartphones.

The strong but lightweight frames for buildings are made from metals such as steel or aluminum.

ART AND JEWELRY

Many rocks and minerals are beautiful, especially in their crystal form. Cleaning, cutting, and polishing them can get them looking their best. People make gemstones and precious metals into jewelry. Artists carve stunning sculptures from rocks such as marble, as well as other minerals such as alabaster and soapstone. Other minerals are ground to a powder and used as colored pigments for making paints for artists.

Many rocks and minerals are beautiful as well as durable. These diamond rings are set with a sapphire, a ruby, and an emerald.

ROADS AND BRIDGES

Gravel, made up of small rocks, forms the base of road surfaces and also supports railway tracks. It also makes an easy and effective covering for driveways, paths, and gardens. One of the most common materials used for building roads, bridges, and other large structures is concrete. It's made from small stones or sand bound together with cement made from limestone and other minerals.

The ancient Romans used rocks for their roads, such as this one in Pompeii, Italy, built over 2,000 years ago.

Without kaolinite, we wouldn't have the glossy paper we use to print photographs, books, and magazines.

INGREDIENTS

Minerals are used as ingredients in lots of everyday products. In many cases, the minerals are ground to a powder before being added to other materials. For example, there is ground-up talc in many cosmetics, as well as paint. The mineral kaolinite is used for making glossy paper and cat litter, and gypsum is used in medicines, porcelain, and some baked goods. And don't forget halite, better known as salt—it's a very common ingredient indeed!

ROCKS AROUND THE WORLD

It's taken billions of years for our planet to take on the form that we know and recognize today. Over time, tectonic plates have moved and shifted, coming together to form continents and then breaking apart. Ocean levels have risen to create vast inland seas, and fallen to reveal the land beneath. But amid all this movement, there are some particularly strong and stable parts of the continental crust that we call cratons. These form the base of all continents and contain their oldest rocks.

ALL CHANGE

Earth is about 4.5 billion years old, but the version of it that appears on maps and globes is much, much younger. Most dinosaurs became extinct at the end of the Cretaceous Period, about 66 million years ago—and that's actually pretty recent when you compare it to the age of the planet. But even then, the continents weren't quite in their current shapes or positions. India, for example, hadn't yet collided with the rest of Asia, and Australia was still in the process of splitting apart from Antarctica.

At the end of the Cretaceous Period, North and South America weren't connected. They came together about 3 million years ago, separating the Atlantic and Pacific oceans.

A stunning coastline in Lefkada, Greece, showing steep limestone cliffs. Earth's landscape continues to change over millions of years as continents move and sea levels shift.

Any modern map is just a snapshot in time. These seven continents were once all joined and may come together again in the future.

TRULY UNIQUE?

Because the continents were once connected, geologists have discovered many similarities in their rocks. However, each continent has its own geology, and there are some minerals that are found only in certain places. Each continent also has its own spectacular landforms and unique weather conditions. Although canyons, cliffs, and arches form in similar ways, each one has its own story to tell. This chapter will take you on a tour of the most amazing natural sights that each continent has to offer.

ROCK FORMATIONS

Earth's geologic history is a never-ending story of new rocks being formed while older rocks are either worn away or melted down. Rivers, winds, and glaciers have scoured the landscape, carving deep canyons and valleys, and sculpting rocks into weird and wonderful shapes. Many of the unusual formations that tourists visit today are the result of millions of years of slow, gradual change.

Delicate Arch in Utah began to form around 65 million years ago. Erosion and weathering continue to change the landscape, so it won't last forever.

NORTH AMERICA

North America has some of the oldest rocks on the planet—more than 4 billion years old—which now lie in an area called the Canadian Shield. Gradually, other rocks collided and joined with this mass of rock to form the continent we know today. Long mountain ranges were pushed up on each side when tectonic plates collided, forcing the rock to push upward—creating the Appalachians in the east and the Rockies in the west.

The Rocky Mountains are the longest mountain range in North America stretching 3,000 miles (4,800 km) from northern Canada to the southern United States. Among the towering peaks are valleys and lakes carved out by rivers and glaciers, such as Saint Mary Lake Glacier National Park, Montana, shown here.

10
GREENLAND
ALASKA
Canadian Shield
CANADA
1
2
3
Rocky Mountains
Morrison Formation
4
5
6
7
UNITED STATES
Appalachian Mountains
MEXICO
9
8
CENTRAL AMERICA

OCEANS AND ICE SHEETS

Even once North America took on a recognizable shape, it didn't always look like it does now. During the time of the dinosaurs in the Mesozoic Era (251–65 million years ago), a large, shallow sea cut through the middle of the continent. More recently, starting about 2.5 million years ago, huge sheets of ice covered its northern half.

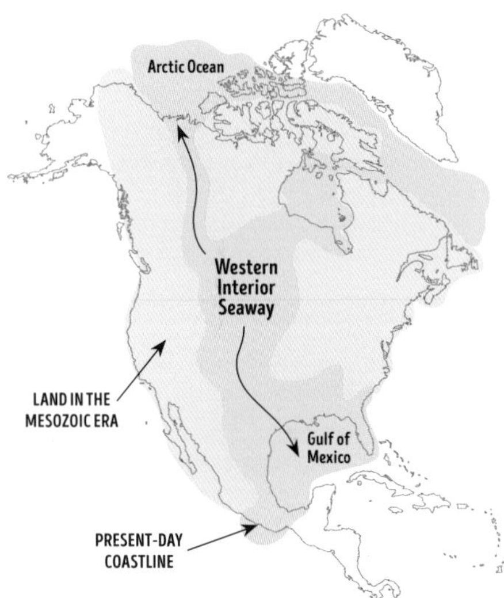

When the dinosaurs roamed Earth, North America was divided in two by the Western Interior Seaway.

The continent of North America began as the Canadian Shield but it now stretches from Greenland in the north to Central America in the south. The Appalachian Mountains date back more than 480 million years, while the Rocky Mountains are quite young and only formed around 55–80 million years ago.

1 ROCHER-PERCÉ

Meaning "pierced rock," this limestone and shale formation (see pages 107–108) stands in the Gulf of Saint Lawrence in Québec. The rock is almost 295 ft (90 m) high and 1,545 ft (471 m) long. It features a natural arch big enough for a boat to sail through. Until 1845, there were two arches, both carved out by the ocean waves. The collapsed arch used to connect the smaller column on the right to the main rock.

2 HOPEWELL ROCKS

Over thousands of years, the huge tides in Canada's Bay of Fundy have carved sedimentary rock into more than 20 free-standing sea stacks. The bases are narrower than the tops because they are still covered at low tide, causing further erosion. The trees and other plants growing at the top give this site its nickname, the "Flowerpot Rocks."

3 CRATER LAKE

The clear blue waters of Crater Lake in Oregon are famous with tourists and photographers. This beautiful lake—the deepest in the USA—formed in a crater left behind when the volcano Mount Mazama collapsed. A volcanic cinder cone known as Wizard Island can be seen poking out of the water. The crater is about 5.5 miles (9 km) wide, and no rivers flow into the lake, so all the water comes from rain or snowfall.

4 DEVILS TOWER

A huge tower of rock thrusts up from the surrounding land in northeastern Wyoming, USA, as made famous by the 1977 film *Close Encounters of the Third Kind*. Known as Devils Tower, this rock has fluted sides and a flat top the size of a football field. It formed when magma pushed up into layers of sedimentary rock, hardening into igneous rock. Much later, when the sedimentary rock eroded, the harder igneous rock remained.

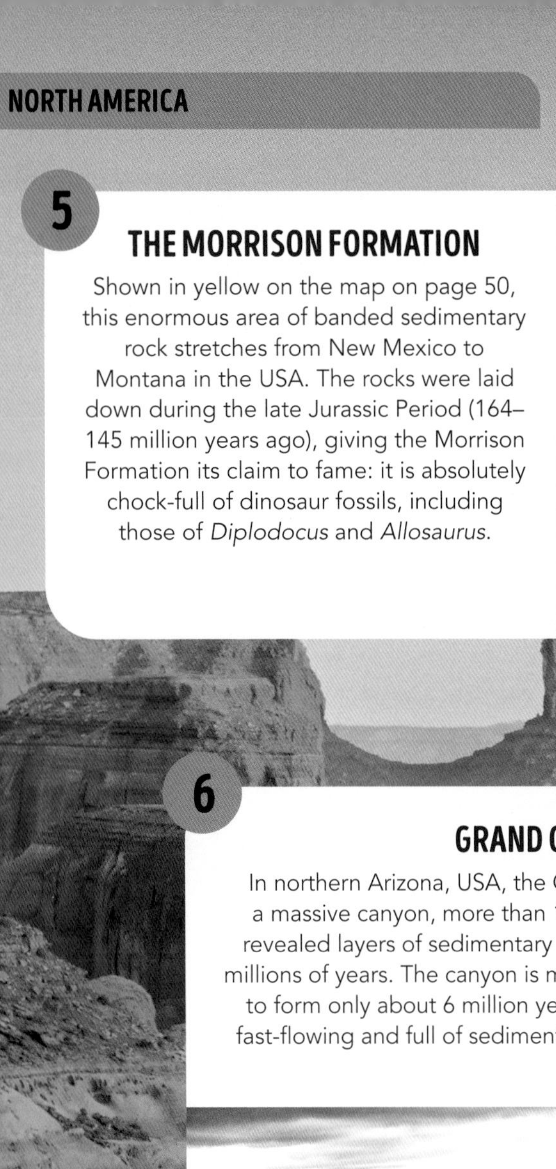

5

THE MORRISON FORMATION

Shown in yellow on the map on page 50, this enormous area of banded sedimentary rock stretches from New Mexico to Montana in the USA. The rocks were laid down during the late Jurassic Period (164–145 million years ago), giving the Morrison Formation its claim to fame: it is absolutely chock-full of dinosaur fossils, including those of *Diplodocus* and *Allosaurus*.

THE BONE WARS

In the late 19th century, a fierce rivalry grew between two paleontologists—Edward Drinker Cope (1840–1897), above, and Othniel Charles Marsh (1831–1899), below. The Morrison Foundation became their excavation battleground. Both men raced to be the first to discover new species and, between them, over 130 new dinosaurs were identified. Many of these are the famous dinosaurs we know so much about today, such as *Stegosaurus* and *Triceratops*.

6

GRAND CANYON

In northern Arizona, USA, the Colorado River has carved out a massive canyon, more than 1.1 miles (1.8 km) deep. It has revealed layers of sedimentary rocks dating back hundreds of millions of years. The canyon is much younger though—it started to form only about 6 million years ago. The river waters were fast-flowing and full of sediment, which scraped away the rock.

7

PETRIFIED FOREST

In the Petrified Forest of Arizona, what look like fallen logs are scattered across the desert ground. They are the remains of trees that grew during the Triassic Period (252–201 million years ago). When the trees died and fell, they were buried. Over time the organic matter was replaced by minerals such as quartz, which kept the shape of the original tree, forming solid rock.

Monument Valley is close to the east rim of the Grand Canyon National Park in Arizona. Its iconic landscape is dominated by giant towering sandstone features that were formed over millions of years by weathering and erosion.

8 HIERVE EL AGUA

It looks like a waterfall plunging off a cliff in southern Mexico, but a closer look shows that the "water" is actually a type of limestone called travertine (see page 109). These falls formed when hot springs bubbled up through cracks in the rocks. The water was saturated with calcium carbonate (the chemical compound that makes up limestone), and, as it ran down the rock face, the minerals hardened into rock.

9 CENOTES

Mexico's state of Yucatán is home to thousands of water-filled sinkholes called cenotes. These form when naturally acidic rain filters down through limestone, dissolving the rock. Over thousands of years, this process carves out huge caves and underground rivers. The caves fill with water and sometimes the top collapses, leaving a hole. With some cenotes, the entire roof has collapsed, so they look like ponds. In others, there is only a small hole leading down to a water-filled cavern.

10 FJORDS OF GREENLAND

It can be hard to see Greenland's rocks—Earth's largest island is largely covered with a thick sheet of ice and snow. But its coastlines are marked by stunning, steep-sided fjords. These landforms are narrow sea inlets that formed when glaciers cut U-shaped valleys in the island's rocks. After the glaciers melted, the sea flooded the channel they had gouged out to create beautiful fjords.

HOW WE USE IT

CATLINITE

Catlinite is a sedimentary rock found only in North America, made from layers of mud. It's brownish-red and soft enough to be easily carved, and it polishes to a smooth, buttery texture. For several hundred years, Native Americans quarried the stone and used it to make ceremonial pipes.

A Native American pipe carved from catlinite in the early 1800s. Catlinite is often known as 'pipestone'.

SOUTH AMERICA

Like all the continents, South America formed from a collection of stable blocks of crust rock called cratons. Five cratons make up the core of the continent, arranged roughly in a line going north to south. Over millions of years, they were joined by other blocks of crust. South America is like a bowl—raised at the edges and shallower and flatter in the middle. Areas where rocks have been pushed up include the Brazilian Highlands in the east, the Guiana Highlands in the north, and the "younger" Andes tower along the west coast.

This glacial lake lies in the Andes of Chile. The Andes is the longest continental mountain range on Earth, extending 4,350 miles (7,000 km) along South America's west coast. The Andes began forming around 30–20 million years ago, as the Nazca oceanic plate subducted beneath the South American continental plate.

LAND OF RICHES

South America has many natural resources, but its geology is behind one of the most important: gemstones! Brazil produces a greater variety of gemstones than any other country in the world. Prospectors mine for diamonds, emeralds, amethyst, aquamarine, tourmaline, topaz, and a green stone called amazonite. Many of these gemstones formed deep underground in rocks called pegmatites.

These beautiful gemstones come from Minas Gerais, a state in southeastern Brazil.

About 50–30 million years ago, Antarctica broke away from South America at a rate of about 1/10 inch a year to form a separate continent. Then about 3 million years ago, a small strip of land formed to connect what is now Colombia with North America.

1 TEPUIS

The landscape of northern South America is dotted with tepuis. These steep-sided, flat-topped mountains have a name meaning "house of the gods" in the language of the local people. They are all that remains of a large sandstone plateau that once covered the area. Over time, the sandstone eroded, leaving the tepuis behind. The animals and plants that live at their tops are completely isolated from the species on the ground below. One of the largest, Mount Roraima (shown below) has cliffs up to 3,300 ft (1,000 m) tall.

HOW WE USE IT

AMETHYST

This beautiful purple stone takes its name from the Greek *amethustos* meaning "not drunk." This is because the ancient Greeks believed that wearing it or drinking from an amethyst cup could protect you from the effects of alcohol. For many centuries, these gemstones were as rare and expensive as diamonds and rubies. Then, huge deposits of amethyst were found in Brazil, which lowered the price and meant that more people could afford it.

This large geode, found in Brazil, is full of amethyst crystals.

2 ANGEL FALLS

Deep in the jungle highlands of Venezuela, a tall tepui rises from the forest floor, and over its side plunges the world's tallest waterfall. The waters of Angel Falls drop for 3,212 ft (979 m)—more than three times the height of France's Eiffel Tower! At roughly the size of Greater London, the tepui's flat top is big enough for a river to cross it, carving out a valley before plunging over the side. The Falls are named after Jimmie Angel (1899–1956), an American aviator and explorer, who spotted them while flying over the area in 1933.

3 CHIMBORAZO

This snow-covered volcano in Ecuador towers over the surrounding landscape. And depending on how you measure it, it's Earth's tallest mountain! At a height of 20,561 ft (6,267 m) above sea level, it's quite a bit shorter than Mount Everest. But it's very close to the Equator. Our planet's rotation creates a noticeable bulge along the Equator, so the highest point of Chimborazo is farther from the center of Earth than Everest's peak!

4 VINICUNCA

The name of this mountain comes from the local Quechua language and means "colored mountain." It's not hard to see why! A range of about a dozen different minerals in Vinicunca's rocks give its slopes vivid, rainbow-like stripes of color. Until fairly recently, the mountain's slopes were covered in snow that concealed its bright colors, but the snow has disappeared due to climate change—good for tourists, but bad for the environment.

5 SALAR DE UYUNI

High in the Andes of southwest Bolivia, a vast plain of glittering white salt stretches for miles, reflecting the blue sky. This is the Salar de Uyuni, the world's largest salt flat, which covers an area about the size of New Jersey. It's all that remains of a prehistoric lake that evaporated, leaving its salt behind to form a flat, brittle crust. The salt often cracks into hexagonal shapes, and this otherworldly landscape has been used as a location for several films.

Seen here in northern Argentina, the mountains of the Altiplano-Puna form second-highest plateau on Earth. The plateau also stretches across western Bolivia, northern Chile, and central and southern Peru.

6 VALLE DE LA LUNA

With a name meaning "Valley of the Moon," this beautiful landscape does look very alien with little in the way of vegetation. Located in the Atacama Desert, one of the driest places on the planet, it's an area of rock and sand that have been carved into shapes by the actions of wind and water. In fact, scientists have used the valley's dry and barren landscape to test out the prototype for a Mars rover!

7 SERRANÍA DE HORNOCAL

Argentina's Serranía de Hornocal is a mountain range that looks like a series of jagged, multicolored teeth. These mountains are part of an eroded limestone formation, and the different colors are due to minerals such as iron oxide, manganese oxide, and copper oxide. The sedimentary rocks that form it were originally laid down during the Cretaceous Period, and dinosaur fossils have been found within them.

8

CONO DE ARITA

Visitors to the Salar de Arizaro, a salt flat in northern Argentina, are often fooled by the cone-shaped rock formation that rises 400 ft (120 m) from its flat surface. At first glance it looks like one of the pyramids built by the ancient Egyptians, but the Cono de Arita has a completely natural origin—it's a small, partially formed volcanic cone. Its dark color makes it appear to float above the lighter-colored salt flats.

9

IGUAÇU FALLS

On the border of Brazil and Argentina, the Iguaçu River plunges off the high ground of the Paraná Plateau, creating a horseshoe-shaped arc of separate waterfalls nearly 2 miles (3 km) long. The river has exploited weaknesses in the rock caused by tectonic faults, and three layers of volcanic basalt rock give the falls a staircase shape. The noise and spray produced by the huge amount of water tumbling down the falls are truly awe-inspiring.

10

SUGARLOAF MOUNTAIN

The conical shape of Sugarloaf Mountain stands at the mouth of Guanabara Bay in Rio de Janeiro, Brazil. This 1,300-ft (396-m) block of gneiss takes its name from its shape, which resembles the pressed loaf shapes that white sugar used to be sold in. It formed underground, probably squeezing into and pushing apart sedimentary layers. Later it was pushed up to the surface while the softer sedimentary layers eroded away leaving just the gneiss.

11

MARBLE CAVES

General Carrera Lake lies across the border of Chile and Argentina, and the stunning Marble Caves are carved out of deposits of marble near the shoreline. This marble was once sedimentary rock formed from the remains of prehistoric sea creatures. Over many years, the movement of the lake's waters carved the marble into pillars and smooth, sweeping shapes. Light reflects off the blue water to paint them in dazzling colors.

AFRICA

The modern continent of Africa is based on a core of five ancient cratons, or blocks of crust rock, that formed more than 2 billion years ago. In the time since then, belts of younger rock have been folded and pushed up to form mountains. Like all continents, Africa has seen great change. At times, parts of it were covered with shallow seas and glaciers—even the Sahara was once hidden by ice!

Although the vast Sahara Desert is best known for its towering sand dunes, most of its landscape is rocky like these sandstone cliffs in Algeria. About 50 to 100 million years ago, a shallow sea covered the region. Scientists have found fossils of marine life that once lived here.

Africa separated from South America about 76 million years ago, when the South Atlantic Ocean was opened up by seafloor spreading. The island of Madagascar was separated from the mainland about 65 million years ago.

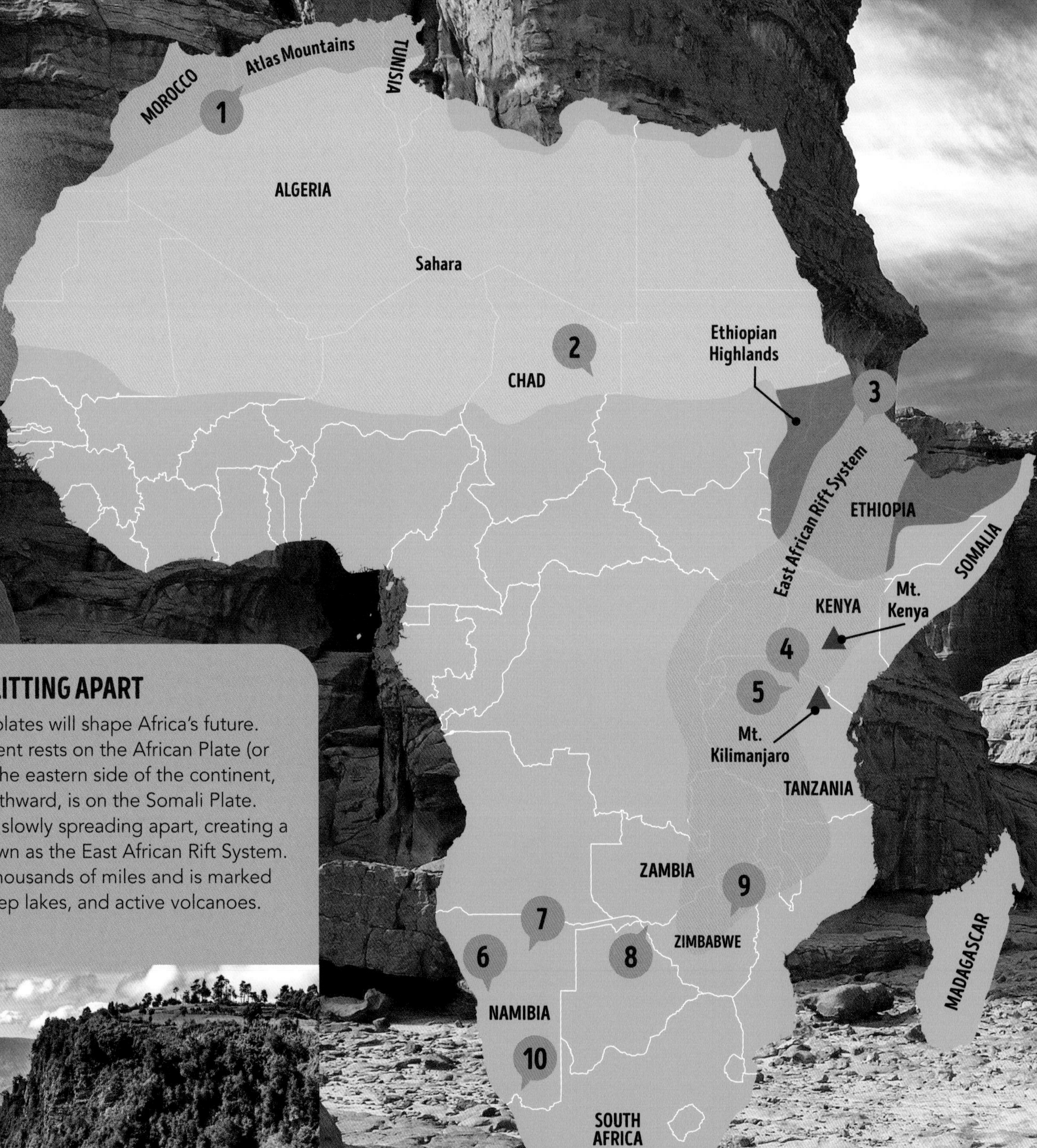

SPLITTING APART

Moving tectonic plates will shape Africa's future. Most of the continent rests on the African Plate (or Nubian Plate), but the eastern side of the continent, from Somalia southward, is on the Somali Plate. These two plates are slowly spreading apart, creating a system of cracks known as the East African Rift System. This stretches for thousands of miles and is marked by steep cliffs, deep lakes, and active volcanoes.

Part of the East African Rift System in Kenya. As the plates move apart, in 5–10 million years Africa could be split in two.

1 ATLAS MOUNTAINS

The Atlas Mountains run for more than 1,200 miles (2,000 km) through Tunisia, Algeria, and Morocco, marking the northwestern edge of the Sahara from the Mediterranean Sea to the Atlantic Ocean—in fact, the Atlantic takes its name from these mountains! They are actually a series of linked mountain ranges. The oldest parts of the southern section are about 300 million years old, while the northern section began to form about 65 million years ago.

2 ENNEDI MASSIF

Also known as the Ennedi Plateau, this region in northeast Chad is part of the Sahara Desert. It's a huge sandstone plateau that has been eroded and carved into a labyrinth of weird rock shapes. Springs and pools in its shaded gorges provide much-needed water for the animals and plants that live there, and for the nomadic herders who pass through. Rock paintings spanning a period of thousands of years show how the region's climate has gradually become drier.

3 DANAKIL DEPRESSION

Located in Ethiopia, the Danakil Depression is one of the strangest landscapes on Earth. This low-lying region lies over a spot where three tectonic plates are slowly spreading apart. This allows heat and minerals from the mantle to reach the surface. There are active volcanoes, lakes of glowing lava, and hot springs that have been dyed green, yellow, and other colors by the minerals in their waters.

HOW WE USE IT

TANZANITE

Africa is famous for diamonds, which are found in the kimberlite rock that forms vertical "pipes" in many places in Africa, as well as around the world. However, there's a different precious mineral that is only found in one part of Africa. Tanzanite is a variety of the mineral zoisite. It is prized as a gemstone with its beautiful blue-violet color caused by small amounts of the element vanadium. It is named after its country of origin, Tanzania.

Tanzanite is highly prized due to its rarity and the way it appears to change color when it reflects light.

4 OLDUVAI GORGE

Located in Tanzania, this long, steep-sided ravine is part of the East African Rift System. Digging through the different layers of rock in the gorge, as seen in this natural butte (see page 32), is like traveling back in time. The layers are about 300 ft (90 m) deep in total and cover a period from about 2.1 million to 15,000 years ago. It is here that scientists found the remains of some of our oldest human ancestors.

5 NGORONGORO CRATER

Tanzania's immense Ngorongoro Crater is what remains of the rim of an ancient volcano. The crater is what's known as a caldera, formed when a large volcano's cone collapsed in on itself after a huge eruption a few million years ago. In places, the crater is nearly 12 miles (20 km) across, and the lush plains within its rim are home to huge numbers of animals including zebra, wildebeest, and buffalo.

Africa's highest mountain, Kilimanjaro, rises from the plains of Tanzania. This dormant volcano hasn't erupted for more than 150,000 years. Its peak was once covered in glaciers, but these are shrinking rapidly due to climate change.

6 SPITZKOPPE

With a name meaning "pointed dome," the Spitzkoppe is one of the most recognized landforms in Namibia. This huge granite dome formed around 120 million years ago as part of an ancient range of volcanoes. It was later buried by sediment that was eventually worn away. Spitzkoppe is a good example of an inselberg (see page 33)—an isolated hill or mountain that has resisted the weathering and erosion of the surrounding plain. The highest peak rises more than 700 m (2,300 ft) above the surrounding land, and the rocks are a popular destination for climbers.

7 HOBA METEORITE

Namibia is home to the largest intact meteorite ever found on Earth. At about 10 ft (3 m) across, it's so big and heavy that it still rests where it landed, about 80,000 years ago. When the Hoba Meteorite was discovered in 1920, only the top part was visible, but farmers soon dug out the rest of it. The meteorite is mainly made of iron and there is no crater surrounding it, so it was likely traveling fairly slowly when it landed.

8 VICTORIA FALLS

On the border between Zambia and Zimbabwe, the Zambezi River plummets over the edge of a basalt plateau and into a deep chasm carved out by water. This is Victoria Falls, the world's largest waterfall in terms of the amount of water that goes over it. At its widest, the falls are more than 1 mile (1.6 km) wide. Because of the noise and spray created by the falling water, it's known as "the smoke that thunders" in the local Sotho language.

9 BALANCING ROCKS

In the Matobo Hills of Zimbabwe, huge boulders balance on top of each other, as though placed there by a giant. But these formations are completely natural! The Matobo Hills are made of granite, and over many years the rock has weathered and eroded, leaving stacks of large boulders. They're a famous landmark in Zimbabwe, and some of the rocks even appear on the country's banknotes!

10 FISH RIVER CANYON

Everyone's heard of Arizona's Grand Canyon, but the Fish River Canyon in Namibia is just as spectacular, even if it only gets a fraction of the visitors! This canyon began to form about 500 million years ago, when a shift in tectonic plates created a deep valley. Erosion and moving glaciers deepened it, and then—starting about 50 million years ago—the Fish River began to carve its way into the valley floor.

11 TABLE MOUNTAIN

It's not hard to see how Table Mountain got its name! This flat-topped mountain towers over Table Bay and the city of Cape Town in South Africa. It's made up of horizontal sandstone layers that once formed the floor of a valley, before being pushed upward. At the top is a fertile plateau, and when the wind comes in from the southeast it forms its very own cloud cover, known as the "Tablecloth."

EUROPE

From a geologist's point of view, Europe is not a continent at all! It's connected to Asia, and the two share the same tectonic plate. Because of this, they are sometimes considered to be a single continent called 'Eurasia'. It was Greek explorers and writers who first divided this vast land into two separate units, based on cultural differences. There is no official boundary where one ends and the other begins, but many people use the Ural Mountains in Russia as a guideline.

Europe has a long and complex coastline with many peninsulas. Here you can see the golden limestone and red clay cliffs of Praia da Rocha in the Algarve, Portugal.

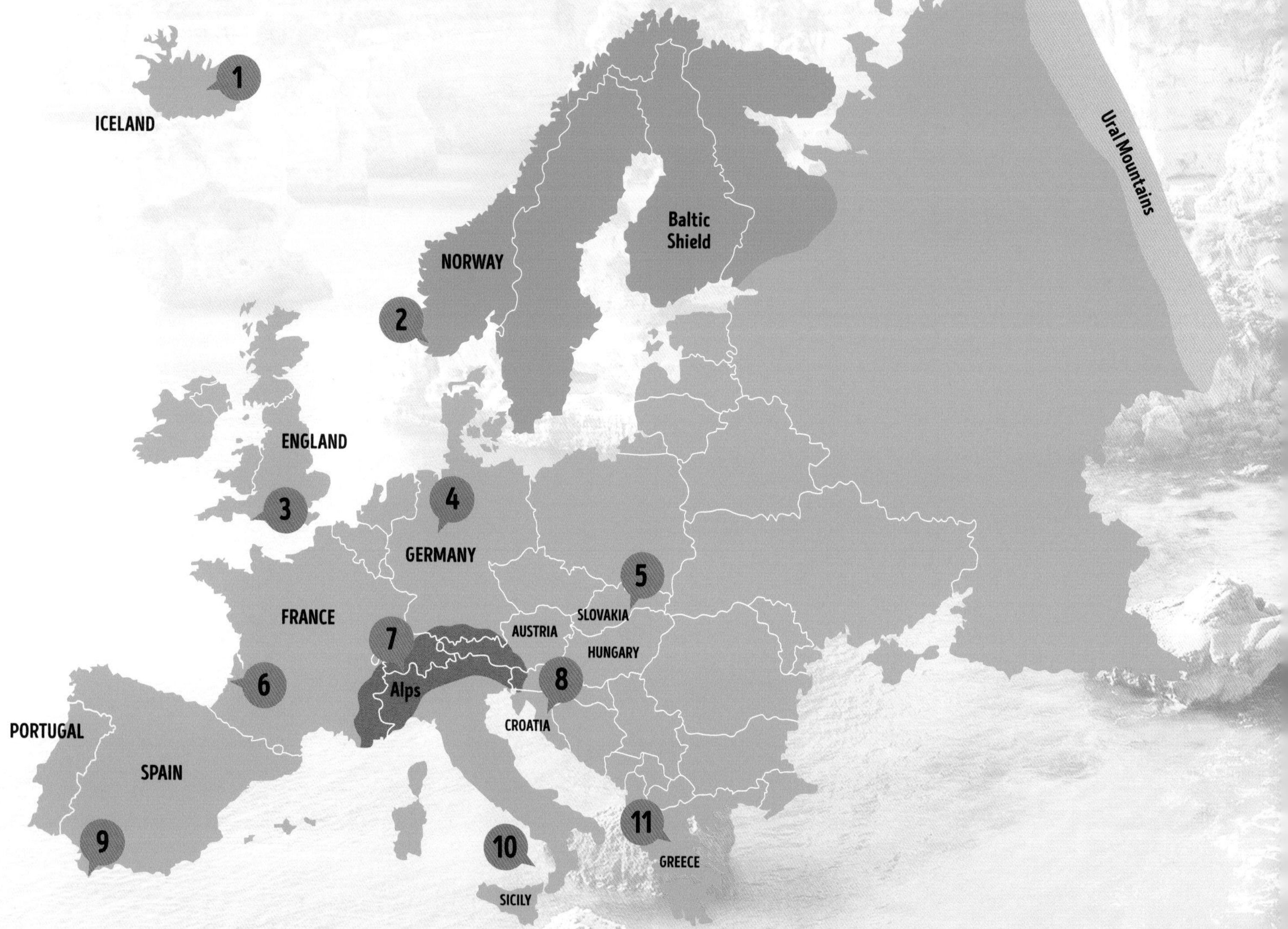

1 ICELAND
Ural Mountains
Baltic Shield
NORWAY
2
ENGLAND
3
4
GERMANY
5
SLOVAKIA
FRANCE
7
AUSTRIA
HUNGARY
6
Alps
8
CROATIA
PORTUGAL
SPAIN
9
10
SICILY
11
GREECE

OLD AND NEW

Europe's oldest rocks date back about 3.8 billion years, and many are found in an area called the Baltic Shield, in modern-day Scandinavia and northwestern Russia. Some of the youngest rocks are in the Alps—a mountain range in central Europe—which began to form about the time that most dinosaurs had died out. In other places, such as Iceland and some Italian islands, new rocks are still forming from volcanic lava. The continent's shape has changed over time. The British Isles, for example, only split from mainland Europe when rising sea levels separated them about 8,500 years ago.

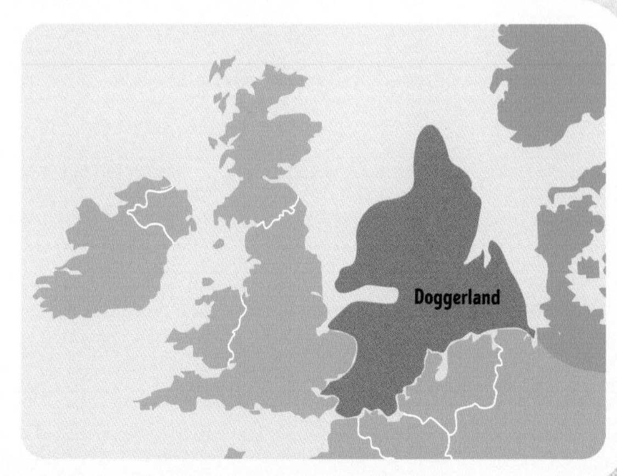

The area of land that once connected Great Britain to the mainland is called Doggerland, and fishing boats often find ancient tools and artefacts from the people who once lived there.

1 ICELAND

The volcanic island of Iceland marks the place where Europe ends and North America begins. It sits atop a divergent plate boundary, where two tectonic plates are pulling apart. This split creates cracks in the land, but they are quickly filled with fresh magma. As well as being on a plate boundary, Iceland is also above a 'hot spot', where hot mantle probably rises all the way from the boundary between Earth's core and the mantle. Iceland is a geologist's dream, with active volcanoes and lava fields alongside geysers (below) and hot springs, all heated from underground.

2 PREIKESTOLEN

With a name meaning 'Preacher's Chair', the Instagram-worthy Preikestolen has become a popular tourist attraction in Norway. This huge cliff of granite (see page 101) and gneiss (see page 112) rises hundreds of metres above a fjord, topping out in a large flat rock platform. However, its days may be numbered—a wide crack that has been there for decades seems to be widening, and the entire platform may one day tumble down into the waters below.

3 LULWORTH COVE AND DURDLE DOOR

Part of the coast in southern England is known as the Jurassic Coast because it has exposed rock layers and fossils dating back to the time of the dinosaurs. The Jurassic Coast includes two features just a short walk apart. Lulworth Cove (below, top), a nearly round body of water bitten out of the coastline, formed when water broke through a crack in the stone of the coastline and eroded the softer rocks inland. Nearby is Durdle Door (below, bottom), a large limestone arch reaching out into the sea.

HOW WE USE IT

BLUE JOHN

The mineral known as blue john is only found in a small area of England, giving it the alternative name 'Derbyshire spar'. It's a rare form of fluorite that shows alternating bands of yellowish and purplish-blue colors. Scientists aren't quite sure what causes the color banding, but it's made blue john a popular stone for carving and polishing. It has often been carved into beautiful vases and goblets that show off the unique banding.

This large piece of polished blue john is a museum specimen measuring about 25 cm (10 in) across.

4

EXTERNSTEINE

In Germany's Teutoburg Forest, huge columns of sandstone reach toward the sky, standing up to 40 m (130 ft) tall. Known as the Externsteine, this formation has been a sacred site for many centuries and still attracts visitors today. The Externsteine formed when sandstone was fractured into blocks by tectonic movement. Then, over time, erosion carved the blocks into columns and other shapes.

5

AGGTELEK KARST CAVES

Europe's largest stalactite cave system is found in the Aggtelek Mountains on the border of Hungary and Slovakia. The caves formed in the last 65 million years, as underground streams carved caverns out of the limestone. There are more than 1,000 caves—some are cold enough to contain ice all year round, while others are filled with fairytale-like formations of stalactites and stalagmites.

6

DUNE DU PILAT

Most people associate sand dunes with large deserts. But on the Atlantic coast of France there is a huge dune—the largest in Europe! It rises more than 100 m (33 ft) above the shore and stretches about 3 km (2 miles). The dune formed when strong winds from the Atlantic Ocean blew sand from a nearby sandbank onto the land. These same winds are slowly blowing the dune farther inland, covering over the neighboring forests.

7

MATTERHORN

It's not the tallest of the Alps, but the Matterhorn may be the most famous peak in that range. The Matterhorn's distinctive triangular peak was shaped by glaciers that once flowed down from it in different directions. Four of them each carved out a valley called a cirque, leaving the triangular summit standing proud in the middle.

Europe's Alpine lakes, like Zeller Lake in Austria, lie in valleys that were formed during the last Ice Age, gouged out by glaciers.

8 PLITVICE LAKES

Croatia's largest national park includes caves and a string of 16 interconnected lakes, many separated by waterfalls. The rocks in this area are largely limestone, which gets dissolved by the waters running over and through it. The calcium carbonate that the waters carry away then gets deposited to form layers of travertine (see page 109). This sedimentary rock forms natural dams that separate the lakes and create the waterfalls.

9 GIBRALTAR

Near the southernmost point of Spain, a small peninsula juts out into the Mediterranean Sea. This is Gibraltar, dominated by a high ridge of limestone and shale that rises up from the land, known as the Rock of Gibraltar. Gibraltar formed from the shells of Jurassic sea creatures, which made up a layer of rock that was later pushed upward when tectonic plates shifted. The limestone is dotted with many caves, including some where early humans once lived.

10 STROMBOLI

The island of Stromboli, off the coast of Sicily, formed about 200,000 years ago in a subduction zone where one tectonic plate is subducting below another (see page 12). This caused volcanic eruptions that eventually built an island—one that is still erupting! Stromboli has erupted nearly constantly for at least 2,000 years, forcing out fountains of lava that can be seen from miles away—giving it its nickname of the 'Lighthouse of the Mediterranean'.

11 METEORA

The Meteora are a series of towering sandstone columns in northern Greece. They likely formed when a sandstone formation was uplifted, creating a plateau marked with cracks. Later weathering left the shapes that are seen today. Standing up to 550 m (1,800 ft) high, for centuries some of these columns have been the site of monasteries, where monks could live a quiet religious life.

ASIA

Asia is a record-breaker—it's Earth's largest continent in terms of area and is home to about 60 percent of the world's population. However, it's also one of the youngest continents, with new land still being created in the east and southeast. Asia has many large mountain ranges as well as active volcanoes, and earthquakes are common in many places.

Asia has a huge range of rocky landscapes, including great sweeps of desert, such as the Gobi, which stretches across parts of China and Mongolia.

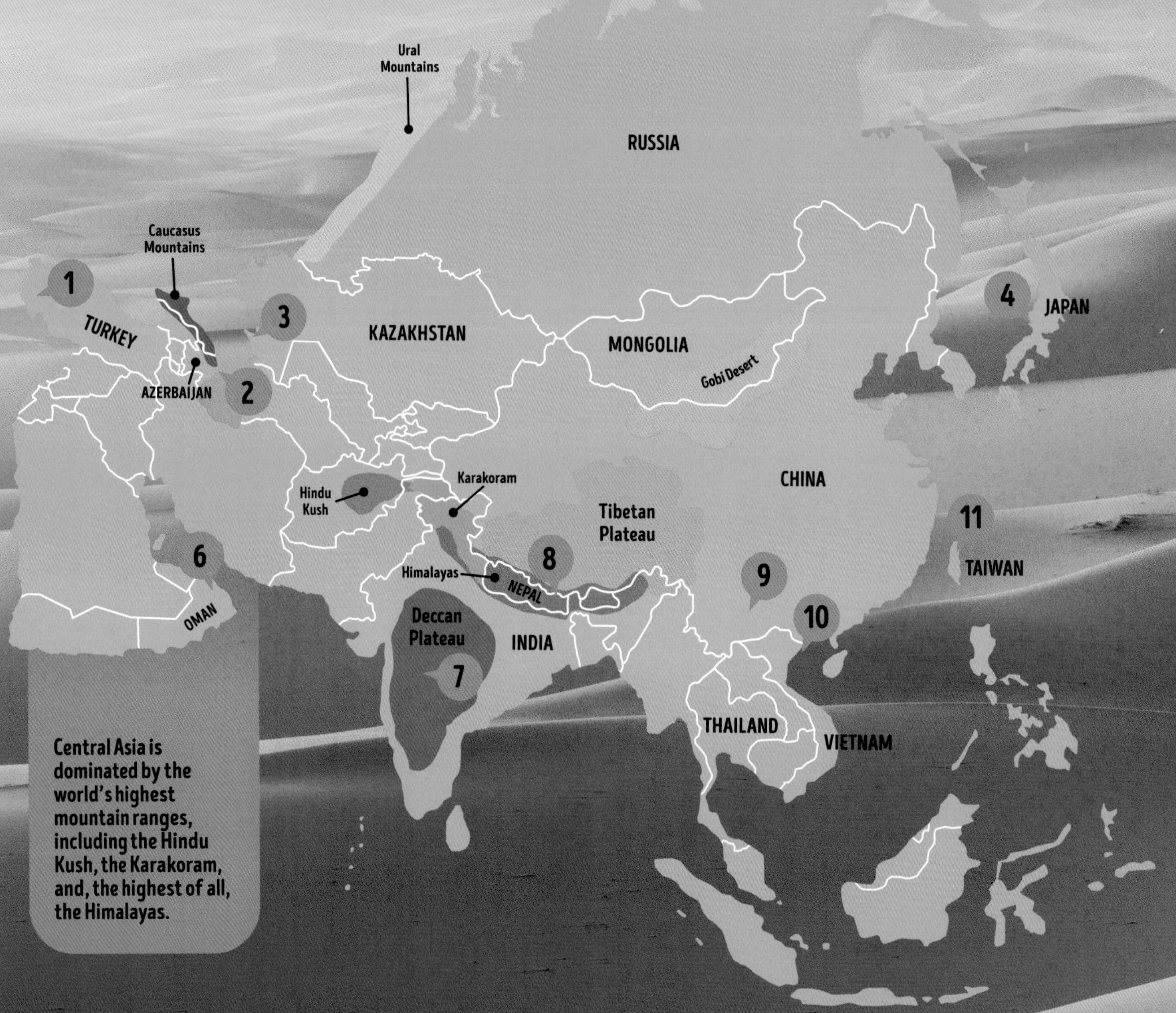

Central Asia is dominated by the world's highest mountain ranges, including the Hindu Kush, the Karakoram, and, the highest of all, the Himalayas.

The Tibetan Plateau formed as a result of the collision between India and Asia, which began about 50 million years ago.

THE ROOF OF THE WORLD

At the heart of Asia is the Tibetan Plateau, Earth's highest and largest plateau. This region covers an area more than seven times the size of Germany and is surrounded by huge mountain ranges such as the Himalayas and the Karakoram. The plateau has a harsh, rugged landscape and an average elevation of over 13,000 ft (4,000 m), but people, plants, and animals all manage to thrive here.

1

PAMUKKALE

In southwest Turkey, waters from a hot spring have created a beautiful landscape of white rocky pools filled with clear blue water. This is Pamukkale, a name that means "cotton palace" in Turkish. The spring waters are rich in calcite, and, as they flowed down the hillside, they laid down travertine rock (see page 109). Over time, this travertine built up to form the pools and petrified waterfalls we see today. People have bathed in the warm waters for thousands of years.

2

MUD VOLCANOES

Most volcanoes erupt lava, but some bubble with hot mud instead. These mud volcanoes are found around the world, but Azerbaijan has more than any other country. Mud volcanoes form when hot water underground mixes with mineral deposits, creating a runny slurry that can then be forced up through a crack in the ground. Some are cool enough to bathe in, but these volcanoes can also release methane gas, which can catch fire.

3

VALLEY OF BALLS

There is a landscape in Kazakhstan that looks like a place where giants would play marbles! The Valley of Balls is dotted with large spherical rocks, some as big as cars. Geologists don't all agree on how they formed. The rocks might have crystallized in volcanic ash, then been revealed when the surrounding rocks eroded. Or they may have been created by sediment forming layers around a hard core. We call these concretions. Whatever the cause, they look amazing!

4

TOJINBO

The rocky Tojinbo cliffs on the Japanese island of Honshu are far from being the world's tallest, but they have an interesting origin. The cliffs formed as a result of volcanic activity about 12 million years ago, when magma mixed with sedimentary rock. The rock we see today is known as a pyroxene andesite, and it has formed tall columns that have since been eroded by the waves.

Towering limestone cliffs dominate the landscape at Railay beach in Krabi, Thailand—a popular spot with rock climbers from around the world.

5

KAMCHATKA

The Kamchatka peninsula sticks out from the far northeastern edge of Russia. Three tectonic plates—the Eurasian, North American, and Pacific plates—meet here. That means that, to a geologist, Kamchatka is incredibly interesting! It's part of the "Ring of Fire" (see page 13), and its many mountains include nearly two dozen active volcanoes, as well as geysers and hot springs. Klyuchevskaya (right), the highest point on the peninsula, is an active volcano.

6

SAMAIL OPHIOLITE

In a few places, rocks from Earth's upper mantle can be pushed up to the surface. These rare rocks are called ophiolites, and geologists love them because they provide clues about rocks deep below the surface. In the Hajar Mountains of Oman, an ophiolite made of rocks from Earth's upper mantle has been exposed. This large, thick area of rock covers much of the northern coast of Oman.

KHADG SINGH VALDIYA (1937–2020)

Khadg Singh Valdiya was an Indian geologist who spent his career studying the Himalayas and teaching the next generation of geologists. He helped use stromatolites—sedimentary rocks formed from ancient bacteria—to estimate the age of some of the rocks of the Himalayas. His research helped to show how tectonic faults shape mountains, and he also studied the minerals and water patterns of the Himalayas.

7

LONAR LAKE

India's Lonar Lake is small and fairly ordinary looking, but it's how it formed that makes it special. It lies on the Deccan Plateau, a huge area of basalt created by volcanic eruptions around the time of the end of the dinosaurs. Geologists originally thought this round lake was a volcanic crater, but they now think it's a crater from a meteorite impact. The lake's waters are both salty and alkaline, and in 2020 microorganisms in the water caused the lake to turn pink!

8

EVEREST

Earth's tallest mountain towers over the border of Nepal and China, standing 29,032 ft (8,849 m) tall. It's known in the Tibetan language as *Chomolungma*, "Goddess Mother of the World," and in Sanskrit as *Sagarmatha*, meaning "Peak of Heaven." It was formed alongside the rest of the Himalayas starting about 30 million years ago and is roughly shaped like a triangular-sided pyramid. The rocks on the top are limestone that formed in the deep sea about 400 million years ago.

9

SHILIN STONE FOREST

This stunning limestone formation is located in Yunnan, a province in southern China. The rock formations are nearly 300 million years old and cover an area about double the size of Washington, DC. They're another example of a karst landscape (see page 64), where water has carved out hollows and channels in rocks such as limestone. The towers in Shilin seem to rise from the ground like petrified trees.

10

HA LONG BAY

This large bay on the coast of Vietnam is dotted with about 1,600 small islands, most of which are uninhabited. Some are little more than limestone pillars jutting up from the sea, but there are also cone-shaped hills, caves, grottoes, and stone arches. Tectonic activity caused cracks in the limestone, and these cracks eroded to form the landscape we see today. It may look very familiar —it has been used as a location for many films.

11

TAROKO GORGE

Located in Taiwan, the Taroko Gorge was formed when the Liwu River carved deep into the area's marble and limestone. While the river carves down, the region is being slowly pushed upward by the movement of tectonic plates. It all makes for a beautiful landscape of cliffs, tunnels, and waterfalls, covered over in many places by a lush forest.

AUSTRALIA AND OCEANIA

Australia, the world's smallest continent, lies in a geographical region known as Oceania. This region includes thousands of islands, both large and small, that dot the southern Pacific Ocean. Australia sits on the Indo-Australian tectonic plate, as do many of the other islands in the region, while the rest sit on the Pacific Plate. The region where the two plates meet is part of the "Ring of Fire" (see page 13), which is prone to volcanoes and earthquakes.

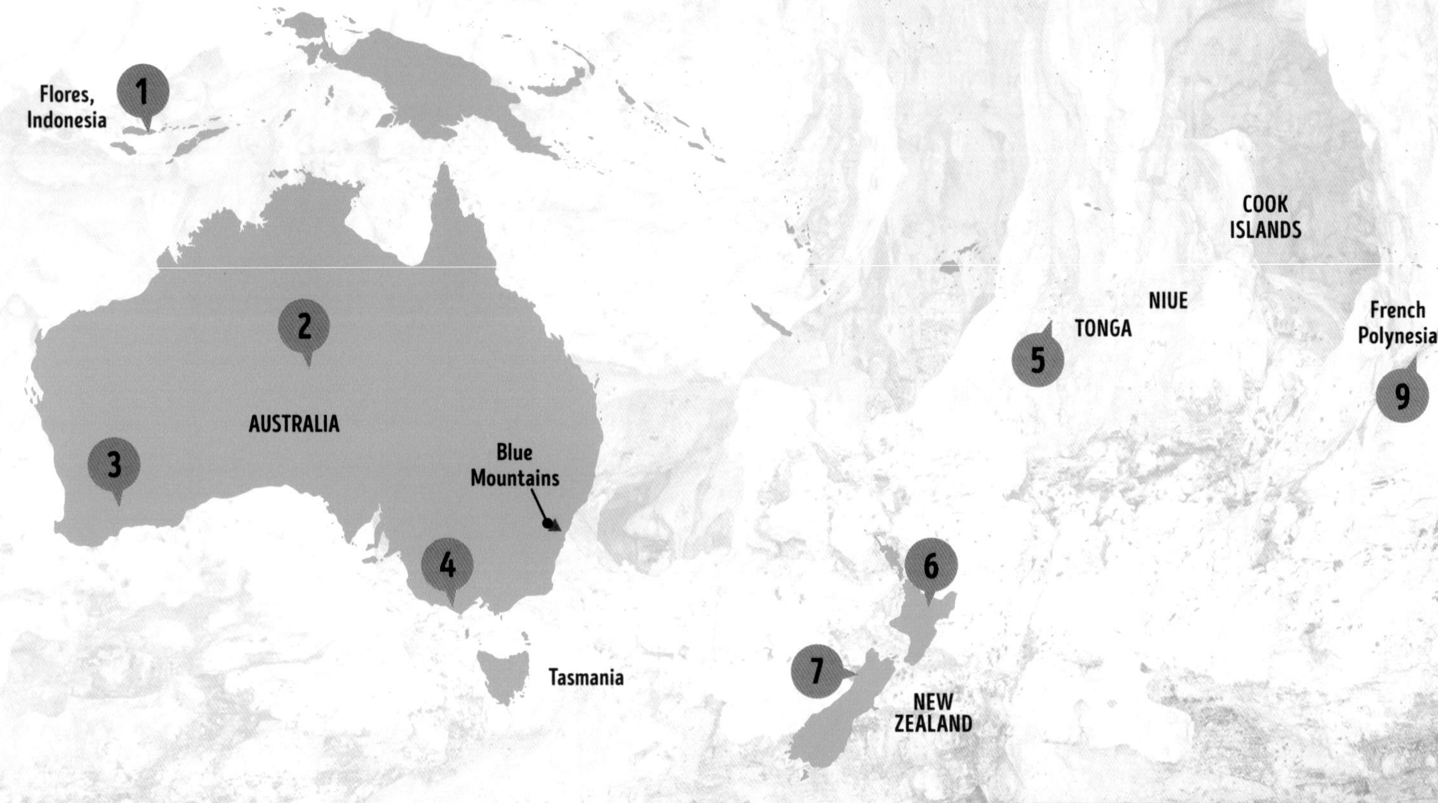

Australia and Oceania have some of Earth's oldest and youngest geographical formations—from ancient rocks that are over 4,000 million years old to more recently formed volcanic islands.

ISLAND FORMATION

The islands of Oceania formed in a variety of ways. Some, such as the Hawaiian islands, are chains of volcanoes that rise from the ocean floor. They formed as the plate moved over a "hotspot" in the mantle. Others, such as Palmerston in the Cook Islands, are formed from rings of coral that build up around old volcanoes as they sink beneath the ocean surface. Many islands are formed above subduction zones (see page 12) as one plate sinks beneath another.

This ring-shaped coral island (atoll) in Bora Bora, French Polynesia, surrounds the cone of an old volcano, which has been completely submerged by the sea.

1 KELIMUTU

Kelimutu, a volcano on the Indonesian island of Flores, has three craters, each with a lake inside. These lakes are all different colors—and the colors can randomly change! The waters can be green, blue, brown, black, red, or milky white—in one year, their colors changed six times. The different colors are due to volcanic activity below the surface, which releases different minerals that color the water.

2 ULURU

Uluru, once known as Ayers Rock, is one of Australia's most famous natural features. This huge block of reddish-orange sandstone rises 1,142 ft (348 m) from the surrounding land. It's huge, but it's just the tip of a larger formation that extends deep underground. Uluru formed from sediment eroded from ancient mountains. The sandstone formed below the sea, but then the sea receded and the block of rock was pushed upward, where we see it today.

The island nation of Niue formed when coral reefs were uplifted to break the water's surface. It has stunning landscapes made of limestone that began as coral.

HOW WE USE IT

MINING OPAL

Australia is famous for opals (see page 147)—about 95 percent of the world's opals come from here! Much of the continent was once covered by a vast inland sea, and its waters seeped down to fill cracks in sedimentary rock, creating perfect conditions for opals to form. People have mined opals in the southern town of Coober Pedy for over a century, often digging underground homes to stay cool in the scorching heat. In the east, the town of Lightning Ridge is known for its valuable black opal. Australian opal is made into jewelry and sold around the world.

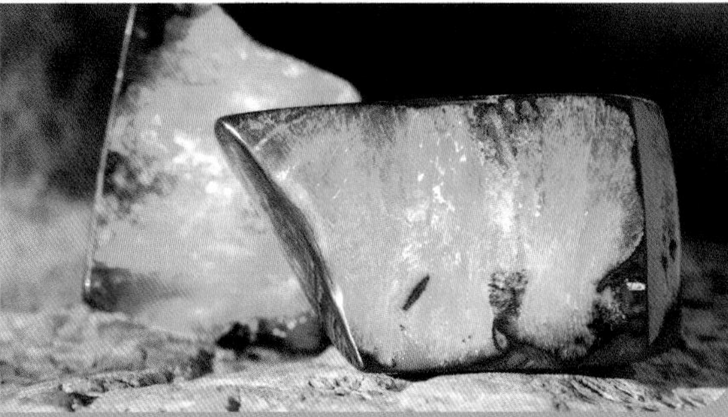

Boulder opal from Queensland is one of the most valuable forms of opal due to its rarity and lustrous colors.

3 WAVE ROCK

You wouldn't expect to see a towering wave hundreds of miles from the sea, but in southwestern Australia there's a rock formation that looks just like one! Wave Rock is the face of a granite cliff. Over millions of years, weathering and erosion have carved it into a curving shape that looks just like a giant ocean wave. The formation stands 50 ft (15 m) high and stretches for around 360 ft (110 m) long. Spring water running down its face has stained it with streaks of red, yellow, and brown.

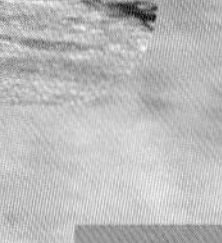

4

TWELVE APOSTLES

Parts of Australia's southern coast are marked by tall limestone cliffs. About 170 miles (275 km) west of Melbourne, a series of sea stacks rise up from the coastal waters. These stacks were once part of the land, but the pounding waves of the ocean gradually wore away limestone to create caves in the cliffs. Over millions of years, the caves eroded further to form arches, which eventually collapsed to form stacks, standing up to 148 ft (45 m) high.

PAWEL STRZELECKI (1797–1873)

Pawel Strzelecki was a self-taught Polish geologist who explored North and South America before traveling to Australia in 1839. He wanted to make a geological survey of the continent, and he explored the southeastern part of the mainland before turning his attention to the island of Tasmania. Strzelecki found deposits of coal and gold and collected many mineral samples. He also claimed and named Mount Kościuszko, the tallest peak on mainland Australia, in honor of a Polish military leader named Tadeusz Kościuszko.

The Blue Mountains in Australia began to form about 50 million years ago, shaped by underlying rocks, uplift, and erosion. The mountains get their name from the eucalyptus forests that span the landscape. Oil in the leaves creates a bluish haze in the hot sunshine.

5

HUFANGALUPE

With a name meaning "pigeon's gate," the natural stone arch of Hufangalupe stands on the Tongan island of Tongatapu. It formed when the roof of a sea cave collapsed, leaving two pillars made of limestone and coral and connected at the top. Ocean waves pound through its 130-ft (40-m) wide opening. Local legend says that it was made when a giant turtle carrying a rock on its back became trapped in a reef. It pushed the rock up out of the water to escape and left the stone arch behind.

6

WAIOTAPU

Located on New Zealand's North Island, Waiotapu is an area where volcanic activity heats water below the ground. The water comes to the surface as hot springs, geysers, or pools of bubbling mud. Minerals in the water, such as sulfur, give the hot springs bright colors (below), and they also form crusts around the edges as water evaporates. A geyser called Lady Knox can shoot water 65 ft (20 m) into the air if a park ranger adds soap, which reduces the surface tension of the water enough to allow it to erupt.

7 PANCAKE ROCKS AND BLOWHOLES

Punakaiki is a small village on the west coast of New Zealand's South Island. Nearby, erosion has formed a striking landscape in the uplifted limestone rock. Different layers eroded at different rates, making the rocks look like stacks of pancakes. The area also has several blowholes, where sea water shoots out of holes in the ground. These holes have underground connections to the ocean, and waves force water through them until it explodes out the top.

8 MACQUARIE ISLAND

Macquarie Island lies far to the south of Australia and New Zealand, about halfway to Antarctica. Home to colonies of penguins and seals, this long, thin island is unique—it's not made of continental crust, but of oceanic crust that is being pushed upward. Macquarie Island is very unusual in that it is made up entirely of an ophiolite—a section of Earth's upper mantle (see page 68) that has been exposed above sea level. Ophiolites are very rare and are almost always found on continents. This makes Macquarie Island doubly rare as the only oceanic island we know of formed from an ophiolite.

9 TOARUTU CAVE

Sometimes known as "the mouth of the dragon," this cave is on the island of Rurutu in French Polynesia. About a million years ago, Rurutu was pushed upward as it passed over a hotspot in the mantle. This created steep cliffs of coral that still circle the island. Over time, erosion carved out caves where people once lived. At Toarutu Cave, limestone pillars remain at the cave's mouth, looking like the fearsome teeth of a giant dragon.

10 KILAUEA

Hawaii is a string of volcanic islands formed as the Pacific Plate passed over a volcanic hotspot. It's home to several extinct or dormant volcanoes, along with six active ones. The youngest one, Kilauea, is the most active of them all! For long periods it erupts almost continuously. This volcano appears as a bulge on the flank of the larger Mauna Loa, but it has its own supply of molten magma. Its eruptions send lava flowing down into the sea.

ANTARCTICA

It's hard to believe that Earth's fifth-largest continent wasn't discovered until about 200 years ago! Antarctica sits at the globe's southern end, surrounded by a stormy ocean full of ice. Now it is cold and barren, but hundreds of millions of years ago, it was connected to Africa, Australia, and South America, and it had a tropical climate and plenty of life. Its current position and icy climate occurred in the last 50 million years.

Most of Antarctica's rocks are hidden beneath vast layers of ice. Only a few hardy animals, such as penguins, can survive in this desolate landscape.

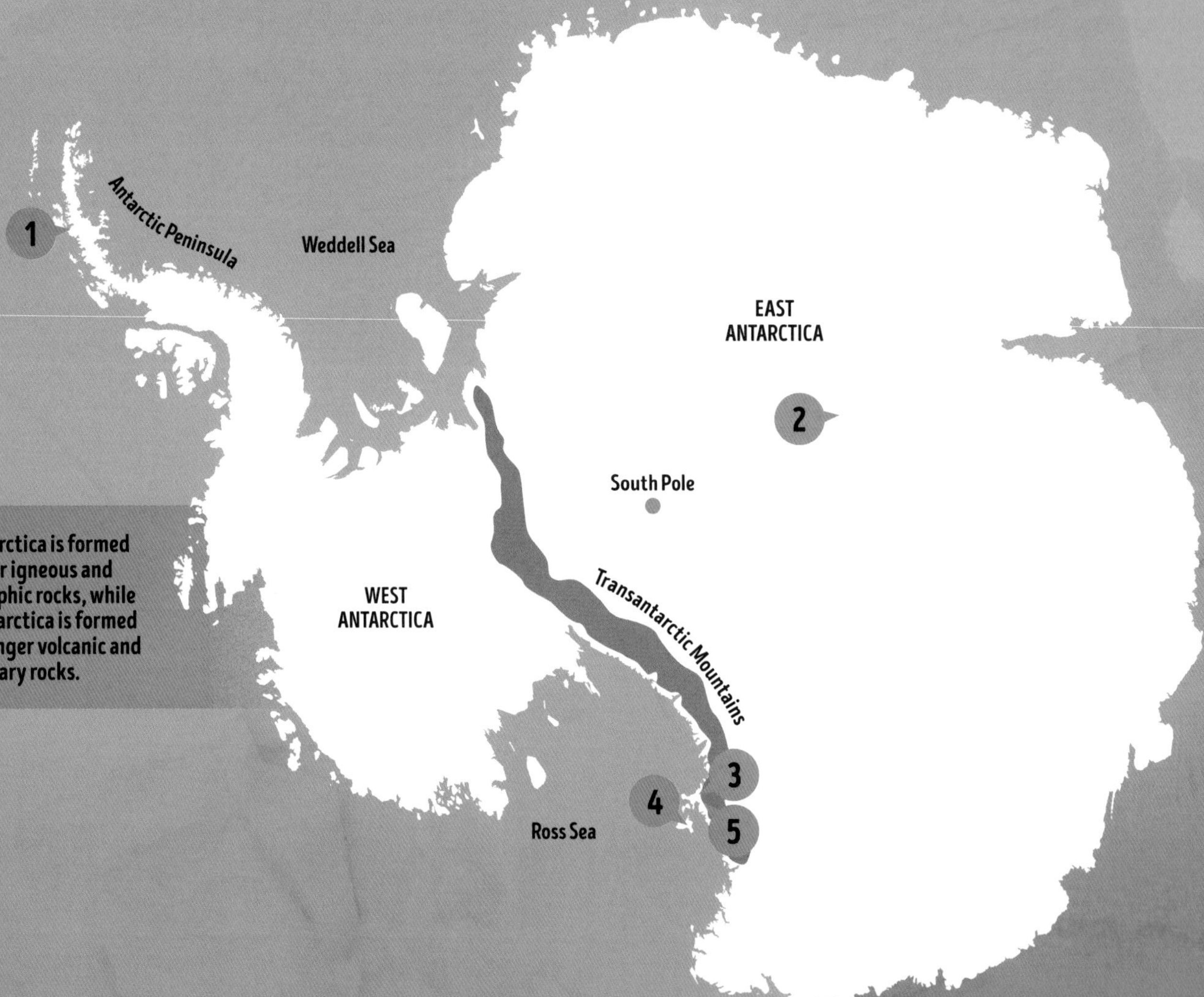

1
Antarctic Peninsula
Weddell Sea
EAST ANTARCTICA
2
South Pole
WEST ANTARCTICA
Transantarctic Mountains
3
4
5
Ross Sea

East Antarctica is formed from older igneous and metamorphic rocks, while West Antarctica is formed from younger volcanic and sedimentary rocks.

SNOWY PEAKS

The Transantarctic Mountains are one of the longest mountain ranges on Earth, stretching for more than 2,000 miles (3,200 km). They form a border between East and West Antarctica. This is the most prominent mountain range on the continent, with the highest peak—Mount Kirkpatrick—reaching 14,855 ft (4,528 m). Made mainly of sedimentary rock, the range began to form about 65 million years ago. The mountains were first crossed by Antarctic explorers in the early 20th century.

1

CAPE RENARD

Antarctica has a long peninsula that juts out into the Southern Ocean. Not far from its tip lies the rocky outcrop of Cape Renard. Cape Renard is the site of a lighthouse as well as two pointy basalt towers topped with ice known as Una Peaks. The taller of the two reaches a height of 2,451 ft (747 m). Cape Renard was named after Alphonse Renard, a Belgian geologist and mineralogist.

2

GAMBURTSEV RANGE

How could you possibly hide a mountain range with peaks standing 9,840 ft (3,000 m) tall? The Gamburtsev Range stretches for more than 745 miles (1,200 km) across Antarctica, but we'll never see it. That's because its peaks are hidden below a thick ice sheet. Scientists used radar and other imaging tools to help us see what these mountains look like.

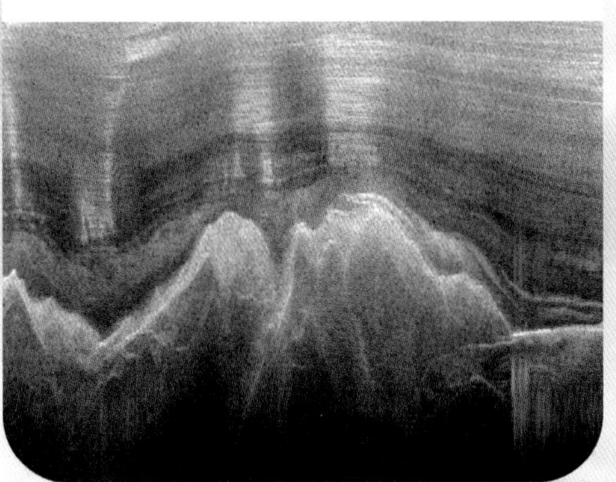

3

BLOOD FALLS

There's a waterfall in Antarctica that looks like a sheet of dripping blood! It's formed by meltwater flowing from beneath one of the continent's glaciers. Below the surface, the water is clear, but when it comes into contact with the air it turns red. This phenomenon mystified scientists for decades. Now they think the color is caused by microscopic iron-rich spheres carried in the flowing water.

4

MOUNT EREBUS

Antarctica may be cold, but there is one place that is always hot—deep inside a volcano! Mount Erebus, located on Ross Island, is the continent's highest active volcano, as well as being the southernmost active volcano on Earth. It has a lava lake in its crater and has been erupting regularly for decades. Scientists recently discovered that its eruptions often force out tiny crystals of gold dust!

5

MCMURDO DRY VALLEYS

If someone asked you where Earth's driest place was, you'd probably think of a sand-filled desert like the Sahara. But in fact, Antarctica is the driest continent, and the McMurdo Dry Valleys are the driest place of all! These valleys are carved out of granite and gneiss, with gravel covering the valley floors. The freezing cold air in Antarctica carries very little moisture, and it hasn't rained (or snowed) here for about 2 million years!

UNDER THE SEA

Oceans cover about 70 percent of Earth's surface, but about 80 percent of their vastness remains unexplored. Scientists study their currents and waves, and the plants and animals that live there. They also study the geology of the sea floor. Just like the land on the surface, the land at the bottom of the ocean is marked by mountains and valleys as well as volcanoes and other structures.

The oceans' great depth and darkness makes exploring the seafloor difficult. Scientists use tools such as sonar and remotely operated vehicles to help learn more.

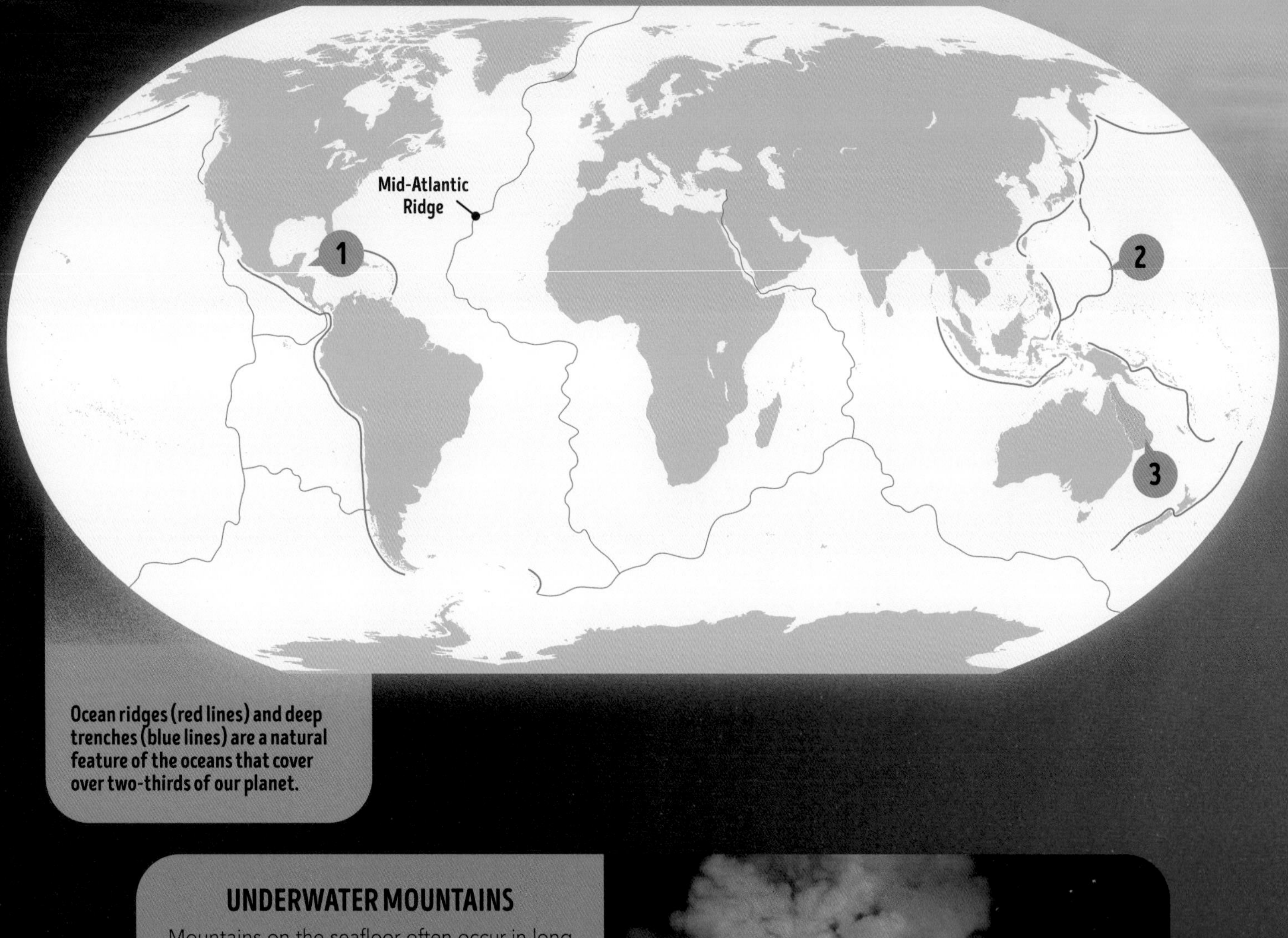

Mid-Atlantic Ridge

1

2

3

Ocean ridges (red lines) and deep trenches (blue lines) are a natural feature of the oceans that cover over two-thirds of our planet.

UNDERWATER MOUNTAINS

Mountains on the seafloor often occur in long chains called ridges. These ridges form along divergent plate boundaries (see page 12), and they all connect to form the world's largest mountain range. This mid-ocean ridge stretches for 40,390 miles (65,000 km)—that's about one-and-a-half times the circumference of Earth! One of the longest sections is the mid-Atlantic ridge, where plates move apart by about 1 inch (2.5 cm) per year. This discovery helped to prove Alfred Wegener's theory of plate tectonics (see page 13).

Some underwater mountains and volcanoes, such as West Mata, 4,000 ft (1.2 km) below the South Pacific Ocean, form at subduction zones.

MARIE THARP (1920-2006)

Marie Tharp was an American geologist who—alongside her colleague Bruce Heezen—produced the first detailed map of the Atlantic seafloor in 1957. Tharp's map showed that the ocean floor was not flat, as many people believed. As a woman, she wasn't allowed at first on the ships that collected the data for her maps, and people dismissed her ideas about the seafloor spreading. In 1977, she and Heezen produced the first world map of the ocean floors.

2 MARIANA TRENCH

The deepest point in the ocean is in the Mariana Trench—a crescent-shaped valley between Indonesia and Japan. It is a subduction zone (see page 12), where the Pacific Plate is pushed under the edge of the Mariana Plate. It drops down to about 36,000 ft (11,000 m) at its deepest point where the water pressure is more than 1,000 times that at the surface. However, some organisms can live even here, including sea cucumbers and shrimplike creatures called amphipods. People have made it down on just a handful of occasions, as the film director James Cameron did in 2012 in his submersible *Deepsea Challenger* (below).

1 GREAT BLUE HOLE

Lighthouse Reef is a coral atoll off the coast of Belize. At at its center is an area of deep-blue water that fills a giant sinkhole. This hole was originally a limestone cave on land. Over time, sea levels rose and the cave was flooded. Its roof eventually collapsed to form the sinkhole that we see today. Measuring more than 1,000 ft (300 m) across and reaching depths of 400 ft (125 m), this sinkhole is a favorite location for scuba divers.

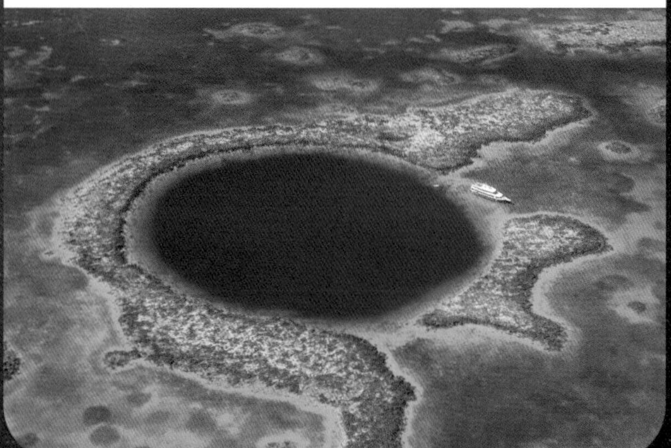

3 GREAT BARRIER REEF

Australia's Great Barrier Reef is the world's largest coral reef, stretching more than 1,800 miles (3,000 km) along the northeastern coast. Made from living coral and teeming with fish and other sea creatures, the reef is the only living thing that is visible from space. The reef is actually a collection of thousands of individual reef systems, and also includes coral islands that rise above the surface. It formed on the submerged hills of a coastal plain as sea levels rose.

BE A ROCK HOUND!

The world is full of interesting rocks, in a huge range of colors and textures. You can buy samples of polished rocks in stores, but wouldn't it be more fun to collect your own? All over the world, amateur geologists head out with their hammers, picks, and magnifiers, looking for interesting specimens. These people are often known as "rock hounds"—and you can be one too!

The exciting thing about rock hunting is you never know what you're going to find!

A FASCINATING HOBBY

Professional geologists have all kinds of high-tech tools to help them explore Earth's rocks, but you don't need any equipment at all to get started, and you don't need to travel into the wilderness either! Just keep your eyes peeled next time you're outdoors. You can find interesting rocks—and sometimes even fossils—in a gravel driveway. The more you find, the more you'll learn.

If you take a close look at the stones landscaping your local park or covering a driveway, you'll see many different shapes, sizes, colors, and textures.

BUILDING A COLLECTION

People collect all sorts of things, such as stamps, coins, and trading cards. Rock hounds collect rocks! They look for samples of minerals they haven't found before, hoping to find something amazing. This chapter will show you how to start building your own collection by going out to search. You'll learn how to identify the rocks you find, and how to display them and get them looking their best.

THE MORE THE MERRIER!

Just like any other hobby, rockhounding is more fun if you do it with friends. There are rockhounding clubs in many places. Is there one near you? They're a great way to meet fellow rock hounds, who are usually willing to share tips and information or help you identify your finds. These clubs often organize rockhounding trips. So why not start your rockhounding journey by joining one? Make sure you ask your parent or guardian's permission first though.

RESPONSIBLE COLLECTING

Being a rock hound is a fun hobby, but it can also be a dangerous one. Rocks are often found in wild or remote locations, and you'll need to use tools to collect and test them. If you want to stay safe, you need to be serious about knowing the risks and how to avoid dangerous situations. You'll also need to know the rules about what you can collect, and where.

There are so many rocks out there to search for and collect, but always check the rules before you take any samples home.

WHOSE LAND IS IT?

Some land is privately owned. That means that it's owned by a person or company, not the government. You need the owner's permission to explore this land, and also to remove any rocks. Check before you go! National and local governments also own huge areas of land—some are set aside as parks or wilderness reserves. They can be great places to hunt for rocks, but they often have strict rules about digging or removing rocks. Sometimes it's not allowed.

If you see an interesting rock and you're not allowed to keep it, you could always take a photo of it instead.

BUDDY UP!

The first rule of rock hunting is never to do it alone. Unless you're just digging in your own backyard, take an adult with you. You should also tell another responsible adult where you're going and when you plan to be back. Keep a mobile phone with you in case of emergencies—and a power bank is a good idea to keep you from running out of charge. The GPS on the phone will also be useful in case you get lost, though always bring a map of the area as a backup.

WHAT YOU NEED

Even if it's warm, wear long pants and long sleeves to protect you from the Sun and rough surfaces. A hat and sunscreen are also essential, as well as food and plenty of water. And don't forget your rockhounding kit!

- special rock hammer
- chisel
- bags and labels for storing your samples
- magnifying glass or hand lens for closer inspection
- gloves to protect your hands
- safety glasses to keep flying chips of rock away from your eyes

STAYING SAFE

The weather can change quickly, especially in mountainous areas. Always check the weather forecast before you go. Do dangerous animals such as ticks, spiders, or snakes live where you're searching? If so, you'll need to take precautions. Rocks can be unstable—loose rocks can shift around, and even solid-looking cliff faces can collapse. Never go into abandoned mine shafts or anywhere else that looks unsafe, and don't work below areas of overhanging rock.

A hard hat is a good addition to a rock-hounding kit, and essential if there's a danger of falling rocks. It's best to be prepared.

WHERE TO LOOK

If you want to find rocks, that's easy—just look around you! There are rocks and pebbles everywhere, even in cities. Many buildings are clad in beautifully polished rocks, and city parks are full of rocks and stones too. But if you want to find interesting and unusual rocks, you might need to go farther afield. Some places are richer in potential finds than others.

Footpaths in the countryside are full of rocks to explore. Over time, the paths wear away, exposing more rocks underfoot.

FRESHLY EXPOSED

The main thing to look out for is exposed rocks, which aren't covered in plants or soil. You don't want to have to dig down into a grassy field! Cliffs and mountains are examples of exposed rock, but you'll find it in many other places too. Look for patches of bare rock or rocks that glint in the sunlight. The longer a rock surface has been exposed to the elements, the more it will be weathered. Some of the original minerals may have changed to other minerals like clays.

Prolonged exposure to air and sunlight can discolor rocks, and so can plants growing on them. Weathering processes also reveal fresher rock underneath.

WATER SITES

Flowing water carries rocks from one place to another. Riverbanks are good places to look, as there will be new rocks turning up all the time. On the inside bends of a river, the current is slower and rocks often accumulate. After a big rainstorm, once the water levels have gone back to normal, is a good time to go. Stream beds are another good place to look, and they are safer, too—sometimes there is no running water at all! Lake and ocean beaches are also good sites.

Low tide after a storm is a good time to explore a beach. The waves will have churned up a lot of new rocks waiting to be discovered!

QUARRIES AND OUTCROPS

Quarries are full of interesting finds—after all, they only exist where there's something worth digging for! They have rock faces that are recently exposed, and these faces can extend down through various layers of different types of rocks. Natural outcrops of rock occur in many different locations, such as cliffs or rocky hillsides. You don't need to climb them; usually what you find at the base will be the same as what's hidden higher up.

At this abandoned marble quarry, heavy machinery has done the hard work of exposing the rock, revealing different colors and textures.

GROUP EXPEDITIONS

Is there a rockhounding club in your local area? If so, give it a try! You'll meet other people who are interested in rocks, and they can share their tips and knowledge. Even better, these clubs usually organize field trips for their members. You may get permission to dig at sites you wouldn't be able to visit on your own, and you'll have company! And the more people there are looking, the more rocks you'll find.

Many parts of the USA have pay-to-dig sites where you are charged a fee to pan for gold or dig for rocks. You get to keep whatever you find.

SAFE AND LEGAL

Rockhounding is fun but it can also be dangerous. Only go rockhounding with a responsible adult. Before you set off, ask yourself two questions: is the area safe, and is it legal? Quarries, roads, and flowing water can have hidden dangers. Always assess an area thoroughly with an adult before you begin. You'll need to know who owns the land. Is it privately owned? Is it public land, such as a park? Searching for rocks and taking them home might not be allowed. With the help of an adult, you can ask for permission from the landowner, or check the park's rules.

Always check for hazards and dangers before you go rockhounding. Look for signs and restrictions, but use your common sense, too.

ON THE HUNT

It's time to start your first rock hunt! You've made a plan for where you're going and you have an adult to take you. You've checked the collecting rules and talked about a safety plan. You've got a bag filled with water, snacks, and equipment. There's only one question left to answer: what will you find?

MAP IT!

A good geologist always keeps careful records for every rock they find, and this includes noting down the rock's location. As you hunt, you should plot your finds on a map. You can draw your own, or print out an online map of the area to mark up. Use a pencil to add any useful landmarks that don't appear on the map. Give each rock you collect a number, and mark that number on the map to show where you picked it up.

LABELING YOUR FINDS

By the end of the day, you may have so many rocks you can't remember which one is which. That's why it's so important to label as you go! You can put each rock in a sealed bag and write the number on the bag with a marker. Or even better, put each rock into a different section of an empty egg carton. You can write the number right on the carton —just don't take all your rocks out at once and get them mixed up!

BREAKING LOOSE

Not all interesting finds will be sitting on the ground, waiting for you to pick them up. If a rock you want is stuck inside a larger piece, you may need to break it free. Use a hammer and chisel to chip away at the rock. Hold the chisel at an angle for the best results. You may have to chisel in a few different places before the rock breaks free. Make sure you wear safety goggles. Gloves can help protect your hands, too. You may also hammer rock to obtain a fresh unweathered surface. But remember you can't use your hammer in all places. Many sites with special geology don't allow hammering at all as it spoils it for others.

CLEANING UP

If you find rocks on a beach, they may already be washed clean. But others might need a bit of work! When you get back home, you could lay out some old newspapers and get a bowl of water. You can use damp paper towels or an old cloth towel to brush away dirt and grit, too. If that doesn't work, a scrubbing brush will give it a really good clean. An old toothbrush can also be useful (but make sure it's one you don't need any more!).

You should never go rock hunting alone. Always bring a trusted adult with you.

HARRISON SCHMITT (1935–)

You can find interesting rocks in your own backyard, but the geologist Harrison Schmitt traveled a lot farther to find his samples—all the way to the Moon! He was part of the Apollo 17 mission in 1972 and is one of only 12 people so far to walk on the Moon. Like earlier crews, he collected rock samples to bring back to Earth. One of them gave scientists evidence that the Moon may once have had a magnetic field.

WHAT IS IT?

Once you have your finds, it's time to work out what kind of rocks they are. You can try this right away while the rocks are still where you found them, or you can investigate further at home. One of the first steps is discovering which of the three main rock types—igneous, sedimentary, or metamorphic (see pages 14–19)—they belong to.

IS IT IGNEOUS?

It's not always easy to identify rocks. Three main clues help us to tell if a rock is igneous. If you want to practice, you could identify some common igneous rocks first, such as granite. As a general rule, igneous rocks are mainly black, white, or gray, and there won't be bands of different colors. Igneous rocks are also very strong. You probably won't be able to break off a piece with your hands. Third, if you can see tiny holes or large grains, that's a clue that the rock is most likely igneous.

Look and feel for three particular clues. This igneous granite, for example, is gray, hard and has large grains.

A magnifying glass or hand lens helps you to identify rocks in more detail. But what a rock feels like is also important.

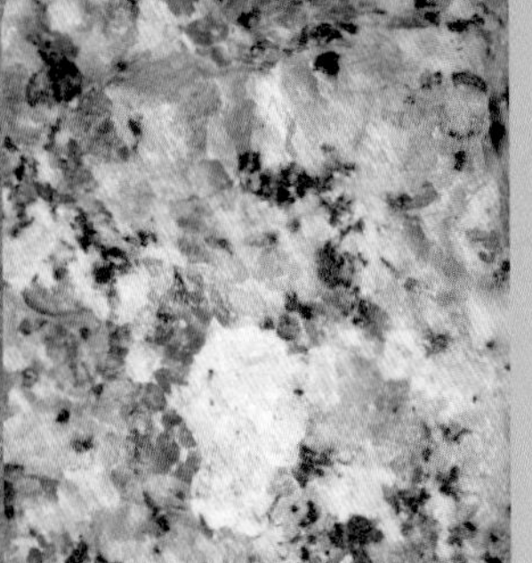

INTRUSIVE AND EXTRUSIVE

Geologists divide igneous rocks into two categories. Extrusive rocks are those made from magma that erupted above the surface as lava and then cooled and hardened. Intrusive rocks are from magma that never made it above ground. It cooled underground, "intruding" into the other rocks already there. Intrusive rocks cooled slowly, which gives them big grains. In extrusive rocks, the grains are much smaller, and you might see tiny holes left by gas bubbles in the lava.

You can usually see the different-sized grains in intrusive rock, such as granite (left). The grains in extrusive rock, such as tuff (right), are more difficult to spot but you can often see the formation of air bubbles.

IS IT SEDIMENTARY?

Sedimentary rocks form when bits of rock or other materials get laid down in layers, and are then squashed until they turn into rock. You can often see the effect of this process when you examine a rock. You could familiarize yourself first with some common sedimentary rocks such as limestone or sandstone. Look for layers or bands of different colors. You might also see bigger fragments of rock surrounded by more fine-grained rock. Many sedimentary rocks are soft enough to break with your hands.

If there are any fossils in the rock, it's almost definitely sedimentary—fossils are rarely found in igneous or metamorphic rock. This shell fossil is trapped in sandstone.

IS IT METAMORPHIC?

Gneiss is a common metamorphic rock you might come across. Metamorphic rocks form deep underground and only appear on the surface where they have been pushed up by tectonic activity. Rocks found in a region of mountains or volcanoes are more likely to be metamorphic. These rocks are very hard—often harder than igneous rocks. You won't be able to break them apart. You might see layers that look like stripes. These layers are sometimes straight, and sometimes wavy like a folded ribbon. Lastly, many metamorphic rocks (but not all of them!) contain flecks of mica (see page 26), which makes them glitter in the light.

Stripes in metamorphic rock, like this sample of schist, are called foliation. They're caused by high temperature and pressure when the rock formed.

INVESTIGATING PROPERTIES

If you want to find out more about your rocks, you need to think like a detective. When solving a crime, detectives look for clues. Each clue gives them another piece of the puzzle. It's the same when examining rocks. The properties and characteristics of the rocks are the clues you need to identify them.

PETROGRAPHY

We know so much about different rocks and minerals today because of the work of countless geologists over the centuries. They studied rocks and kept detailed records of their properties. This is called petrography, and you can do it too! As you examine your finds, take careful notes. They may help you to spot patterns and similarities.

Petrographers often look at very thin slices of rock under a microscope to see their structure, such as this sample of granite.

FLORENCE BASCOM (1862–1945)

At a time when few universities took women students, Florence Bascom earned two bachelor's degrees and a master's before becoming just the second American woman to earn a PhD in geology. She later founded the geology department at Bryn Mawr, a women's college in Pennsylvania, and worked for the US Geological Survey, where she analyzed rocks and published scientific papers about them.

The gravel and shingle of Charmouth Beach, southern England, makes a great place to search for fossils. When the sea erodes the sedimentary rocks of the cliffs by the beach, fossilized remains are often left on the shore.

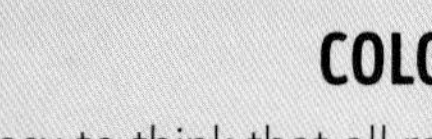

COLOR

It's easy to think that all rocks are brown or gray. But in fact, rocks and minerals can come in a whole rainbow of colors! Many rocks are multicolored, showing the different minerals within them. A rock's color can be a clue to its identity. You'll need to clean off any soil to see its true color. Splitting a rock open is often the best way to see its true color, but this can be dangerous—always ask an adult to help, and take safety precautions.

Washing rocks can help to reveal their colors, which are caused by the different minerals they contain.

TEXTURE

When geologists talk about a rock's texture, they don't just mean what it feels like to touch. A rock's texture has more to do with how big its grains are and how they are arranged—and you can see this more easily than you can feel it. Rocks are often described as "fine-grained" or "coarse-grained." Have a close look at your rock samples. Can you see the different grains? Are they big or small? Are they all the same size, or are some bigger than others?

Igneous granite rock (left) has coarse grains, and mottled colors show the different mineral crystals it contains, while shale (right) is a fine-grained sedimentary rock.

A SURPRISE INSIDE?

A geode is a rock with a hollow space inside that contains beautiful crystals. On the outside, these rocks look fairly ordinary. But if you look carefully, there are clues that something spectacular is hidden inside. Geodes (see page 29) are usually found in deserts or near lakes, streams, or riverbeds. They are round and bumpy, and they feel lighter than other rocks of that size.

A professional can use a special saw to cut open a suspected geode, like this one containing amethyst (see page 144).

DIGGING DEEPER

The more you learn about your rock and mineral samples, the closer you'll get to identifying them. After all, many different minerals have similar colors or textures. To tell them apart, you'll have to dig a little bit deeper and look at other properties as well.

HARDNESS

A mineral's hardness depends on its structure. Geologists use the Mohs scale, which goes from 1–10, to measure a rock's hardness. You test a sample by trying to scratch it with something else. Use a variety of different substances, such as those shown below—start with the softest and work up. Once you find a material that won't leave a scratch, that gives you a rough idea of the mineral's score on the Mohs scale.

MOHS HARDNESS SCALE

INCREASING HARDNESS

1 **Talc**

2 **Gypsum**

← Fingernail

3 **Calcite**

← Copper coin

4 **Fluorite**

5 **Apatite**

← Knife/glass

6 **Orthoclase**

← Steel

7 **Quartz**

8 **Topaz**

9 **Corundum**

10 **Diamond**

If your sample is scratched by a copper coin, but not by a fingernail, its hardness on the Mohs scale would be about 3.

FRIEDRICH MOHS (1773–1839)

The German geologist Friedrich Mohs was interested in science from a young age, and began his career in mining. He later found a job identifying the different samples in someone's rock collection. Mohs began to develop new ways of identifying minerals and classifying them into groups, based on their physical properties. One of these properties was hardness, and it led him to develop the scale of hardness that is now named after him.

STREAK

Many minerals leave a mark when rubbed against a white porcelain tile. This is called its streak, and the color of the streak can help to identify the mineral. Why not try doing a streak test yourself? You'll need an unglazed porcelain tile, called a streak plate, which you can buy online. The shiny porcelain tiles in kitchens and bathrooms are glazed, so they won't work. Make sure to rub firmly, and remember that only minerals with a Mohs number of less than seven will leave a streak—harder ones will just scratch the streak plate. The directory in this book will tell you what streak colors to look out for!

A pyrite streak test leaves a blackish mark. This is a good way to distinguish pyrite or "fool's gold" (see page 119) from real gold!

LUSTER

To check a sample's luster, all you need is your eyes! This term refers to how a rock —and the minerals inside it—reflect light. Luster can be described in many ways: dull (not reflective), greasy, metallic, pearly, silky (soft, shiny fibers), vitreous (glassy), waxy, adamantine (brilliant shine), and resinous (resin-like shine). Also check whether the mineral is transparent (you can see through it), translucent (light shines through it), or opaque (no light shines through).

Aventurine is a type of translucent quartz known for its sparkle. This sample has been cleaned and polished.

CLEAVAGE

Depending on the way the crystals inside them are arranged, some minerals will break along flat surfaces when you hit them with a hammer. This property is called cleavage. Try putting a sample in a cardboard box, pop your safety glasses on, and hit it with a hammer until it breaks. What does the broken area look like? Some minerals will fracture in one direction to form flat sheets, while others will fracture in two or more to form different shapes. Some minerals don't show cleavage at all!

Muscovite (top) fractures in one direction, while feldspar fractures in two directions to form blocks.

At a first glance, many rocks look the same, but you can check for some unique properties using a hand lens or magnifying glass to help identify them.

FURTHER TESTS

By now, you've probably gotten closer to identifying your samples by testing them for color, cleavage, and other properties. But you can take things even further! There are additional tests you can do, which will get you working like a real geologist as you use science to solve the mysteries of the rocks.

In a laboratory setting, geologists can carry out a range of tests to find out more about the different properties of rock samples.

A piece of cork floats in water while a stone sinks, because they have different densities.

DENSITY

An object's density is how much it weighs in relation to its size. Something like a sponge is not dense at all—a brick of the same size would be much heavier. Finding an object's density tells you how tightly its atoms are packed together, which can provide a clue to what minerals a rock contains. Geologists usually test for specific gravity (or "relative density"). This compares a substance's density to the density of a known standard, usually water. This book's directory (see pages 96–155) lists the specific gravity of different rocks.

TESTING SPECIFIC GRAVITY

An experienced geologist can make a pretty good guess of a sample's density just by holding it in their hand, but to be more exact, you can test for specific gravity (or relative density). To do this you'll need a digital scale and a measuring cup. First, weigh the sample in grams (g) and make a note —this is the sample's mass. Now fill the measuring cup with enough water to cover the sample, and note the measurement in milliliters (ml)—note that 1 milliliter equals 1 cubic centimeter (cc).

Put the sample in and the water level will rise. Take the new measurement, then subtract the original amount of water to get the volume of the sample. Then divide the sample's mass by its volume to find the density. To find the specific gravity, divide the density of your sample by the density of water. The density of pure water (at 39.2 °F or 4 °C) is 1 g/cc, so dividing by one means your sample's density value will be the same as the specific gravity.

Specific gravity is useful because you can compare the densities of samples that have been measured in different units.

A FAMOUS TEST

In around 250 BCE, the Greek mathematician Archimedes was the first person to test specific gravity. The local king had given a craftsman gold to make a crown. The crown weighed the same as the gold he'd provided, but the king suspected the craftsman had replaced some of the gold with an equal weight of silver, which is cheaper and less dense. He sought the help of his cousin Archimedes, who thought about the problem until one day, getting into his bath, he noticed that the water level went up. He tested the crown and found it displaced more water than pure gold of the same weight, which meant the crown had more volume, proving that the craftsman had used some silver. Legend says that Archimedes was so excited by his discovery, he ran naked into the street, shouting "Eureka!"—which means "I have found it!"

THE ACID TEST

Some types of rocks will fizz or bubble when exposed to acid. This is a clue that they contain carbonate, a compound made up of carbon and oxygen. Geologists use a strong but dangerous acid called hydrochloric acid, but you can stay safe by using a weaker acid such as lemon juice or vinegar. Place your rock in a glass or plastic bowl, put on your safety glasses, and drip a few drops of lemon juice or vinegar onto the rock. You may need to use a magnifying glass to see any fizzing. You could also try scratching the rock to make a little powder, which can help create a stronger reaction.

This magnetite lodestone attracts the iron in these paper clips, just like a magnet!

MAGNETISM

Try holding a fridge magnet near your rock sample. Is it attracted to the magnet? If so, that's a sign that it contains iron, or minerals containing iron. One of these is magnetite, a very commonly found mineral. In the right circumstances it can become a magnet itself, attracting other piece of iron. Natural magnets like these—called "lodestones"—were how ancient people discovered magnetism.

LOOKING THEIR BEST

Once you've tested and identified your rock samples, it's time to put them on display! It's worth taking a bit of time to get your samples looking their best so you can show them off to your friends and family—and perhaps inspire them to go rockhounding too.

CLEAN IT UP

Out in nature, rocks can get caked in dust and dirt. If you haven't done so already, clean your rocks by soaking them in a bowl or bucket of hot, soapy water. Then you can scrub away the grit and dirt with a scrubbing brush or old toothbrush. It may take a few rounds of soaking and scrubbing to get them nice and clean, especially if they have crevices for dirt to get wedged in. If a rock is covered with delicate crystals, then this is probably as far as you should go —you don't want to risk damaging the crystals.

SANDING SMOOTH

If your rock is hard enough, you may want to sand it to make it smooth. Choose a coarse sandpaper and start rubbing. As you work, keep the rock wet by dipping it in water occasionally. Once you've stopped making progress, switch to a slightly finer sandpaper. Gradually move to finer and finer sandpaper to get a smoother finish.

Sandpaper comes in different grades. They're based on the size of the grit used to coat the paper.

These polished semi-precious stones make a colorful collection at this market stall in Tibet, China.

ROCK TUMBLERS

Sanding a rock, especially a hard one, is tough physical work, so some people use a rock tumbler to do the hard work for them! These machines tumble stones with grit until they're smooth, but they are noisy, and they take days to do the job. You may know someone with a rock tumbler, or you may be able to borrow one from a rockhounding group. You should check before you tumble—rocks like agate and quartz are good for tumbling, but softer, large-grained rocks will often just crumble.

The stones that you see in gift shops have usually been through a rock tumbler, like this one, to smooth and polish their surfaces.

TIME FOR A POLISH

Once a stone is smooth, you can make it shine by giving it a polish. Use a square of heavy fabric, such as denim, and rub the rock until it begins to shine—or show luster, if you want to talk like a geologist! Be patient and keep at it. Once you've done all you can with the cloth, you can polish it further with a special rock polish, which you can buy online. Some people like to polish their rocks with a little mineral oil to give them a wet, shiny look.

ON DISPLAY

It's time to put your rocks on display! You might be able to find a cardboard box or tray that's already divided into compartments, or you may have a plastic box for storing beads. You can also make your own dividers by cutting an old cardboard box into strips and slotting them together. Add some sponge or cotton wool for padding before you position your rocks. It can be useful to label each sample to show what type of rock it is and where you found it!

DIRECTORY OF ROCKS AND MINERALS

Geologists have identified thousands of different rocks and minerals. This directory will provide a guide to around 100 of them. Some are common, and others are more rare—but all of them are fascinating! You can also use this directory to help identify rocks found on your rockhounding trips.

Rocks and minerals come in different shapes and sizes, with varying textures and colors too. Flick through this directory to find something new, or try rock hunting yourself first to see what you can discover!

ROCKS, MINERALS, AND MORE

This directory is divided into sections, based on different categories of rocks and minerals, and you'll see the category listed at the top of each page. There are rocks, which contain a mixture of different minerals, followed by native elements—those few elements, such as gold, that naturally occur in their pure form. Then there are minerals in different families, followed by minerals and other substances that we use as gemstones.

Lazurite

Lapis lazuli

Rocks are made up of minerals, and they often share properties with the minerals they contain. For example, the mineral lazurite is what gives the metamorphic rock called lapis lazuli its rich blue color.

HOW TO USE THIS GUIDE

You can use this guide simply to learn more about the incredible world of rocks, minerals, and gemstones. Or, if you've followed the advice in the *Be a Rock Hound!* chapter, you can browse through this directory to see if any of the photos match your own samples. If you have an idea of what your sample might be, you can also search the index to find the correct entry. Take a look at the photographs, as well as the fact file information such as color, luster, and hardness. Does your sample match? If it's not a perfect match, could your sample be a different member of the same category?

Try some of the tests on pages 86–93 to find the properties of your samples.

How Each Entry Works

The heading at the top of the page shows what category the rocks or minerals belong to.

A photo shows you what the rock or mineral can look like in its natural form.

The fact file provides information on its properties and how it got its name. The properties of each entry will vary, depending on whether the sample is a rock, native element, mineral, or gemstone.

The properties here include cleavage, streak, hardness, specific gravity, and luster. These are all described in more detail on pages 90–91, with explanatory vocabulary on pages 98–99.

BORATE MINERALS

BORAX

Borax is a compound of boron, sodium, oxygen, and water molecules. It forms when water containing borate compounds (see page 25) evaporates, especially in dry regions. It's often found in dry lake beds or salt flats.

FACT FILE

- **Name:** from the Arabic *buraq*, meaning "white"
- **Color:** colorless, gray, or white
- **Cleavage:** perfect
- **Streak:** white
- **Hardness:** 2–2.5
- **Specific gravity:** 1.7
- **Luster:** vitreous to earthy

Borax

USING BORAX

The borate compounds in borax have natural cleansing and deodorizing properties, so they're often used in household cleaning products. For similar reasons, borax is also used in hand soap and some tooth-whitening products. Other uses of borate compounds include as an insecticide to get rid of ants, as a soil nutrient to help crops grow, and as an aid in welding and soldering metals.

Borax is a key ingredient in homemade slime. It helps to link glue molecules together.

The ruins of an old borax works stand in Death Valley, California, where this "white gold" was once mined.

Some entries include a warning symbol, if the sample is toxic or extra care is needed.

The text gives further information on the rock or mineral and how we use it.

TALK LIKE A GEOLOGIST

Geologists use a lot of special terms that aren't part of everyday speech—it can sometimes feel like you're speaking a different language! Reading a reference guide to rocks and minerals might be confusing at first if you don't know the lingo. But here are some words you can learn, which will get you talking like a geologist in no time.

The more you learn about rocks and minerals, the more you'll begin to sound like a professional geologist out at work in the field!

WHY DO MY SAMPLES LOOK DIFFERENT?

You might notice that in some entries there are pictures of a mineral that look very different from each other. How can one mineral look so different? One of the main differences is whether the mineral is part of a rock, or whether it is growing alone or in groups of single crystals that are large enough to be distinct. A mineral can also sometimes occur in different colors, depending on tiny amounts of other substances that can change from one sample to the next.

Check your samples carefully against all the information provided. You may have a match, even if it doesn't look just like the picture.

CRYSTAL TYPES

Sometimes a geologist will describe a sample as being "massive." This sounds like it should be really big, but in fact it's kind of the opposite. If a rock or mineral is massive, that just means that it forms a mass with no structure such as layers or crystal shapes. Minerals are sometimes also described as "microcrystalline"—this means that their individual crystals are too small to see without a microscope, so they look like a solid mass.

Chalcedony is a microcrystalline variety of quartz (see page 144) with crystals too small to see, giving it a smooth, waxy appearance.

CLUES FROM CLEAVAGE

Looking at minerals' cleavage is one way that geologists can tell them apart. Cleavage is just the way that a mineral breaks when you hit it with a hammer, and it depends on the way that its atoms are arranged. Minerals with no cleavage will shatter, but those with cleavage will break apart with a flat edge. Here are some words that geologists use to describe cleavage:

Term	What it means
perfect	cleaves without leaving rough surfaces
imperfect	cleaves with a mostly smooth surface with some rough patches
poor (or distinct)	cleaves but leaves a mostly rough surface
indistinct	the cleavage is so poor that it's hardly noticeable
none	broken surfaces are fractured and rough

TALKING ABOUT LUSTER

A mineral's luster is a way of describing what the surface looks like and how it reflects light. A mineral such as pyrite or gold has a shiny, opaque luster that is described as metallic. Non-metallic luster can be divided into several different subcategories. Here are some of the most common ones:

Term	What it means
vitreous	shiny and glassy, like a piece of broken glass
adamantine	glassy, but more brilliantly reflective than vitreous luster
resinous	looking like the hardened resin secreted by trees
pearly	looking like the surface of a pearl
greasy	looking as though it's coated with a thin layer of oil or grease
waxy	looking smooth like wax, and opaque or slightly translucent
silky	with tightly packed fibers that give the appearance of silk fabric
dull	not shiny or reflective; often rough or porous

BASALT

Basalt is a very common rock formed by volcanic eruptions—more than 90 percent of all volcanic rocks are basalt. This rock forms when runny lava cools very quickly. The rapid cooling gives it a fine-grained texture.

FACT FILE

- **Name:** from the Latin *basaltes*, meaning "very hard stone"
- **Rock type:** igneous
- **Color:** dark gray to black
- **Texture:** fine-grained
- **Found:** worldwide, especially on the ocean floor

The basalt columns of Giant's Causeway, Ireland, formed when lava flowed through cracks in the ground and cooled quickly.

BASALT EVERYWHERE

Although basalt is very common, much of it is never seen. That's because it makes up most of the world's ocean floors! Some volcanoes on the seabed erupt so much that they create islands made of basalt (such as Hawaii). It's one of the most abundant rocks on the Moon (that's what the dark patches are made of) and it also forms volcanoes on Mars and Venus.

About 25 percent of the near side of the Moon is basalt.

DIORITE

Diorite forms when underground magma cools slowly. It is similar to granite, but darker in color and contains less silica. Some people call it "salt and pepper" rock because it's often made of black and white speckles. It's sometimes also called "black granite."

FACT FILE

- **Name:** from the Greek *diorizein*, meaning "to distinguish," because it is easy to identify
- **Rock type:** igneous
- **Color:** mottled black or dark green with gray or white
- **Texture:** medium-grained to coarse-grained
- **Found:** worldwide, especially at the roots of mountains

Diorite forms the base of many mountains, such as Ben Nevis, the highest peak in Scotland.

HARD AND DURABLE

Diorite is a very hard stone, but ancient people became skilled at carving and polishing it. The Egyptians and Sumerians used it to carve statues of rulers. People also carved diorite into stone jars, and the Inca of South America used it as a building stone. Many ancient objects made from diorite still exist today because the stone is so hard-wearing.

This diorite statue of Gudea, a Sumerian ruler of present-day southern Iraq, was carved in the 22nd century BCE.

GRANITE

Granite is an intrusive rock, meaning that it forms underground from cooling magma. It's very common all over the planet, forming the base of every continent. Many of Earth's oldest rocks are granite.

FACT FILE

- **Name:** from the Latin *granum*, meaning "grain," because of its obvious grains
- **Rock type:** igneous
- **Color:** pink, white, gray, or red with darker specks
- **Texture:** medium-grained to coarse-grained
- **Found:** worldwide, especially in continental crust

MAIN MINERALS

Granite comes in different types, but all are mainly made up of feldspar, quartz, and mica (see page 26). Feldspars make up the bulk of granite, and they are often pink, white, gray, or cream colored. The mica in granite can give it a shimmery shine.

The speckles and sparkles in granite are especially noticeable when it is cut and polished.

This Spanish quarry is a source of granite—one of the country's most abundant natural stones.

GRANITE IN BUILDINGS

Granite has been cut into blocks for building for thousands of years. It's also cut into thin slabs and polished. Granite slabs can make durable worktops or facing stones that line buildings on the inside and outside, giving them an elegant, polished appearance.

Granite kitchen worktops are popular because this stone is heat-resistant and hard to scratch.

USING GRANITE

Like diorite, granite is hard. People have used it for carving things that they want to last, such as temples, pyramids, and statues of pharaohs in ancient Egypt. Some Roman aqueducts built from blocks of granite are still standing today. Granite has been used to build bridges, and hard-wearing granite paving slabs line many roads.

The presidents on Mount Rushmore in South Dakota are carved from a granite mountain.

OBSIDIAN

Obsidian is an extrusive igneous rock. It forms above the ground when lava cools and hardens so quickly there is not enough time for crystals to form. This gives it a smooth, glassy texture.

FACT FILE

- **Name:** from the Latin *obsidius*, the name of an ancient Roman explorer who supposedly discovered it
- **Rock type:** igneous
- **Color:** usually black, sometimes with white spots or a swirl of brown; other colors are very rare
- **Texture:** glassy, with no visible grains
- **Found:** worldwide, but only near recently active volcanoes

ROCK OR GLASS?

You'll often hear obsidian called volcanic glass. It forms in a similar way to the glass we make for windows and tableware—by molten material cooling too rapidly for crystals to form. This means that obsidian's texture is what geologists call "amorphous." It doesn't have a regular crystalline structure, like minerals do.

If lava flows into cold sea water, it often cools and hardens quickly enough to form obsidian.

SNOWFLAKES AND COLORS

Most obsidian is black, but tiny traces of other elements can turn it brown or green. A mix of brown and black obsidian swirled together is called "mahogany obsidian." Obsidian can even be blue, red, orange, or yellow, though this is rare. Over time, obsidian's structure can change. Small quartz crystals appear, making white blotches that look like snowflakes.

The red-brown colors in "mahogany obsidian" are caused by iron oxide, while "snowflake obsidian" contains quartz crystals (silicon dioxide).

Snowflake obsidian

Mahogany obsidian

Obsidian is found in volcanic regions and forms in lava that is rich in lighter elements such as silicon, oxygen, and aluminum.

WEAPONS AND TOOLS

Like all glass, obsidian is brittle. When it breaks, it forms a smooth, curved surface with a very sharp edge. People have chipped away at obsidian for thousands of years to make knives, spear points, and arrowheads. In fact, some surgeons today still use obsidian blades on their scalpels, as they are sharper than steel blades!

This 15th century polished obsidian mirror was made by the Aztecs. They believed they could use such objects to see into the world of the gods.

PERIDOTITE

Peridotite is a general term for a rock containing mostly olivine (see page 138) with most of the remainder being pyroxene (see page 26). This is the most common rock found in the upper mantle, and it's found in the oceanic tectonic plates.

FACT FILE

- **Name:** from the name of the gemstone peridot
- **Rock type:** igneous
- **Color:** apple-green to brown or black
- **Texture:** coarse-grained
- **Found:** worldwide, but more common underground

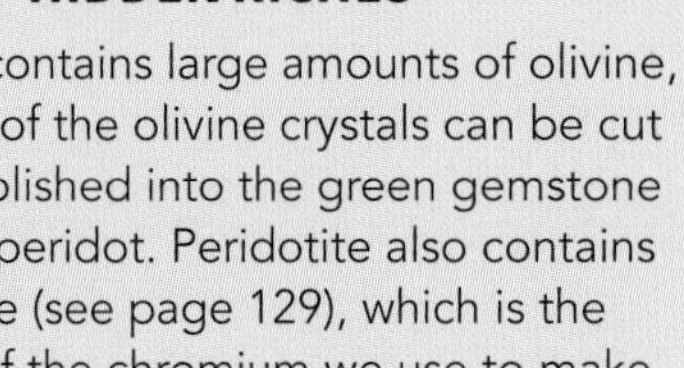

HIDDEN RICHES

Peridotite contains large amounts of olivine, and some of the olivine crystals can be cut out and polished into the green gemstone known as peridot. Peridotite also contains chromite (see page 129), which is the only ore of the chromium we use to make stainless steel. A variety of peridotite called kimberlite sometimes contains diamonds!

Deep-seated volcanic eruptions can bring kimberlite to Earth's surface, sometimes carrying diamonds with it!

This rock outcrop near Niihama City, Japan, is made from peridotite. Fresh peridotite is a greenish-brown color due to the olivine it contains but when it weathers it turns medium brown.

PUMICE

In some volcanic eruptions, the lava is saturated with gas. It's forced out as molten froth and, when it cools, bubbles of gas become trapped in the newly formed rock. These bubbles give pumice its distinctive spongelike appearance.

FACT FILE

- **Name:** from the Latin *pumex*, meaning "foam"
- **Rock type:** igneous
- **Color:** white, gray, tan, or black
- **Texture:** glassy and porous, like a sponge
- **Found:** worldwide, especially in volcanic regions

LIGHT BUT STRONG

Pumice is often mixed with concrete to make lighter building blocks. The air spaces in pumice are good for insulation, too. Pumice is very abrasive, even when it's ground to a powder, so people have used it to scrub and scour for centuries. Pumice is also useful to gardeners. When it's mixed with soil, it stores moisture and nutrients, releasing them slowly. It also helps to add oxygen to the soil.

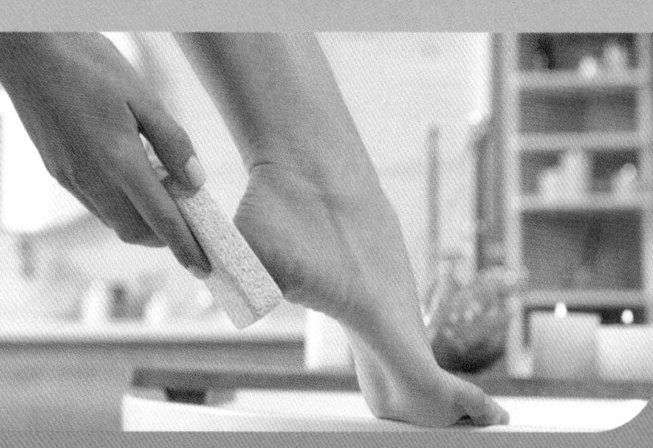

Pumice stones are used to scrape away dead skin. Some soaps also contain ground pumice.

The empty pockets in pumice make it so light that it will float on water. Sometimes pumice travels across oceans!

RHYOLITE

Rhyolite is similar to granite (see page 101), but it forms above the ground rather than below it. It forms from thick, slow-moving lava, and it often piles up into large lava domes. The same magma that forms rhyolite can also form pumice (see page 103), if it has enough gas trapped inside it when it erupts.

FACT FILE

- **Name:** from the Greek *rhyax*, meaning "lava stream"
- **Rock type:** igneous
- **Color:** pink or gray
- **Texture:** very fine-grained
- **Found:** worldwide, often near volcanoes along continental edges

BIG AND SMALL

Rhyolite often has a very fine-grained texture. Sometimes, however, it can be what geologists call "porphyritic," with a mix of small and large crystals. Rocks like these form when magma cools slowly underground, allowing large crystals to form. Then the magma erupts, and the uncrystallized portion of it cools quickly with a fine-grained texture, trapping the larger crystals, as shown below.

These cliffs in Corsica are porphyritic rhyolite—a mix of fine-grained rock and large crystals called phenocrysts.

The Novarupta volcano in southern Alaska formed during the largest volcanic eruption of the 20th century. After the eruption, a lava dome of rhyolite plugged the vent of the volcano.

TUFF

When a volcano erupts, it often ejects out ash and other minerals. These materials shoot into the air and eventually fall to the ground. There, they are compacted into a layer of rock. This is what's known as tuff.

FACT FILE

- **Name:** from the Latin *tofus*, meaning "porous rock"
- **Rock type:** igneous
- **Color:** brown or gray
- **Texture:** fine-grained
- **Found:** worldwide, near the locations of explosive eruptions

TUFF DEPOSITS

Thick deposits of tuff form around the bases of volcanoes. Geologists can often find stacked-up layers from different eruptions. Tuff is softer and easier to work than many other rocks, and in Italy the Romans carved it into blocks for buildings and bridges. It's also widely used in Armenia and parts of Germany.

These famous statues known as *moai*, on Easter Island in the southeastern Pacific Ocean, were carved from tuff.

The rocks of Jeju Island, South Korea, are full of tuff deposits. The bands of colors come from different volcanic eruptions.

BRECCIA

Sedimentary rocks are described as "clastic" if they're made up of broken pieces, or "clasts," of pre-existing rocks. These pieces are usually visible within the rock. Breccia is one of these clastic rocks. It's a generic name for a clastic rock made up of the jagged pieces of older rocks.

FACT FILE

- **Name:** from the Italian *breccia*, meaning "loose gravel" or "rubble"
- **Rock type:** sedimentary
- **Color:** various
- **Texture:** coarse-grained, with large, angular fragments
- **Found:** worldwide, wherever rock debris collects

FORMATION

Breccia can form anywhere that rock debris piles up. This might be at the base of a rock outcrop that's weathered by wind, or in a place where flowing water deposits rock particles. Over a long time, the smaller particles fill the spaces between the fragments, and everything gets bound together to form a new rock.

The clasts in breccia can be a fraction of an inch across or several feet, like these at Titus Canyon, California.

Breccia is often named for the type of rock that its fragments came from, such as this "marble breccia."

CONGLOMERATE

Conglomerate is similar to breccia, and the two rocks form in similar ways. The main difference is that the particles of old rock in conglomerate have a rounded shape, while in breccia they are more angular.

FACT FILE

- **Name:** from the Latin *conglomerare*, meaning "to roll together"
- **Rock type:** sedimentary
- **Color:** various
- **Texture:** coarse-grained, with rounded fragments
- **Found:** worldwide, wherever flowing water deposits rock debris

MIX AND MATCH

The rock pieces in conglomerate got their rounded shape from being tumbled in flowing water, so conglomerate is found in places where water flows (or once flowed). It's often described as pebble, cobble, or boulder conglomerate, based on the size of the pieces. In some conglomerate, the pebbles are all a similar size, but in others they're a mix of different sizes.

Shingle on beaches could eventually form into conglomerate if it's buried and turned into rock.

The rounded fragments of different rocks in conglomerate are held together by silica, calcite, or iron oxide.

COAL

Most rocks are made of minerals, but coal is unusual in that it formed from the remains of dead plants that lived millions of years ago. In swampy areas, the low oxygen levels in the water kept dead plants from decaying. The plants were eventually buried, forming a thick seam of material that gradually turned into the rock we call coal.

FACT FILE

- **Name:** from the Old English *col*, meaning "glowing ember"
- **Rock type:** sedimentary
- **Color:** black or brownish-black
- **Texture:** coarse-grained
- **Found:** worldwide

SLOWLY CHANGING

Over millions of years, heat and pressure turned the underground layers of plant matter into rock. The coal goes through different stages during this time. Once it has formed rock, it's known as lignite. Bituminous coal is next, with more carbon and less oxygen and hydrogen. The final stage is anthracite. This is considered to be a metamorphic rock because heat and pressure have changed it so much.

An artist's impression of plants living 300 million years ago, which formed much of the coal we have today.

Coal is mined around the world and burned as a fuel. The largest reserves are in the USA, Russia, China, Australia, and India.

SILTSTONE

Siltstone forms where layers of silt are deposited by flowing water. Over time, the layers then get compacted and turned into rock. Siltstone is less common than sandstone or shale, which form in similar ways. It also tends to form in thinner layers.

FACT FILE

- **Name:** possibly from the Old Swedish *sylta*, meaning "mud"
- **Rock type:** sedimentary
- **Color:** various
- **Texture:** fine-grained
- **Found:** worldwide, wherever flowing water deposits rock debris

WHAT IS SILT?

Silt is not a specific material. Whether a substance is classified as silt depends on the size of its particles. Silt particles are smaller than those in fine sand, but bigger than those in clay. The particles can be micas, feldspars, quartz, or other materials (see page 26). As a result, siltstone comes in a wide range of colors, including gray, brown, and reddish-brown.

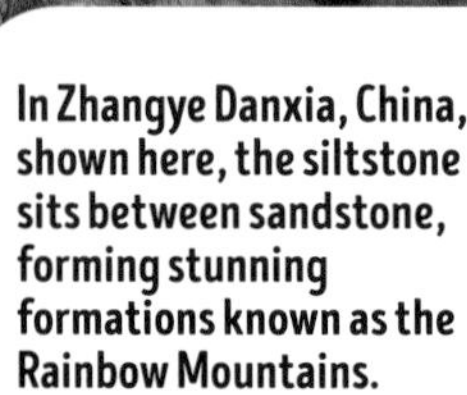

In Zhangye Danxia, China, shown here, the siltstone sits between sandstone, forming stunning formations known as the Rainbow Mountains.

Robotic rovers have found sedimentary rocks on Mars, including what we think is siltstone.

LIMESTONE

Limestone comes in many different forms, including chalk, but all are made of calcium carbonate. Limestone is often found exposed at the surface, where rainwater slowly dissolves it into weathered shapes.

FACT FILE

- **Name:** comes from the lime (calcium oxide) it produces when burned (Old English *lim* means "sticky substance")
- **Rock type:** sedimentary
- **Color:** white, gray, or pink
- **Texture:** fine-grained
- **Found:** worldwide, especially in shallow parts of the ocean floor

LIVING ROCK?

Limestone can form in one of three ways. Some limestone forms when calcium carbonate that was dissolved in water precipitates, or comes out of the solution, and accumulates to form rock. Limestone can also form when water evaporates, such as the formation of stalagmites and stalactites. Other limestone forms from the remains of sea creatures. Their shells and skeletons are rich in calcium carbonate, and when they die their remains get buried to form thick layers of limestone.

Some corals create exoskeletons of calcium carbonate, which slowly build up to form reefs.

Large deposits of chalk, such as these cliffs on the Danish island of Møn, often contain fossils of prehistoric sea creatures.

CAVE ROCKS

Many caves form when water wears away limestone underground. These caves can also form new limestone. Water seeps down into the cave from above. It's saturated with minerals, including calcium carbonate. When the water evaporates, the calcium carbonate is left behind. It hardens into pillars that create eerie formations. This type of limestone is known as travertine (see page 109).

Luray Cavern in Virginia is full of limestone stalactites and stalagmites.

USING LIMESTONE

Limestone is incredibly versatile—we may use it in more different ways than any other rock. It's easy to mine and is widely used as a building stone. Limestone is also crushed to form the base layer of roads and railways. Burning it produces lime, which we need to make cement. It's even fed to chickens as a dietary supplement to help them produce strong eggshells!

The prehistoric White Horse of Uffington, England, was made by scraping earth away to reveal the chalk below.

SANDSTONE

Sandstone is one of the most common sedimentary rocks, found all over the world. It's formed from layers of small, sand-sized grains that are deposited by flowing water. Over time, the tiny gaps between the grains fill with a chemical "cement"—usually calcium carbonate or silica.

FACT FILE

- **Name:** from its sand-sized grains
- **Rock type:** sedimentary
- **Color:** various, including brown, yellow, red, gray, and white
- **Texture:** medium-grained
- **Found:** worldwide

The colored bands of "Old Castle Rocks," a sandstone outcrop in the Palatinate Forest, Germany. Red sandstone gets its color from the iron oxide it contains.

CLUES TO THE PAST

Sandstone often has bands of color, and erosion caused by wind or water can carve it into beautiful formations. By looking carefully at sandstone samples, geologists can often see structures—such as ripple marks or mud cracks—that provide clues about the conditions when the rock formed. Layers of sandstone can also conceal fossils of prehistoric plants and animals.

In the ancient city of Petra, buildings were carved into a sandstone cliff in the 3rd century BCE.

SHALE

Shale forms in a similar way to sandstone, but from smaller, clay-sized grains. It's basically mud that has turned into rock, so it's part of a group of sedimentary rocks known as mudrocks. Shale is different from other mudrocks because it's made up of thin layers that can split apart, forming thin slabs.

FACT FILE

- **Name:** possibly from the Old German *schale*, meaning "shell" or "slice"
- **Rock type:** sedimentary
- **Color:** often black or gray but also green, red, yellow, or brown
- **Texture:** fine-grained with thin layers
- **Found:** worldwide

These colorful layers of shale are found in the Caucasus region, which lies between the Black Sea and the Caspian Sea.

USING SHALE

Some deposits of shale, buried deep underground, are sources of oil and natural gas. The mud that they were made from contained tiny particles of organic matter (the remains of dead plants and animals), which turned into oil or gas after millions of years of heat and pressure. Shale can also be ground into a fine powder and mixed with water to make clay that can be shaped into bricks, tiles, and plant pots.

Oil companies drill deep underground to reach the shale layers where crude oil is found.

TRAVERTINE

Travertine is a variety of limestone. Unlike many limestones, travertine is not made from the remains of prehistoric organisms. Instead, it forms when water that is rich in calcium carbonate evaporates, leaving the minerals behind. This often happens in caves and hot springs.

FACT FILE

- **Name:** from the Italian *travertino*, meaning "a kind of building stone"
- **Rock type:** sedimentary
- **Color:** white or cream in its pure form, but impurities can make it yellowish or rusty
- **Texture:** fine-grained
- **Found:** worldwide, in caves or near mineral springs

CARBON CAPTURE

Calcium carbonate is dissolved in spring water, and the chemical trigger that makes it separate out to form rock is usually a change in the water's carbon dioxide levels. Most travertine forms when carbon dioxide is lost to the atmosphere, like the bubbles fizzing out of a can of cola. But some types form when the water absorbs carbon dioxide from the atmosphere—effectively sucking up this greenhouse gas!

Travertine is often cut and polished to make beautiful kitchen worktops or hard-wearing tiles.

Over thousands of years, the waters of these hot springs at Yellowstone National Park have formed travertine terraces.

FLINT

Flint is a hard, tough substance that forms as nodules within beds of limestone. It's made of very fine-grained quartz that has replaced part of the limestone, or filled in holes left by animals or fossils. Flint is very hard and usually remains long after the surrounding rock has weathered away.

FACT FILE

- **Name:** from the Old English *flint*, meaning "chip" or "splinter"
- **Rock type:** sedimentary
- **Color:** usually gray or black with a white outer covering
- **Texture:** fine-grained
- **Found:** worldwide, wherever flowing water deposits rock debris

USING FLINT

A freshly broken piece of flint has a smooth, almost glassy appearance. When struck sharply, a piece of flint will break into sharp-edged pieces. Prehistoric people learned how to shape it into scrapers, axes, knife blades, and other tools. People have also used flint to start fires, as it gives off sparks when struck against a piece of steel. It was part of the firing mechanism in early guns.

In England, farmers have traditionally built houses using lumps of flint cleared from their fields.

Because it is so tough, gravel containing flint is often used in driveways.

MARBLE

Marble forms when limestone recrystallizes due to heat and pressure. This stone can be polished smooth to give it a beautiful shiny appearance, which is why it's been used as a luxury building stone for thousands of years.

FACT FILE

- **Name:** from the Greek *marmaros*, meaning "shining stone"
- **Rock type:** metamorphic
- **Formed from:** limestone and dolomite
- **Color:** mainly white
- **Texture:** fine to coarse-grained
- **Found:** worldwide, particularly China, India, Italy, Spain, United States

In this marble quarry in Italy, dynamite has loosened the marble from the quarry walls and the stone has been cut into blocks. The blocks can then be cut into thin slabs to be transported to where it's needed.

BUILDING BLOCKS

Marble is quarried for use as a building stone. It can be cut into blocks to form the structure of buildings. Polished marble slabs are also used for interior walls and floors, and it can be shaped into decorative features, such as columns and fireplaces.

The Taj Mahal in India is made from pure white marble.

COLOR RANGE

Pure marble is white, but impurities can give it other colors, ranging from green, pink, and brown to grey and even black. These mineral impurities were originally layers of other minerals that were embedded in the original limestone, and when the rock recrystallized, they remained as bands of color. Common mineral impurities found in marble include quartz, mica, graphite, iron oxides, and even small crystals of pyrite.

Pink marble (left) usually contains iron and feldspar, while yellow and brown colors (right) are caused by iron oxide.

SCULPTING WITH MARBLE

Pure white marble was the material of choice for ancient Greek and Roman sculptors, as well as many later artists. It's relatively soft, making it easier to carve. It also has a waxy look once polished, which makes sculptures of people look more lifelike.

Michelangelo's *David*, completed in 1504, stands over 16 ft (5 m) tall and was carved from a single block of marble.

SLATE

Slate is the metamorphic rock formed from shale (see page 108), and the two look quite similar. You can tell them apart by hitting the rock with a hammer—shale will make only a dull sound, but slate will "ring."

FACT FILE

- **Name:** from the Old French *esclate*, meaning "to split or splinter"
- **Rock type:** metamorphic
- **Formed from:** mudstone or shale
- **Color:** various
- **Texture:** fine-grained
- **Found:** worldwide, particularly Spain, Brazil, United States, Canada, China

TOUGH TILES

Microscopic crystals inside slate rock are all aligned in the same direction, meaning that slate can be split into thin, flat sheets. This property has made slate incredibly useful, and for many centuries people have been using it for floor and roof tiles. Slabs of polished slate form the base of many pool tables. Unlike wood, the rock will not warp so the playing surface remains perfectly level and even.

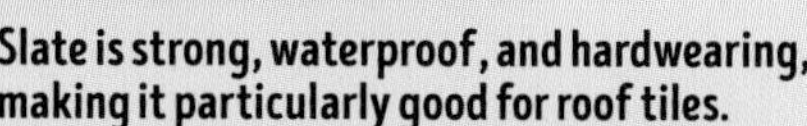

Slate is strong, waterproof, and hardwearing, making it particularly good for roof tiles.

A natural slate outcrop in Spain, the world's largest producer and exporter of natural slate.

QUARTZITE

This metamorphic rock forms when sedimentary sandstone is subjected to intense pressure. In its pure form, quartzite is usually white or gray. However, impurities from other minerals can give it a wide variety of different colors.

FACT FILE

- **Name:** from its main mineral, quartz
- **Rock type:** metamorphic
- **Formed from:** sedimentary sandstone
- **Color:** various
- **Texture:** large, coarse grains surrounded by fine grains
- **Found:** worldwide, particularly Canada, United States, Ireland

SOLID AND STRONG

Quartzite is very hard, and prehistoric people used it to make stone axes. The ancient Egyptians sculpted it into statues and stone coffins. Today it is polished and used for walls and flooring, as well as kitchen worktops. Quartzite can also be crushed and used to build roads.

This quartzite statue of the Egyptian pharaoh Osorkon I was carved in the 10th century BCE.

A quartzite outcrop in Minnesota where the rock was historically used as a building stone.

AMPHIBOLITE

Amphibolite often forms in places where two tectonic plates push together and mountains have formed. The heat and pressure turn igneous or sedimentary rocks into metamorphic rock. This process often forms thin layers within the rock.

FACT FILE

- **Name:** from the Latin *amphibolus* ("ambiguous") because of the variety in this mineral group
- **Rock type:** metamorphic
- **Formed from:** igneous rocks such as basalt and gabbro, or clay-rich sedimentary rock
- **Color:** black, brown or green
- **Texture:** coarse-grained
- **Found:** worldwide, where intrusive igneous rocks form

HARD AND VERSATILE

Amphibolite is hard, heavy, and tough. Ancient people used it to make stone axes for cutting down trees and working the wood. It has also been used to make hard-wearing gravestones. Today it is often crushed and used as a base in road building, or to support railway tracks.

Polished amphibolite can be used for decorative features. It's often called "black granite."

Cape Ortegal on the Galician Coast, Spain, is a mountainous peninsula of amphibolite rock.

GNEISS

The name of this rock is pronounced "nice," and it has distinct bands of different minerals. These bands are often folded, though the folds are often only visible in large areas of rock. Gneiss usually forms at convergent plate boundaries, where two tectonic plates push against each other.

FACT FILE

- **Name:** from the Old High German *gneisto*, meaning "spark," because of its sparkly appearance
- **Rock type:** metamorphic
- **Formed from:** often from shale (under heat and pressure) but also from some igneous rocks
- **Color:** gray, pink, or white with bands of darker gray or black
- **Texture:** coarse-grained
- **Found:** worldwide

SPARKLY BANDS

Gneiss is often rich in feldspar and quartz, as well as mica, which can give it a sparkly appearance similar to granite. Feldspar and quartz occur in the pale bands, and different feldspars can sometimes give gneiss a pinkish color. The dark bands are often made up of a mineral called hornblende. The bands formed as a result of extreme heat and pressure during the metamorphic process.

Some gneiss has a salt-and-pepper effect, while other types have wide, clearly defined bands of color.

Hard-wearing paving stones are often made of gneiss and granite. Gneiss looks similar to granite, but you can see its minerals are separated into light and dark bands.

SCHIST

Schist is similar to gneiss in many ways, but with one major difference: it can be broken into thin slabs. A rock's ability to be broken this way is called schistosity. If schist continues to metamorphose under heat and pressure, it will lose its schistosity and turn into gneiss.

FACT FILE

- **Name:** from the Greek *schistos*, meaning "split"
- **Rock type:** metamorphic
- **Formed from:** sedimentary rocks such as shale or mudstone, or igneous rocks
- **Color:** black, silvery gray, blue, green
- **Texture:** coarse-grained
- **Found:** worldwide, in places where intrusive igneous rocks formed

HIDDEN TREASURES

Schist's tendency to split means that it's not usually strong enough to use in construction. However, it is valuable in another way—as a source of gemstones. Many different gemstones that tend to form in metamorphic rocks are often found in schist. These include emerald, garnet, sapphire, ruby, and black and blue stones called staurolite and tanzanite.

This schist sample is embedded with garnets (red) and staurolite (black).

Some traditional stone walls are made by stacking up slabs of schist, like this wall found in Portugal's Douro Valley.

ECLOGITE

Eclogite is similar in composition to basalt, and is usually a mix of pyroxene (see page 26) and red garnet. The beautiful mix of green pyroxene, red garnet, and white quartz gives eclogite its nickname: the Christmas rock.

FACT FILE

- **Name:** from the Greek *ekloge*, meaning "choice" or "selection"
- **Rock type:** metamorphic
- **Formed from:** igneous rocks rich in iron and magnesium
- **Color:** mottled red, white, and green
- **Texture:** coarse-grained
- **Found:** worldwide, especially United States, Norway, Australia, Brazil, West Africa

SURFACE OR MANTLE?

Eclogite forms when igneous rock rich in magnesium and iron is subjected to intense pressure and relatively high heat. These conditions exist deep underground, in the upper layers of the mantle. As a result, eclogite mainly occurs underground and is relatively rare on the surface. It can form from oceanic crust that is subducted about 25 miles (40 km) deep into the mantle.

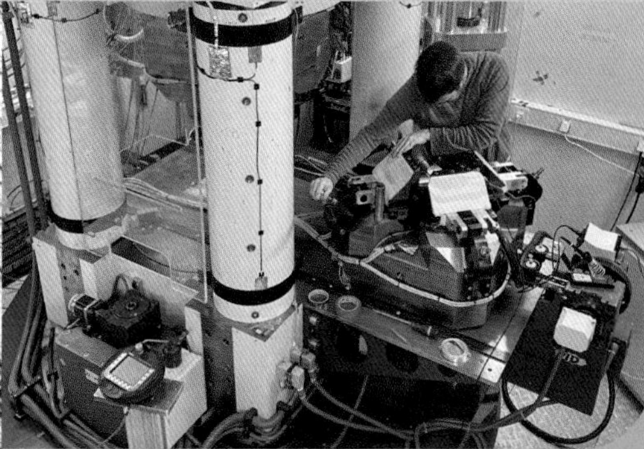

This geologist is using a high pressure press to test the properties of eclogite found deep within Earth.

When eclogite is viewed under a microscope, you can clearly see the different colored grains.

GOLD

Humans have always been fascinated by gold. Its shiny yellow appearance led the Inca of South America to call it the "tears of the Sun." We have been making gold into jewelry, art, and coins for thousands of years.

FACT FILE

- **Name:** from the Old English *gold*, which came from an older word meaning "to shine"
- **Color:** shiny, bright yellow
- **Cleavage:** none
- **Streak:** shiny yellow
- **Hardness:** 2.5–3
- **Specific gravity:** 19.3
- **Luster:** metallic

FLAKES AND NUGGETS

Gold is a chemical element as well as a mineral. It doesn't react easily with other elements to form compounds, so it is often found in nature in its pure form. It can form regular crystal shapes, but this is rare. Gold is more often found as tiny flakes or scales, or as irregularly shaped nuggets. Most nuggets are small, but there are whoppers too—the biggest ever found weighed nearly 175 lb (80 kg)! Flakes and nuggets can be melted down and used for jewelry.

This solid gold necklace dates from the 4th century BCE. It was discovered in a burial mound in Ukraine in 1971.

USING GOLD

Aside from being beautiful, gold is extremely versatile. It is tough and durable, yet malleable enough to hammer into shape. It's good at conducting both heat and electricity. These properties give it a huge range of uses. Gold has long been used for fillings in teeth. Today it is used in electrical devices such as smartphones. Tiny amounts of gold on window glass reflect sunlight and keep buildings cool.

Space satellites are fitted with ultra-thin layers of gold foil to control their temperature in orbit and to protect them from radiation.

You can sometimes see thin veins of gold embedded in other rocks. These formed when hot fluids flowed through cracks deep in Earth's crust.

STRIKING IT RICH

Because gold is so valuable, countless people have dedicated their lives to finding it. They might use metal detectors to hunt for nuggets, or use pans to sieve out tiny flakes in rivers or streams. Word of big finds spreads quickly, and may cause a "gold rush" as people from all over the world flock to the area to see if they can find some for themselves.

Today, large companies operate most open-cast gold mines, like this one in New Zealand.

SILVER

Like gold, silver is often found in its natural form. However, it is also found mixed with other metals or locked inside different minerals. Today we get much of our silver as a by-product when the ores of other metals are processed.

FACT FILE

- **Name:** from the Old English *seolfor*, meaning "silver" or "money"
- **Color:** silvery, or grayish-black when weathered
- **Cleavage:** none
- **Streak:** silver white
- **Hardness:** 2.5–3
- **Specific gravity:** 10.1–11.1
- **Luster:** metallic

USING SILVER

Silver is a bit harder than gold, but it can still be hammered out thin or made into wire. It does react with other elements, such as sulfur, and this reaction is what causes a layer of tarnish on silver cutlery or jewelry. For many decades, silver was used to make chemical compounds that were used in photographic film.

Coins used to be made of silver, as it is hard-wearing but soft enough for designs to be imprinted on the metal.

Because silver conducts electricity so well, silver-based inks and films are often used to make circuit boards.

COPPER

Copper is easily found when it is in its natural state, and it's probably the first metal that humans learned to hammer into shape. The ancient Egyptians melted it and cast it in molds, and later people learned to mix it with tin to produce bronze, which is stronger.

FACT FILE

- **Name:** from the Old English *coper*, originally from the Greek name for Cyprus (where it was mined)
- **Color:** light reddish-brown, but turns green or black over time
- **Cleavage:** none
- **Streak:** light rose
- **Hardness:** 2.5–3
- **Specific gravity:** 8.9
- **Luster:** metallic

COPPER TODAY

Nuggets of native copper were sometimes found in streams, where the element's shiny metallic appearance made it easy to spot. Today, most copper is produced from ores. At large mines, machines dig out rocks that contain up to 1 percent copper, then smelt them to obtain the metal. Copper is used for plumbing pipes and wiring for computers, telephones, and other electrical items.

Copper is the most common metal used in wiring. The average car contains 1.5 miles (2.5 km) of copper wire!

Many coins were once made of solid copper, and today some are still coated with a thin layer of copper.

ARSENIC

Arsenic is a semi-metal—it has properties in common with some metals, but other properties that are more like those of non-metals. It is widely found mixed with other elements in minerals such as orpiment (see page 121), but it can also sometimes be found in its pure natural form.

FACT FILE

- **Name:** from the Persian *zarnik*, meaning "gold-colored"
- **Color:** silver-white or gray
- **Cleavage:** perfect
- **Streak:** white or gray
- **Hardness:** 3.5
- **Specific gravity:** 5.7
- **Luster:** metallic

DANGER!

Arsenic is NOT a mineral that you should add to your collection. It's highly toxic and in the past it was widely used as a pesticide—and sometimes as a murder weapon too! If you see a piece of what you think might be arsenic when out rockhounding, don't handle it. It's been phased out of most pesticides and insecticides, for safety.

Arsenic is still used in some electronic devices but the amounts are tiny enough to be safe.

Arsenic is often released at hydrothermal sites, such as the El Tatio geyser in Chile, where water heated underground spews out.

BISMUTH

Bismuth is found in the same group of the periodic table as arsenic, but it can look very different. Its natural color is pinkish, but when exposed to air it turns iridescent, shimmering in a rainbow of colors. However, this is only temporary, and when it tarnishes further, the bismuth will become dark gray.

FACT FILE

- **Name:** from the Old German *wis mat*, meaning "white mass"
- **Color:** silvery pink, or iridescent or silvery-gray when tarnished
- **Cleavage:** perfect
- **Streak:** gray
- **Hardness:** 2–2.5
- **Specific gravity:** 9.7–9.8
- **Luster:** metallic

IS IT REAL?

It is rare to find bismuth in its pure, natural state. However, scientists often grow crystals of pure bismuth in a laboratory. These crystals form unusual "hopper" shapes, which look like hollow pyramids. They grow in a spiral formation, each one stepping up from the one before. These brightly colored crystals look like something made on a 3-D printer, but they are pure bismuth!

Lab-grown bismuth is often coated so that it won't tarnish and lose its bright rainbow colors.

Bismuth is often found in lead ores, such as this galena, so it is produced as a by-product of lead mining.

GRAPHITE

You won't see graphite listed on the periodic table, but it's a pure form of the element carbon. Diamonds are another pure form of carbon, but they're nothing like dull gray graphite. Both substances are made up of nothing but carbon atoms, but the atoms bond together in different ways.

FACT FILE

- **Name:** from the Greek *graphein*, meaning "to write"
- **Color:** black
- **Cleavage:** single sheet
- **Streak:** shiny black or grey
- **Hardness:** 1–2
- **Specific gravity:** 2.2
- **Luster:** metallic or dull

DIFFERENT STRUCTURE

In graphite, the carbon atoms are organized in flat sheets—each is one atom thick—as shown in the diagram below. The sheets stack up but aren't really connected to each other, so a small amount of force can make them slide over one another. Graphite often forms as crystals or flakes within metamorphic rocks. It can also form from the metamorphism of coal.

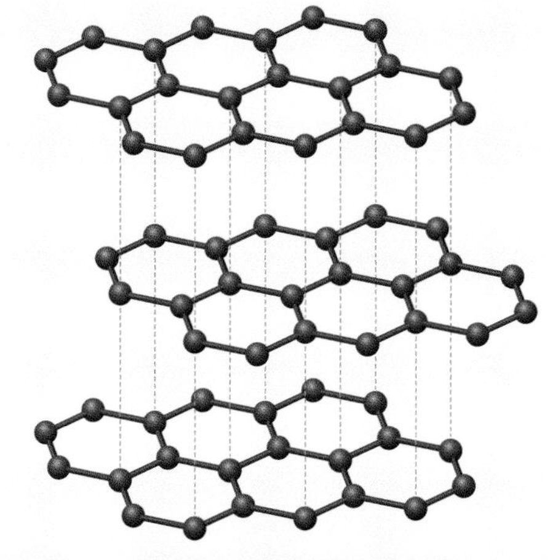

The "lead" in pencils is graphite. Its structure lets it rub off easily as you scrape the pencil across paper.

SULFUR

Sulfur is one of the more abundant elements found in Earth's crust. Most of this sulfur is locked up in compounds with other elements —in fact, sulfide minerals make the next category in this directory! But sulfur can also be found in its native form. Solid sulfur can form from volcanic gases, so deposits of it are often found near volcanic vents.

FACT FILE

- **Name:** from the Anglo-French *sulfere*, meaning "sulfur" or "hellfire"
- **Color:** yellow
- **Cleavage:** none
- **Streak:** white
- **Hardness:** 1.5–2.5
- **Specific gravity:** 2.1
- **Luster:** dull or greasy

BURNING STONE

In the past, pure sulfur was often known as "brimstone," which means "burning stone" because it burns easily, and in the Bible it's associated with Hell. In prehistoric times, it was used for cave paintings. Today, it is mined and made into sulfuric acid, which is an important ingredient in the processes that form other chemical products.

Sulfur's deep-yellow crystals come in many different shapes and arrangements.

Lassen Volcanic National Park, California, is full of the vibrant colors and pungent smells of sulfur deposits.

CHALCOPYRITE

Chalcopyrite is a mineral made up of copper, iron, and sulfur. It's the world's most important ore of copper, but its brassy yellow color can make it look more like gold, and it's sometimes called "fool's gold" as a result.

FACT FILE

- **Name:** from the Greek *khalkos*, meaning "copper"
- **Color:** brassy yellow or iridescent
- **Cleavage:** distinct
- **Streak:** greenish-black
- **Hardness:** 3.5–4
- **Specific gravity:** 4.2
- **Luster:** metallic

CHANGING COLOR

Chalcopyrite can form from igneous rock. It also forms in regions with hydrothermal activity. When first exposed, chalcopyrite is shiny and gold-colored, but over time it weathers and becomes a dull gray-green. But if there is acid present, the chalcopyrite can develop an iridescent sheen, with shades of violet and blue.

Some chalcopyrite samples sold in shops have been treated with acid to give them more vivid colors.

Chalcopyrite has been mined near a Spanish River, the Rio Tinto, for thousands of years. High levels of iron have turned the water red.

GALENA

Galena is another important ore, but it's an ore of lead and silver, not copper. It's been smelted to obtain lead for at least 8,000 years and may have been the first ore ever smelted by humans because it has a low melting point. Galena is found in igneous rocks as well as metamorphic and sedimentary. Because galena contains poisonous lead, you should wear gloves to handle it, and don't scrape it or inhale any dust.

FACT FILE

- **Name:** from the Latin *galena*, meaning "mix of silver and lead"
- **Color:** gray or silvery
- **Cleavage:** perfect
- **Streak:** lead gray
- **Hardness:** 2.5
- **Specific gravity:** 7.6
- **Luster:** metallic

CUBIC CRYSTALS

When freshly broken, a piece of galena shows cleavage in three different directions that meet at right angles. This is because its crystals are often cube-shaped. Because it has so much lead, which is a very heavy element, galena will feel heavy (high density) when you pick it up. One of the main uses of the lead obtained from galena is in the lead-acid batteries made for car engines.

Freshly broken galena crystals are a bright silvery color that will tarnish over time to a dull gray.

You can see galena glinting in these rock samples that contain the iron ore pyrite (fool's gold) and the lead ore galena (silvery).

MOLYBDENITE

Molybdenite is a compound of sulfur and the element molybdenum. In the past, people often confused it with lead. It forms hexagonal crystals with a metallic sheen that make it resemble graphite, though molybdenite is shinier and has a higher specific gravity.

FACT FILE

- **Name:** from the Greek *molybdos*, meaning "lead"
- **Color:** black or gray
- **Cleavage:** perfect
- **Streak:** greenish- or bluish-gray
- **Hardness:** 1–1.5
- **Specific gravity:** 4.7
- **Luster:** metallic

USEFUL ORE

Molybdenite is the main ore of the element molybdenum. Molybdenum is tough with a very high melting point, so it's often alloyed with other metals in order to pass on these properties. Molybdenum alloys are strong enough to be used for spacecraft parts! Molybdenite often also contains small amounts of rhenium, one of the rarest elements.

Adding small amounts of molybdenum to steel makes it stronger, harder, and more resistant to corrosion.

Most of the rhenium extracted from molybdenite is used to make the super-strong turbine blades in jet engines.

PYRITE

Pyrite looks even more like gold than chalcopyrite does, so it is also often called "fool's gold." However, it's easy to tell gold and pyrite apart if you know what to look for. Pyrite is hard and brittle—if you try to hammer it into shape like you would with gold, it will break. It also has a blackish streak while gold has a gold streak.

FACT FILE

- **Name:** from the Greek *pyrites*, meaning "stone of fire"
- **Color:** pale brassy yellow
- **Cleavage:** none
- **Streak:** greenish- or brownish-black
- **Hardness:** 6–6.5
- **Specific gravity:** 5.0
- **Luster:** metallic

SHINY CUBES

Pyrite naturally forms cube-shaped crystals, which can have faces over an inch across. Pyrite can also form eight- or twelve-sided crystals. And although pyrite has none of the properties that make gold so valuable, the two minerals often form together, so finding pyrite is sometimes a sign that there is gold nearby.

Golden pyrite crystals. Pyrite was named after the Greek word *pyr* ("fire") because it produces a spark when struck with iron.

Pyrite can be shaped into beads and jewelry, but it tarnishes easily if it's exposed to moisture.

SPHALERITE

Sphalerite is a compound of zinc, iron, and sulfur that's found in many different types of rocks. It's useful as an ore of zinc, which is used to galvanize (coat) iron and steel and stop them from rusting. Zinc is also alloyed with copper to produce brass.

FACT FILE

- **Name:** from the Greek *sphaleros*, meaning "deceptive," because it was often mistaken for galena
- **Color:** black, brown, yellow, gray, orange
- **Cleavage:** perfect, in six directions
- **Streak:** brown to light yellow
- **Hardness:** 3.5–4
- **Specific gravity:** 3.9–4.1
- **Luster:** metallic, resinous, or adamantine

Sphalerite (seen here as the colors brown to cream) is often found alongside other minerals such as galena and pyrite. When a sample is cut and polished, you can see the circles and swirls of the different minerals.

VARIED APPEARANCE

Sphalerite often forms in places where hot, acidic fluids rich in zinc come into contact with carbonate rocks. It can usually be seen as crystalline flecks in rocks, and sometimes also forms larger crystals. Thanks to differences in trace elements in the mineral, sphalerite crystals can be a transparent reddish-brown, opaque black, or green and glassy. Larger crystals cleave in six directions, forming perfect faces.

Sphalerite crystals come in different colors. These green-glassy sphalerite crystals are called cleiophane.

CINNABAR

Thanks to its bright red color, cinnabar is easy to spot, but keep your distance—this mineral is toxic, so you shouldn't handle it. It's the main ore of the toxic element mercury. It often forms as a coating on other rocks, but cinnabar can occasionally form larger crystals.

FACT FILE

- **Name:** from the Persian *zinjirfrah*, meaning "dragon's blood"
- **Color:** red
- **Cleavage:** perfect
- **Streak:** scarlet
- **Hardness:** 2–2.5
- **Specific gravity:** 8.0
- **Luster:** adamantine to dull

Most cinnabar is described as "massive" (see page 98), meaning that the grains are so small that you need a microscope to see them.

DEADLY RED

Before people realized how toxic mercury was, powdered cinnabar was often used as a pigment because of its vibrant red color. The pigment made from cinnabar was often known as "vermilion" or "Chinese red," and it was used to make paints or lacquers. Cinnabar was also used as medicine—either swallowed or rubbed on the skin—but probably did more harm than good!

These carved vases date from China's Qing Dynasty (1644–1911). The deep red is a cinnabar lacquer.

STIBNITE

Also known as antimonite, stibnite is a compound of sulfur and antimony, and it's the main ore of antimony. This semi-metal is often added to lead to harden it, especially for use in batteries. Antimony is also used in soldering and in semiconductors for electronic devices.

FACT FILE

- **Name:** from the Latin *stibium*, meaning "antimony"
- **Color:** gray or black
- **Cleavage:** perfect
- **Streak:** dark gray
- **Hardness:** 2
- **Specific gravity:** 4.6
- **Luster:** metallic

CRYSTAL NEEDLES

Stibnite can form impressive crystals. They're long, thin prisms that are often striated—that is, marked with long, parallel streaks or lines. The crystals often look like black or grey needles, radiating out from a point. Some stibnite crystals can be very large. Specimens have been found measuring 24 in (60 cm) long!

When added to fireworks, antimony extracted from stibnite produces a bright blue color.

ORPIMENT

Orpiment is a compound of arsenic and sulfur (see pages 116–117), and, because arsenic is toxic, that means orpiment is too. If you spot a sample that you think might be orpiment, don't handle it.

FACT FILE

- **Name:** from the Latin *auri*, meaning "gold," and *pigmentum*, meaning "paint"
- **Color:** yellow
- **Cleavage:** perfect
- **Streak:** pale yellow
- **Hardness:** 1.5–2
- **Specific gravity:** 3.5
- **Luster:** resinous

MINERAL TWINS?

Orpiment is closely related to realgar, another arsenic-sulfur compound. Realgar is red but equally toxic. In the past, both minerals were regularly ground up to make pigments—red for realgar and golden yellow for orpiment. People also used both minerals for cosmetics and traditional medicine, and they still do in a few places, even though both substances will cause harm.

Realgar (red) and orpiment (yellow) are often found together in the same mineral deposits.

This hot spring in New Zealand has waters saturated with orpiment, which forms orange deposits along the shoreline.

STANNITE

This mineral is a compound that contains copper, iron, tin, and sulfur, and sometimes trace amounts of the element germanium. It's usually found in its massive form (see page 98), with tiny grains coating a surface, although sometimes it forms larger crystals.

FACT FILE

- **Name:** from the Latin *stannum*, meaning "tin"
- **Color:** gray or black
- **Cleavage:** indistinct
- **Streak:** black
- **Hardness:** 4
- **Specific gravity:** 4.4
- **Luster:** metallic

Old mine buildings in Cornwall, England, show where stannite and other ores were once dug out of the ground.

CORNISH TIN

Stannite is an important ore of tin. It was first discovered in Cornwall, England, where copper and tin have been mined for thousands of years. Tin was relatively rare, but it was needed to make bronze (a stronger alloy of copper and tin) for weapons and tools. Cornwall was rich in tin ores such as stannite, and the tin and copper produced there were traded all over the world.

This bronze dagger from Eastern Europe dates from 2400–1300 BCE.

PYRARGYRITE

This deep red mineral is often known as "ruby silver" because of its color and the fact that it is a source of silver. It's a compound of silver, antimony, and sulfur that starts off red but darkens to gray when exposed to light. Smaller crystals are more likely to be red and translucent.

FACT FILE

- **Name:** from the Greek *pyros*, meaning "fire" and argyros, meaning "silver"
- **Color:** deep red to gray
- **Cleavage:** distinct
- **Streak:** purple-red
- **Hardness:** 2.5
- **Specific gravity:** 5.8
- **Luster:** adamantine

The Cerro Rico ("Rich Mountain") silver mine in Bolivia. Miners began extracting silver ores such as pyrargyrite in this region in the 1500s.

PRISMATIC CRYSTALS

Pyrargyrite crystals usually form in a pattern described as prismatic, a type of monoclinic crystal (see page 29). Prismatic is a term that geologists use for crystals that are shaped like prisms, with four or more sides that are similar in length and width. Prismatic crystals are often long and relatively thin, and if you cut a cross-section of one, it would look like a regular polygon, with sides of roughly equal length.

AZURITE

This beautiful blue mineral is in the carbonate family. It's formed from three oxygen atoms arranged around a carbon atom. Azurite also contains copper, and it is often found alongside malachite, another copper-based mineral with a green color rather than blue.

FACT FILE

- **Name:** from the Persian *lazhuward*, meaning "blue"
- **Color:** bright or dark blue
- **Cleavage:** perfect
- **Streak:** blue
- **Hardness:** 3.5–4
- **Specific gravity:** 3.8
- **Luster:** glassy or dull

BLUE CRYSTALS

Azurite forms when waters rich in carbon dioxide seep into the ground and react with copper ores. The water dissolves copper from the ore and carries it to a new location, where azurite crystals form. Azurite is an ore of copper. Its beautiful blue color meant that, in the past, it was often powdered and used as a pigment. Today, it is still cut and polished for jewelry.

Azurite crystals (shown here among green malachite crystals) often form in small round balls known as "blueberries."

CERUSSITE

Most examples of this mineral are colorless or whitish-gray, but impurities from elements, such as copper, can color it blue or green. Cerussite is an important ore of lead, and it was once the source of the "white lead" used in lead-based paints.

FACT FILE

- **Name:** from the Latin *cerussa*, a type of white lead-based pigment
- **Color:** white, gray, blue, or green
- **Cleavage:** distinct
- **Streak:** white
- **Hardness:** 3–3.5
- **Specific gravity:** 6.5
- **Luster:** adamantine or glassy

TWINNED CRYSTALS

Cerussite can form very cool-looking crystals. They often "twin," meaning that two grow together in a symmetrical way. This can produce crystals shaped like stars or snowflakes, or even hearts. But remember that, no matter how amazing the crystals look, they still contain lead—so you should wear gloves and never scrape them or breathe in their dust.

These cerussite crystals were found in Slovakia.

CALCITE

Calcite is one of the most abundant minerals on Earth's surface. It's the mineral form of calcium carbonate —made of calcium, carbon, and oxygen—and it's the main mineral making up rocks such as limestone and marble.

FACT FILE

- **Name:** from the Latin *calx*, meaning "lime" (calcium oxide)
- **Color:** white or colorless
- **Cleavage:** perfect
- **Streak:** white
- **Hardness:** 3
- **Specific gravity:** 2.7
- **Luster:** glassy

These chalky limestone cliffs in Corsica are mainly composed of calcium carbonate.

ONE MINERAL, MANY FORMS

Most calcite occurs in its massive form (see page 98), making up the bulk of limestone and marble deposits. However, calcite can also form beautiful crystals in a variety of shapes. Some of these crystals can be twinned to form symmetrical shapes. Calcite can also form "sand calcite," where the calcite crystals grow in a sandy environment, and grains of sand are included within the crystals.

Over the centuries, flowing thermal waters in Pamukkale, Turkey, have left beautiful calcite stalactites behind.

ALABASTER AND SUNSTONES

Calcite is relatively soft and easy to carve, and the ancient Egyptians turned it into statues as well as bowls and jars. These included the canopic jars used to store the organs when a body was mummified. The Vikings used transparent calcite crystals as "sunstones" to help them find their way. The calcite splits light to make a double image that could show the position of the Sun, even when it was hidden behind clouds.

This ancient Egyptian statue is carved from calcite. The stone was often called alabaster, but to a geologist, alabaster is a form of the mineral gypsum.

USING CALCITE

Calcite is one of the most widely used minerals, mainly in the form of limestone and marble. It's used in buildings around the world. Calcite also has the ability to neutralize acids, so farmers spread crushed calcite on their fields to improve the soil, and antacid tablets for indigestion and heartburn also contain calcite. The white color of powdered calcite makes it useful for paints and pigments.

Chickens are often fed crushed calcite as a calcium supplement in their grain, to help them form their eggshells.

DOLOMITE

Dolomite is a carbonate mineral that contains both calcium and magnesium. The same name is also used for a sedimentary rock, similar to limestone, that is made up mainly of the mineral dolomite. When limestone contains dolomite, it's called dolomitic limestone.

FACT FILE

- **Name:** from the French geologist Déodat de Dolomieu who described it
- **Color:** white, cream, or colorless
- **Cleavage:** perfect
- **Streak:** white
- **Hardness:** 3.5–4
- **Specific gravity:** 2.8–2.9
- **Luster:** glassy

CLOSE COMPANIONS

Dolomite is often found in places where there were once hydrothermal vents, forcing out hot, mineral-rich water. Other minerals such as sphalerite, galena, and chalcopyrite (see pages 118–120) form in similar environments, and they're often found alongside dolomite. Many dolomite crystals are shaped like slanting cubes but they sometimes have curved faces.

Dolomite crystals often form a crust on other rocks or minerals, such as this sample of sphalerite.

The Dolomites are a mountain range in Italy. They're part of the Alps and are named after the dolomite they contain.

MAGNESITE

Magnesite often forms when rocks rich in magnesium react with water containing dissolved carbon dioxide. It's rare for magnesite to form large, distinct crystals. More often it's massive in form (see page 98) or made up of thin sheets. It can also be fibrous, with long, thin crystals.

FACT FILE

- **Name:** from the magnesium that it contains
- **Color:** white, gray, brown, or colorless
- **Cleavage:** perfect
- **Streak:** white
- **Hardness:** 3.5–4.5
- **Specific gravity:** 3.0
- **Luster:** dull and chalky but sometimes glassy

FEEL THE HEAT

Magnesite is an important ore of magnesium, and when it's heated it will separate into magnesium oxide and carbon dioxide. Magnesium oxide has a very high melting point, which makes it useful. Bricks made from magnesium oxide are used to line kilns for firing pottery, as well as industrial ovens and blast furnaces for smelting ore.

When firing pottery, kilns can reach extreme temperatures of 2,500 °F (1,400 °C) or more.

An open-cast magnesite mine in Karagaysky, Russia.

MALACHITE

Malachite is an example of a mineral that is both beautiful and useful. Historically, it was an important ore of copper, while its rich green color, banded patterns, and smooth texture made it popular for decoration and as a gemstone.

FACT FILE

- **Name:** from the Greek *malachitis*, meaning "mallow," because its color was like the leaves of the mallow plant
- **Color:** green
- **Cleavage:** perfect
- **Streak:** pale green
- **Hardness:** 3.5–4
- **Specific gravity:** 3.9–4.0
- **Luster:** adamantine

HOW IT FORMS

Malachite forms underground, but usually fairly close to the surface. The mineral is the result of copper ores weathering and oxidizing (reacting with oxygen). A string of chemical reactions turn copper minerals such as chalcopyrite or bornite into malachite. Malachite can also form in places where hot water rich in copper minerals flows through fractures in the surrounding rocks. The copper minerals precipitate out (see page 28) to form malachite deposits.

Malachite is rarely found as a crystal, but it can form bright green, fibrous crystals in the right conditions.

ORES AND PIGMENTS

Ancient people mined malachite as an ore of copper, but it is rarely used as an ore now. That's because we have found better, cheaper ores—malachite is more valuable for other purposes! It's one of the oldest green pigments, and was used in paintings in Egyptian tombs, dating back thousands of years. It has been used less as a pigment since the 1600s, as people found other materials that would give a vivid green color.

The Arnolfini Portrait **(1434) by Jan van Eyck, used malachite for the woman's green dress.**

Malachite sometimes forms with rounded segments, like a bunch of grapes. Cutting and polishing it reveals the bands.

BEAUTIFUL MALACHITE

Malachite not only has a gorgeous green color, but it also shows a distinctive banded pattern when cut and polished. It can be polished to a high sheen, so throughout history it has been carved into beads and gems. Some people wore malachite because they believed it had healing powers. The mineral is also cut into thin slabs and used as an inlay material in furniture and architectural features.

The banding in malachite has a seemingly random pattern, but is caused by the chemical reactions that help it to form.

SIDERITE

This widespread mineral is a compound of iron, carbon, and oxygen. It's often found as part of sedimentary deposits where it forms thin beds, often layered among seams of shale or coal. It can also be found in metamorphic and igneous rocks.

FACT FILE

- **Name:** from the Greek *sideros*, meaning "iron"
- **Color:** yellowish to dark brown
- **Cleavage:** perfect
- **Streak:** white
- **Hardness:** 3.5–4
- **Specific gravity:** 3.9
- **Luster:** vitreous to pearly

RICH IN IRON

By weight, iron makes up nearly half of siderite, so this mineral has been an important iron ore. It is not contaminated with sulfur or phosphorus, as some other iron ores are. It has also been used as a pigment to produce a brownish-yellow color. Siderite crystals are too soft and brittle to be used as gemstones, but it is popular with rock collectors because of the range of different crystal types it produces.

This siderite sample from eastern Slovakia has a triclinic crystal formation (see page 29).

Siderite crystals can sometimes take the form of small, densely-packed lenses or blades.

RHODOCHROSITE

Rhodochrosite is a carbonate mineral that contains manganese as well as carbon and oxygen. Its pure form is pink, but it can also come in gray or brown, caused by impurities from elements such as iron, magnesium, calcium, or zinc.

FACT FILE

- **Name:** from the Greek *rhodokhros*, meaning "rosy color"
- **Color:** rosy pink, gray, or brown
- **Cleavage:** perfect
- **Streak:** white
- **Hardness:** 3.5–4
- **Specific gravity:** 3.6
- **Luster:** vitreous to pearly

PRETTY IN PINK

The beautiful pink color of rhodochrosite, combined with its rarity, has made it prized as a gemstone. It occasionally forms large, transparent crystals, suitable for cutting. However, most rhodochrosite is difficult to cut because of its perfect cleavage, and it is so soft it is difficult to polish easily. Rhodochrosite also occurs in a granular form, and this is often cut into slabs and polished to show off its bands.

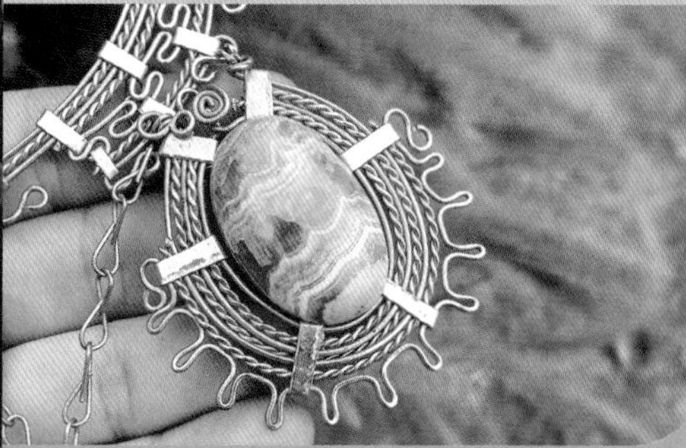

Rhodochrosite jewelry has pretty pink bands, but this gemstone needs to be treated with care.

This mine in Poland is a source of silver, zinc and lead. Rhodochrosite is often found near silver deposits, and some silver mines produce it as a by-product.

BORAX

Borax is a compound of boron, sodium, oxygen, and water molecules. It forms when water containing borate compounds (see page 25) evaporates, especially in dry regions. It's often found in dry lake beds or salt flats.

FACT FILE

- **Name:** from the Arabic *buraq*, meaning "white"
- **Color:** colorless, gray, or white
- **Cleavage:** perfect
- **Streak:** white
- **Hardness:** 2–2.5
- **Specific gravity:** 1.7
- **Luster:** vitreous to earthy

The ruins of an old borax works stand in Death Valley, California, where this "white gold" was once mined.

USING BORAX

The borate compounds in borax have natural cleansing and deodorizing properties, so they're often used in household cleaning products. For similar reasons, borax is also used in hand soap and some tooth-whitening products. Other uses of borate compounds include as an insecticide to get rid of ants, as a soil nutrient to help crops grow, and as an aid in welding and soldering metals.

Borax is a key ingredient in homemade slime. It helps to link glue molecules together.

ULEXITE

Ulexite has a similar composition to borax, and the two minerals are often found in the same locations. Ulexite can form as a lumpy crust or as puffs of hairlike crystals that look a bit like cotton wool balls. But in some cases the mineral's thin, fibrous crystals are arranged in a way that gives it a rare but very cool property.

FACT FILE

- **Name:** from the German chemist who discovered it, Georg Ulex
- **Color:** colorless or white
- **Cleavage:** perfect
- **Streak:** white
- **Hardness:** 2.5
- **Specific gravity:** 2.0
- **Luster:** vitreous to silky

Ulexite is a useful source of boron, which is an ingredient in the brightly colored glazes that decorate pottery.

THE TELEVISION STONE

Ulexite is opaque (not see-through) but sometimes when it takes a fibrous form, the tiny crystals are all aligned in parallel. These colorless crystals form a flat slab that looks like slightly cloudy glass. The tiny fibers reflect light internally, the same way as the glass in fiber optic cables do. If you place a piece of ulexite on a printed image, it will transmit that image to the other side. That's why this mineral is nicknamed the "television stone"!

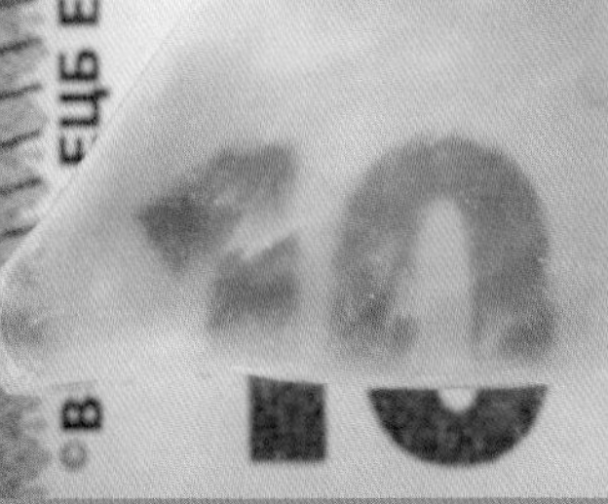

This effect only works with the fibers end-on. If the ulexite is on its side, you won't see the image!

CHROMITE

Oxide minerals contain oxygen, which is bonded to one or more metals or semi-metals. In chromite, the oxygen is bonded to iron and chromium. This mineral is the main ore of chromium, which can be alloyed to other metals to improve their hardness and used as a protective coating on others.

FACT FILE

- **Name:** from the Greek *chromos*, meaning "color"
- **Color:** dark brown or black
- **Cleavage:** none
- **Streak:** brown
- **Hardness:** 5.5
- **Specific gravity:** 4.5–4.8
- **Luster:** metallic

HARD TO PIN DOWN

Chromite can be easily confused with other metallic ores. It can sometimes be slightly magnetic, like magnetite (see page 130), while many of its properties are similar to those of another oxide mineral called ilmenite. To make a positive identification, geologists have to look carefully at all of its different properties, including streak, hardness, and specific gravity.

Chromite (black) is often sandwiched between other types of rock, as shown in this outcrop in South Africa.

Adding chromium to iron and carbon produces stainless steel, which doesn't corrode or rust like plain steel made of just iron and carbon. This is useful for cutlery!

CHRYSOBERYL

This mineral is a compound of beryllium, aluminum, and oxygen. It's too rare to be useful as an ore of beryllium, so it is mainly used as a gemstone instead. This mineral is a master of disguise—gems made from it can be different colors and have very different appearances.

FACT FILE

- **Name:** from the Greek *chrysos*, meaning "gold," and *beryllios*, meaning "crystal"
- **Color:** green or yellow
- **Cleavage:** distinct
- **Streak:** colorless (harder than the streak plate, see page 91)
- **Hardness:** 8.5
- **Specific gravity:** 3.7
- **Luster:** vitreous

BEAUTIFUL GEMS

Chrysoberyl is nearly as hard as corundum (the mineral name for ruby and sapphire), which makes it valuable as a cut gemstone. The most common variety is pale yellow or green. Another variety, called alexandrite, can change color! In daylight it looks green, but under an old-fashioned incandescent bulb, it will look red. A third variety shows a "cat's eye" effect, where a polished stone shows a band of light that seems to move below the surface.

The cat's eye effect is caused by the way that parallel fibers within the crystal structure reflect light.

Chrysoberyl was first discovered and mined in Russia's Ural Mountains. A variant of it, alexandrite, takes its name from a Russian tsar.

HEMATITE

Consisting of iron and oxygen, hematite is an important ore of iron. It's one of the most abundant minerals in the topmost layers of Earth's crust, and it can be found all over the world in sedimentary, metamorphic, and igneous rocks.

FACT FILE

- **Name:** from the Greek *haima*, meaning "blood," because of the red color of some specimens
- **Color:** gray or black, often reddish
- **Cleavage:** none
- **Streak:** bright red or brownish-red
- **Hardness:** 5–6
- **Specific gravity:** 5.3
- **Luster:** metallic to earthy

Hematite nodules like these often form in sedimentary rocks from the oxidation of iron sulfide minerals, such as pyrite.

HIDDEN RED

Samples of hematite can be shiny or dull, and come in red, black, gray, or silver. The mineral also has many different crystal habits (see page 29). However, a sample of hematite will always produce a reddish streak, even if the sample you're testing looks a different color entirely! This is probably the most important clue for identifying hematite. Although it contains a high proportion of iron, hematite is only very weakly magnetic, if at all.

MAGNETITE

Magnetite is also made up of iron and oxygen, but in different proportions. It has a very high iron content and is the most used ore of iron. It's also powdered and mixed with liquid to make a dense sludge that helps separate coal after mining.

FACT FILE

- **Name:** from the Greek *magnetis*, after Magnesia, the place where it was first found
- **Color:** black or brownish-black
- **Cleavage:** none
- **Streak:** black
- **Hardness:** 5.5–6.5
- **Specific gravity:** 5.2
- **Luster:** metallic

Magnetite is a component of emery, a rock that is ground up and used as an abrasive in sandpaper and nail files.

LODESTONES

Magnetite is best known for its magnetic properties. Samples of magnetite will be attracted to a magnet, but some specimens are magnets themselves! Called lodestones, these natural magnets were discovered in ancient times. Because magnets align with Earth's magnetic field, they were used to make compasses. Scientists think that these samples of magnetite may have become magnetized after being struck by lightning.

A lodestone will naturally attract objects made of iron, such as these paper clips.

RUTILE

Rutile is made up of titanium and oxygen, and it's one of the most important ores of titanium. This metallic element is light but strong, so it's used to make aircraft, spacecraft, and ships. Titanium is also added to strengthen the materials used to make golf clubs and fishing rods.

FACT FILE

- **Name:** from the Latin *rutilis*, meaning "red" or "glowing"
- **Color:** reddish-brown or black
- **Cleavage:** good
- **Streak:** black, pale brown, yellow, or reddish
- **Hardness:** 6–6.5
- **Specific gravity:** 4.2
- **Luster:** adamantine to metallic

FROZEN NEEDLES

Crystals of rutile are long and prism-shaped, and they often show parallel lines called striations. Tiny, needle-shaped crystals of rutile can also grow within other minerals, such as quartz. Sometimes these needles are easy to see, and the crystals can either be thinly branching or closely packed. Tiny rutile crystals can also be found in rubies and sapphires, where they reflect light from the inside of the stone.

Visible red and golden rutile crystals can be seen in this "rutilated quartz" from Pakistan.

Rutile is often mined from heavy mineral sands, a type of sedimentary deposit containing tiny pieces of weathered igneous and metamorphic rocks.

SPINEL

The word "spinel" can have several different meanings. It's the name of a mineral made of magnesium, aluminum, and oxygen. It's also the name of a group of related minerals with a similar crystal structure. Lastly, "spinel" can refer to spinel crystals used as gemstones.

FACT FILE

- **Name:** from the Latin *spinella*, meaning "thorn"
- **Color:** nearly any color in the spectrum
- **Cleavage:** none
- **Streak:** colorless (harder than the streak plate, see page 91)
- **Hardness:** 7.5–8
- **Specific gravity:** 3.6
- **Luster:** vitreous

RAINBOW STONE

Spinel's hardness makes it suitable for cutting and polishing. It is unusual among gemstones because it can be found in nearly any color of the rainbow, as well as black, gray, or colorless. The different colors are caused by trace elements within the crystal—for example, chromium produces red and cobalt makes it blue. In the past, blue and red spinels were often mistaken for sapphires or rubies.

The red stone at the front of this British crown is called the "Black Prince's Ruby," but it is actually a spinel.

Spinel is mined in the Hindu Kush mountains of Afghanistan. It can also be found in southeast Asia and Australia.

CRYOLITE

Cryolite is an example of a halide mineral, where a metal bonds to one of the halogen elements (see page 25). It contains sodium, aluminum, and fluorine and has a translucent, icelike appearance.

FACT FILE

- **Name:** from the Greek *kryos*, meaning "frost," and *lithos*, meaning "stone"
- **Color:** white or colorless
- **Cleavage:** none
- **Streak:** white
- **Hardness:** 3
- **Specific gravity:** 3.0
- **Luster:** vitreous to greasy

The town of Ivittuut in Greenland was built to mine the natural cryolite deposits, but no more remains.

RARE BUT VALUABLE

Aluminum is the most abundant metal in Earth's crust, but we hardly used it before the late 1800s because it was so difficult to extract from its ores. However, two chemists then discovered that if you dissolve aluminum oxide in molten cryolite and apply an electric current, molten aluminum metal is released. The discovery made cryolite very valuable, but supplies of this rare mineral eventually ran out. We now use a synthetic version instead.

Aluminum foil is commonly used in the kitchen as a covering and because it helps to retain heat.

FLUORITE

Also known as fluorspar, fluorite is made up of calcium and fluorine. Fluorite is used in the chemical and metal industries, as well as in the making of glass and ceramics. Fluorite has four directions of perfect cleavage, so its crystals often break into pieces with an octahedral (eight-sided) shape.

FACT FILE

- **Name:** from the Latin *fluere*, meaning "to flow," because it melts easily
- **Color:** can appear in most colors, or colorless
- **Cleavage:** perfect
- **Streak:** white
- **Hardness:** 4
- **Specific gravity:** 3.0–3.3
- **Luster:** vitreous

Fluorite often forms intergrowing cubic crystals of purple, green, or yellow, though blue crystals are sometimes seen.

LIGHT SHOW

Have you ever seen ultraviolet (UV) lights make a white shirt "glow"? These lights give off ultraviolet light, which our eyes can't see. However, some substances—including fluorite—absorb the UV energy and re-emit it at a different wavelength, which we can see. This makes the material appear to glow, often in vibrant colors. This property was called fluorescence, because it was first observed in the mineral fluorite.

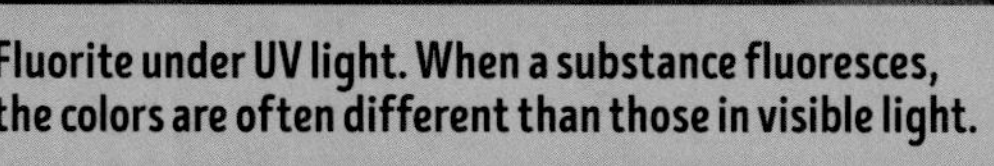

Fluorite under UV light. When a substance fluoresces, the colors are often different than those in visible light.

HALITE

You may never have heard the name "halite," but it's a mineral you come into contact with nearly every day. It's salt! The chemical name for table salt is sodium chloride. What we call "rock salt" is just a rock made up mainly of halite.

FACT FILE

- **Name:** from the Greek *hals*, meaning "salt"
- **Color:** colorless to white; sometimes also yellow, gray, or red
- **Cleavage:** perfect
- **Streak:** white
- **Hardness:** 2.5
- **Specific gravity:** 2.2
- **Luster:** vitreous

SOURCES OF SALT

Halite is usually found within sedimentary rocks, where it formed when sea water or salty lake water evaporated, leaving salt crystals behind. People have mined these underground salt deposits for thousands of years. Halite can also form a salt dome, where a mound or column of halite pushes upward, punching through the surrounding sediment layers. These underground domes can rise up for hundreds of yards or more.

Spain's Cardona salt mountain is made almost entirely of rock salt. This mine is now a visitor attraction.

The Dead Sea between Israel and Jordan is extremely salty, and deposits of halite form along its shoreline.

SYLVITE

Sylvite is similar to halite, although it is made up of potassium and chlorine, rather than sodium and chlorine. The two minerals have the same crystal shape and share some of their properties. That's no surprise, as they are often found together.

FACT FILE

- **Name:** from its old name as a medicine, *sal digestivus Sylvii* (salts of Sylvius, a doctor in the 17th century)
- **Color:** colorless to white, often with a yellow or red tint
- **Cleavage:** perfect
- **Streak:** white
- **Hardness:** 2.2
- **Specific gravity:** 2.0
- **Luster:** vitreous

PLANT POWER

Like halite, sylvite forms cube-shaped crystals that are often interlocking. This mineral often occurs in very dry areas where salty water once flowed. It's usually found alongside gypsum as well as halite. Because it contains potassium, sylvite is most useful as a raw material for producing fertilizers that contain a potassium compound called potash. Plants need potassium to make their own food through the process of photosynthesis.

Small traces of the mineral hematite can give sylvite a reddish or pinkish color.

Sylvite crystals were first discovered on Mount Vesuvius in Italy, where they were formed by volcanic activity.

GYPSUM

Gypsum is the most common sulfate mineral, and contains calcium, sulfur, and oxygen along with water. It often formed in large beds after salty oceans evaporated. When seawater evaporates, gypsum is usually the first mineral to separate out. It's normally quite easy to identify as you can scratch it easily with your fingernail.

FACT FILE

- **Name:** from the Greek *gypsos*, meaning "chalk" or "plaster"
- **Color:** colorless, white, pink, yellow, or gray
- **Cleavage:** perfect
- **Streak:** white
- **Hardness:** 2
- **Specific gravity:** 2.3
- **Luster:** vitreous to pearly

ONE MINERAL, MANY HABITS

Gypsum is a chameleon mineral, appearing in several different forms. We call transparent gypsum "selenite," and some people wrongly use this name for gypsum in general. Crystals can be blocky, flat and bladed, or long and thin. A variety called "satin spar" contains parallel fibers, while a fine-grained, massive variety (see p98) is called alabaster. "Desert rose" is the name given to flat, round crystals arranged like flower petals.

"Satin spar" gypsum has long, parallel fibers that give it a smooth and silky texture.

In New Mexico, white sand made from gypsum has been blown into huge dunes, covering a large area.

CAVE OF THE CRYSTALS

In 2000, miners in Mexico discovered an underground cave filled with giant selenite crystals (the name we give to transparent gypsum). The spiky shape of the crystals led some people to call it the "Cave of Swords." They formed when mineral-rich waters deposited crystals that built up over time. After tourism caused damage to the crystals in the Cave of Swords, the cave was allowed to re-flood naturally.

The gypsum crystals in the Cave of Swords are some of the largest natural crystals ever found, with some measuring 40 ft (12 m) long.

USING GYPSUM

Gypsum is an extremely useful mineral. Its main use is in buildings, where it's a component of plaster and cement. Gypsum is also used to make panels of plasterboard in walls and ceilings. It's powdered and sprinkled on soil to improve its structure, and it's added to water for use in brewing beer. People even used to carve its alabaster form into sculptures, although its softness made it fragile.

Gypsum is a useful building material. It gives this plasterboard stability and rigidity and is also fire-resistant.

BARITE

Sometimes spelled "baryte," barite is a mineral containing barium, sulfur, and oxygen. It takes its name from the Greek word for "heavy" because it is unusually dense for a non-metal. Most of its uses rely on this heaviness.

FACT FILE

- **Name:** from the Greek *barys*, meaning "heavy"
- **Color:** colorless, white, light blue, gray, or beige
- **Cleavage:** perfect
- **Streak:** white
- **Hardness:** 2.5–3.5
- **Specific gravity:** 4.5
- **Luster:** vitreous to pearly

THAT'S HEAVY!

One of the main uses of barite is to make a high-density mud for drilling oil and gas wells. As the drill cuts into the ground, the mud is pumped down the drill hole and then returns to the surface. The mud cools the drill bit and carries any rock cuttings back up to the surface. Barite is also used as a paint pigment, and it's added to rubber to make mud flaps for trucks that are heavy enough not to blow around.

Barite has been added to these playing cards to make them heavier, stiffer, and easier to deal.

Barite crystals can grow in sand, trapping sand grains inside the crystals to form flower-like shapes known as "barite roses."

CELESTINE

Also called celestite, this mineral's sky-blue crystals are why it takes its name from the Latin word for the heavens. However, this mineral can also appear in a range of different colors, and it comes in many forms, including fibrous, massive, or granular (see page 29).

FACT FILE

- **Name:** from the Latin *caelestis*, meaning "heavenly"
- **Color:** colorless, white, reddish, pink, pale blue, pale green, or brown
- **Cleavage:** perfect
- **Streak:** white
- **Hardness:** 3–3.5
- **Specific gravity:** 4.0
- **Luster:** vitreous to pearly

USING CELESTINE

Celestine is made of strontium, sulfur, and oxygen and is often found in sedimentary rocks alongside gypsum and halite. It's an important source of strontium, which is used in the production of glass, ceramics, and batteries. Celestine is sometimes cut as a gemstone, even though it's fairly soft and easily chipped. Some people believe that celestine crystals have healing powers, although there is no scientific proof that they actually work.

Although strontium gives celestine crystals their blue color, when added to fireworks it burns red.

This cave in Ohio is really just a giant geode (see page 29) lined with huge celestine crystals.

APATITE

Apatite is not a single mineral, but a group of closely related minerals with similar makeup and physical properties. All contain calcium as well as a phosphate (a chemical group made of phosphorus and oxygen). Some apatite also contains fluorine, chlorine, carbon, or hydrogen.

FACT FILE

- **Name:** from the Greek *apatao*, meaning "to deceive," because it is easily mistaken for other minerals
- **Color:** most colors of the spectrum as well as colorless
- **Cleavage:** indistinct
- **Streak:** white
- **Hardness:** 5
- **Specific gravity:** 3.1–3.2
- **Luster:** vitreous to waxy

Phosphorite is a phosphate-rich sedimentary rock that contains as much as 80 percent apatite. This is a tunnel in an old phosphorite mine.

PHOSPHOROUS SOURCE

Apatite is found as a component of phosphorus-rich sedimentary rocks. They are mined as a source of phosphorus, which is used for fertilizer and animal feed as well as in the chemical industry. Apatite crystals are hexagonal, and most of them are green, but they can also be found in other colors such as blue or purple. Because of its attractive colors, apatite is sometimes cut as a gemstone, even though it is fairly brittle.

The phosphorus in apatite ignites easily. It is used on the striking surface on a box of matches.

PYROMORPHITE

Along with its phosphate (see apatite above), pyromorphite contains chlorine as well as enough lead that it is sometimes mined as a lead ore. It is often green, but it can also be found in shades of yellow, brown, or orange.

FACT FILE

- **Name:** from the Greek *pyr*, meaning "fire," and *morphe*, meaning "form"
- **Color:** green, yellow, orange, or brown
- **Cleavage:** poor
- **Streak:** white
- **Hardness:** 3.5–4
- **Specific gravity:** 7.0
- **Luster:** resinous

A lead mine in Tullah, Australia. Pyromorphite is often found alongside lead deposits.

MINERAL SERIES

Pyromorphite is part of a mineral series with mimetite and vanadinite. A mineral series is a group of minerals that all have the same crystal structure. The only difference is the elements that they contain. All three minerals contain chlorine and lead, but where pyromorphite has a phosphate, vanadinite has vanadium and mimetite has arsenic.

WAVELLITE

Wavellite is a phosphate mineral that also contains aluminum, hydrogen, fluorine, and water. It was first found and described in Devon, England, but it has since been found in other places around the world, including the United States, India, and Czechia.

FACT FILE

- **Name:** after the British geologist William Wavell who found it
- **Color:** colorless, white, reddish, pink, pale blue, pale green, or brown
- **Cleavage:** green or white
- **Streak:** white
- **Hardness:** 3.5–4
- **Specific gravity:** 2.4
- **Luster:** vitreous to resinous

COIN CRYSTALS

Wavellite is often found in the form of spherical lumps that are usually some shade of green. However, when these spheres are cracked in half, the mineral's crystal structure is revealed. The crystals are long and thin, and radiate out from a central point. This gives the rock the appearance of a coin or sea urchin. These unusual-looking minerals are popular with collectors.

Some rockhounds refer to wavellite as "cat's eye" because of its distinctive crystal pattern.

Wavellite has been found among the rocks and mountains of the Ouachita National Forest, Arkansas.

AUTUNITE

Autunite is a relatively soft phosphate mineral that contains calcium and uranium oxide alongside water and a phosphate group. It often forms green crystals that stand on edge, giving a sample a scaly appearance.

FACT FILE

- **Name:** from the French town of Autun, where it was first found
- **Color:** pale green or yellow
- **Cleavage:** perfect
- **Streak:** pale yellow
- **Hardness:** 2–2.5
- **Specific gravity:** 3.1–3.2
- **Luster:** vitreous to pearly

HANDLE WITH CARE

Autunite samples often look pretty cool, and they look even cooler under ultraviolet (UV) light, when they glow with a bright yellowish-green color. However, the uranium that autunite contains is radioactive, meaning that autunite samples are radioactive too. Radiation is dangerous to humans, so samples must be stored safely and handled as little as possible.

Autunite is radioactive and highly fluorescent. Under ultraviolet light, it glows lime green.

The uranium obtained from autunite can be used as fuel in this nuclear power plant in Suffolk, UK.

OLIVINE

Olivine is a group of minerals containing magnesium or iron alongside silicon and oxygen. These minerals are found in igneous rocks such as basalt, gabbro, and peridotite. It can form either above ground or below the surface, when lava or magma cool and crystallize.

FACT FILE

- **Name:** from its olive green color
- **Color:** usually olive green but sometimes yellow or brown
- **Cleavage:** imperfect
- **Streak:** white or colorless
- **Hardness:** 6.5–7
- **Specific gravity:** 3.2–4.4
- **Luster:** vitreous

GREEN BEAUTY

Olivine is one of the most common minerals in Earth's upper mantle, but it is rarer at the surface, mainly because it weathers easily. There is also olivine on Mars and in many asteroids. Here on Earth, the rock doesn't have many uses in industry. However, it can form translucent green crystals that we know as the gemstone peridot. People as far back as the ancient Egyptians have treasured this beautiful green stone.

The sand on this beach in Hawaii has a green tint, thanks to the presence of olivine that eroded from the nearby volcanic rocks.

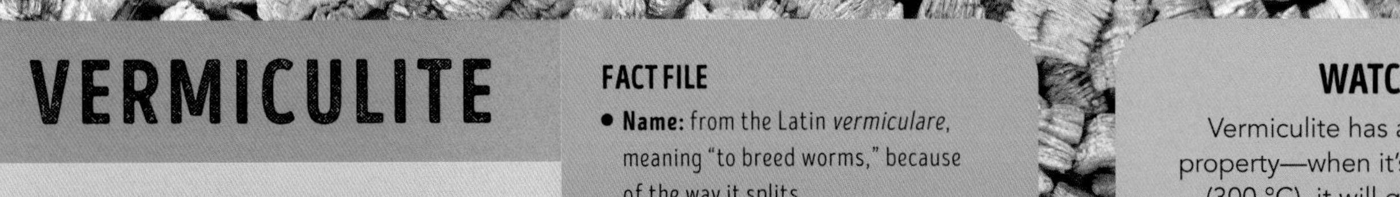

VERMICULITE

Vermiculite is a group of minerals that resemble mica. Deposits of these minerals are often found with volcanic rocks rich in magnesium and silicate minerals. Vermiculite often takes the form of thin sheets that are interlayered with other claylike minerals.

FACT FILE

- **Name:** from the Latin *vermiculare*, meaning "to breed worms," because of the way it splits
- **Color:** grayish-white or golden brown
- **Cleavage:** perfect
- **Streak:** white, yellowish, colorless, or light brown, depending on the type
- **Hardness:** 1–2
- **Specific gravity:** 2.4–2.7 (in its non-exfoliated form)
- **Luster:** greasy to vitreous

WATCH IT GROW

Vermiculite has a weird but very useful property—when it's heated to about 570 °F (300 °C), it will quickly expand to up to 20 times its original thickness. It expands so much that it exfoliates, meaning that its layers split apart. In this expanded form, vermiculite is very light, which makes it useful. It's used as insulation in houses and as a packing material for sending packages, and it's also mixed with concrete to provide insulation.

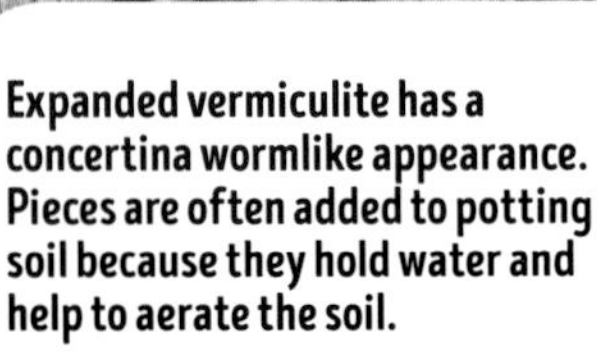

Expanded vermiculite has a concertina wormlike appearance. Pieces are often added to potting soil because they hold water and help to aerate the soil.

At high temperatures, thin flakes of vermiculite (left) expand rapidly, causing the layers to split apart (right).

MICROCLINE

This common feldspar mineral is found in many different types of rocks, including igneous granite, metamorphic gneiss, and weathered pieces of it help make up various sedimentary rocks. Microcline can be massive (see page 98), and it can also form large crystals several yards long.

FACT FILE

- **Name:** from the Greek *mikros*, meaning "small," and *klinein*, meaning "to slope"
- **Color:** white, pale yellow, or blue-green
- **Cleavage:** perfect to good
- **Streak:** white
- **Hardness:** 6–6.5
- **Specific gravity:** 2.6
- **Luster:** vitreous or dull

TWINNED CRYSTALS

Crystals of some minerals are twinned, which means that two crystals grow together in a series of repeated layers. Sometimes crystals are often multiple twinned, with several twins aligned in a similar pattern. This is what happens in microcline, and the twinning produces lines at right angles, which give some samples a cross-hatched "tartan" appearance (shown magnified below). Microcline is mainly used in the production of glass and ceramics.

The blue-green form of microcline is often called amazonite and is cut and polished as a gemstone. This is an amazonite necklace from Peru.

TALC

Talc comes in at 1 on the Mohs scale of hardness (see page 90), making it the softest mineral. This metamorphic mineral rarely forms crystals, but it's often found as fibrous or foliated masses (see page 19). This gives it a sheet structure similar to that of mica.

FACT FILE

- **Name:** from *talq*, the Persian name for the mineral
- **Color:** green, white, yellow, brown, or colorless
- **Cleavage:** perfect
- **Streak:** pale yellow
- **Hardness:** 1
- **Specific gravity:** 2.7
- **Luster:** vitreous to pearly

Talc is ground to make talcum powder, which is widely used in cosmetics, baby powders, and foot powders.

IT'S EVERYWHERE

You may have talcum powder in your bathroom cabinet, but this mineral has many other uses. It's used as a filler in plastics and ceramics to strengthen them. It's also added to paint and paper to make them whiter and brighter. Because it absorbs oils, talc is also used in beauty products. When it forms in compact masses, it's called soapstone, which is soft and easy to carve, and has a slightly soapy or greasy feel.

Soapstone has been used for this carving in Kenya where the stone comes in different colors.

STAUROLITE

Staurolite is often found alongside garnet, muscovite, and kyanite—all of these minerals form under similar temperature and pressure. This silicate mineral, which contains iron and magnesium along with silicon and aluminum, often forms when shale undergoes metamorphism (see page 18).

FACT FILE

- **Name:** from the Greek *stauros*, meaning "cross"
- **Color:** brown, reddish- or yellowish-brown, black
- **Cleavage:** indistinct
- **Streak:** colorless (harder than the streak plate)
- **Hardness:** 7–7.5
- **Specific gravity:** 3.7
- **Luster:** vitreous to resinous

Staurolite crystals are found in many locations around the world, including in the mountains of the Gotthard Pass in the Swiss Alps.

CROSS ROCKS

Crystals of staurolite are six-sided and twinned. The two crystals often form at a 60-degree angle, but sometimes they form a 90-degree angle instead, to make a cross shape. Because the cross is a Christian symbol, these crystals are often made into jewelry or good luck charms. Aside from being sold as souvenirs, staurolite has few uses. However, finding it provides an important clue for geologists about the history of the surrounding metamorphic rock.

The natural crosses formed by staurolite crystals are often known as "fairy crosses."

KYANITE

Kyanite often forms long crystals like flattened blades. It can be found in rocks such as schist or gneiss, and it has many uses. Kyanite has high heat resistance and is used for making porcelain that will hold its shape at high temperatures, such as in spark plugs.

FACT FILE

- **Name:** from the Greek *kyanos*, meaning "dark blue"
- **Color:** blue, green, or black
- **Cleavage:** perfect
- **Streak:** white or colorless
- **Hardness:** 4.5–5 or 6.5–7
- **Specific gravity:** 3.6
- **Luster:** vitreous

Kyanite comes in many shades of blue, from light to greenish to dark, but kyanite crystals can also be black or pale green. Black kyanite (shown here) is found in Brazil, Mexico, Russia, and the USA.

TWO STRENGTHS

Kyanite used to be known as "disthene," from Greek words meaning "two strengths." This is because its crystals show two different hardnesses, based on the direction you test them. When you scratch kyanite crystals along the long axis, they will be harder than if you scratch them at a right angle to that. Kyanite is chemically identical to the minerals andalusite and sillimanite, but it forms at a higher temperature and pressure.

Kyanite makes an attractive blue gemstone, but it is difficult to cut because of its different hardnesses.

EPIDOTE

Epidote is the name of a silicate mineral as well as the name of a group of related minerals that have similar composition. The mineral epidote is usually found in metamorphic rocks such as marble or schist, or in veins in granite.

FACT FILE

- **Name:** from the Greek *epidosis*, meaning "increase," because one side of the prism is longer than the others
- **Color:** pistachio green, brownish-green, or black
- **Cleavage:** perfect in one direction
- **Streak:** colorless or gray
- **Hardness:** 6–7
- **Specific gravity:** 3.4
- **Luster:** vitreous to resinous

Epidote crystals like these are highly desirable amongst collectors. They are lustrous, elongated, and interconnected.

FEW USES

In its massive form (see page 29), epidote can be translucent green. It also sometimes forms prism-shaped crystals with long, thin, parallel streaks. Epidote isn't really used in industry. However, a rock called unakite contains significant amounts of green epidote alongside pink orthoclase. The mottled pink-and-green appearance makes this rock popular as a tumbled stone (see page 95), and it is sometimes made into jewelry or carved into small figurines.

This polished unakite bracelet shows intricate patterns of green epidote and pink orthoclase.

DIOPSIDE

Diopside is part of the pyroxene group of silicate minerals containing calcium and magnesium. It's abundant in the mantle, but less of it is found at the surface. It is also found in many meteorites that fall to Earth. This mineral can form beautiful emerald-green crystals that are sometimes used as gemstones.

FACT FILE

- **Name:** from the Greek *dis*, meaning "twice," and *opse*, meaning "face"
- **Color:** light or dark green, white, or colorless
- **Cleavage:** distinct in two directions
- **Streak:** white or pale green
- **Hardness:** 5.5–6.5
- **Specific gravity:** 3.3
- **Luster:** vitreous

This close-up image shows diopside crystals. Trace amounts of chromium give some diopside crystals their emerald-green color.

DIAMOND CLUE

The most important use of diopside is helping to find diamonds. Diamonds originate in the mantle and are pushed up to the surface in vertical structures of igneous rock known as pipes. Although pipes may be a few hectares in size, they are hard to find. However, they contain plenty of diopside, so diamond hunters search the surface, looking for grains of emerald-green diopside as a clue to where a diamond-rich pipe might be.

A lot of earth has been excavated in this diamond mine in Siberia. Diopside is a clue to where to dig.

RHODONITE

This pretty rose-red mineral was once mined as an ore of the metal manganese, but now, thanks to its color, is mainly used for decoration. Samples of rhodonite are tumbled and polished or made into beads or small figurines.

FACT FILE

- **Name:** from the Greek *rhodon*, meaning "rose"
- **Color:** pink or red
- **Cleavage:** perfect
- **Streak:** white
- **Hardness:** 5.5–6.5
- **Specific gravity:** 3.5–3.7
- **Luster:** vitreous to pearly

INGREDIENT LIST

Rhodonite is a silicate mineral that also contains iron, magnesium, calcium, and manganese. However, not all rhodonite samples are exactly the same, and these elements can be present in different proportions. Samples with a higher proportion of calcium oxide are usually gray or brown, and are called "bustamite." Those that contain zinc oxide are pink, red, or browny-black and are known as "fowlerite."

Rhodonite is fairly rare, and samples of large, distinct crystals are even rarer.

Rhodonite is often found alongside black manganese oxides. The manganese oxides fill any gaps or cracks in the rhodonite, giving a mottled black and pink appearance.

MUSCOVITE

Muscovite is the most common member of the mica group of minerals. Micas are soft silicate minerals that can be split into very thin, flexible plates. Ground mica has a pearly luster, and it is often used in cosmetics to give them a pearly sheen.

FACT FILE

- **Name:** from its old name, "Muscovy glass"
- **Color:** colorless, silvery, or brown
- **Cleavage:** perfect
- **Streak:** white or colorless
- **Hardness:** 2.5–3
- **Specific gravity:** 2.8
- **Luster:** vitreous to pearly

MUSCOVY GLASS

Muscovite takes its name from Muscovy, an old name for Russia. Sheets of muscovite are thin enough to be transparent and can be wide enough to fill a window opening. In Russia, muscovite was often used in place of glass for windows, so in England this mineral became known as "Muscovy glass." Today, sheets of muscovite are more likely to be used in scientific tools and electrical devices.

These muscovite windows from Russia date from the late 17th century when muscovite was cheaper than glass.

Muscovite is an important rock-forming mineral, and is often found in granite. Muscovite gives this granite sample a silvery sheen.

ORTHOCLASE

Orthoclase is one of the most common rock-forming minerals in Earth's crust, and on the Mohs scale (see page 90) it is the example given for a hardness of 6. It's found all over the world, where it often appears as the pink component of many granites.

FACT FILE

- **Name:** from the Greek *ortho*, meaning "straight" and *klasis*, meaning "fracture"
- **Color:** white, gray, pink, yellow, or colorless
- **Cleavage:** perfect
- **Streak:** white
- **Hardness:** 6
- **Specific gravity:** 2.5-2.6
- **Luster:** vitreous to pearly

USING ORTHOCLASE

Orthoclase is used in making glass and also ceramics—as an ingredient in both the ceramic base material and the glazes used to coat it. Ground orthoclase is also used as an abrasive in scouring powders and polishing mixes. Some orthoclase crystals are fine enough to be cut into gemstones. One variety of orthoclase is known as moonstone (see page 150). Its blue sheen makes it a popular gemstone.

Huge crystals of orthoclase have been found in the Sandia Mountains of New Mexico.

Scientists have found orthoclase in samples of igneous rocks brought back from the Moon. Orthoclase has also been found on Mars.

LABRADORITE

Labradorite is a feldspar mineral that can be found in igneous, sedimentary, and metamorphic rocks. It's often found in gneiss, basalt, and gabbro, as well as in a type of intrusive igneous rock known as anorthosite.

FACT FILE

- **Name:** from Labrador in Canada, where it was first found
- **Color:** gray, white, or colorless with blue-green iridescence
- **Cleavage:** perfect
- **Streak:** white
- **Hardness:** 6-6.5
- **Specific gravity:** 2.7
- **Luster:** vitreous to pearly

THE SCHILLER EFFECT

Raw labradorite can often appear gray or white, but when the light hits it right, it turns a shimmery blue-green. This is called the "schiller" effect, after a German word meaning "shimmer." The colors come from inside the stone—light enters the top layer and reflects off a twinning crystal surface within the stone. Looking at it, you see the color of the reflected light. Different twinning surfaces within the stone create a range of different colors.

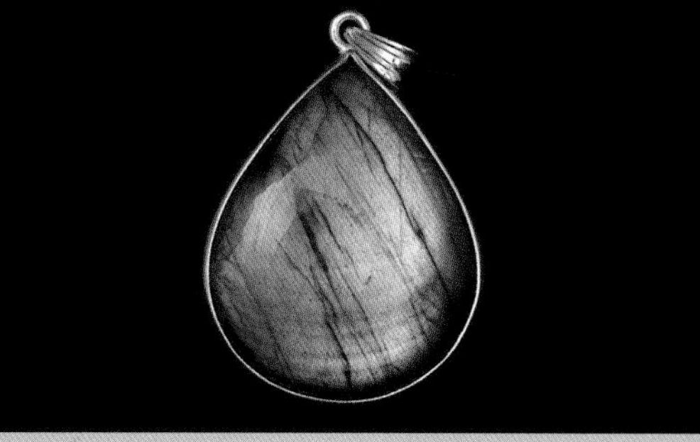

Because of its beautiful shimmering colors, labradorite is often polished and used as a gemstone.

Labradorite was originally discovered near the town of Nain off the east coast of Labrador, Canada.

QUARTZ

The mineral quartz is a master of disguise. Although it is simple in composition, containing a mixture of silicon and oxygen, it comes in many forms that can look completely different from each other. Many of these forms are well-known under different names, but they're all quartz.

FACT FILE

- **Name:** from the German *quarz*, which came from a Czech word meaning "hard"
- **Color:** colorless, pink, orange, purple, brown, or black
- **Cleavage:** none
- **Streak:** white
- **Hardness:** 7
- **Specific gravity:** 2.7
- **Luster:** usually vitreous; some varieties are waxy or dull

QUARTZ IS EVERYWHERE

After feldspar (see page 26), quartz is the most abundant mineral in Earth's crust. It's a component of many rocks. There is quartz in igneous rocks such as granite, and metamorphic rocks such as gneiss, schist, and quartzite. It is fairly resistant to weathering, but it is still very common in many sedimentary rocks, such as sandstone and shale. Most quartz originally formed when it crystallized from cooling magma.

Cathedral Rock in Australia is a series of large granite boulders, all of which contain quartz.

ROCK CRYSTAL

In addition to being a component of many rocks, quartz also occurs in large crystals. One of these is rock crystal, a colorless and transparent variety of quartz. Our word "crystal" comes from the Greek *krystallos*, meaning "ice," because ancient scientists thought that clear quartz crystals such as rock crystal were a form of water ice that stayed solid, even when no longer cold. It's so clear that it was used for many years to make lenses.

Rock crystal can form crystals that are as clear as glass. They have a long hexagonal shape that comes to a point at the end.

COLORED QUARTZ

Small traces of various elements can give translucent quartz crystals different colors. For example, aluminum produces the brown color of smoky quartz, while titanium, iron, or manganese can give rose quartz a delicate pink color. Traces of iron turn amethyst purple, ranging from pale lavender to vivid purple. These beautiful colored crystals are often cut and used as gemstones.

The aluminum or iron in citrine makes this type of quartz yellow. It is rare in nature, but heating smoky quartz can result in the same color.

The sand that covers many of the world's beaches is mainly made up of tiny quartz crystals.

QUARTZ WITH INCLUSIONS

Quartz crystals often trap other minerals inside them when they form. Rutilated quartz contains tiny "needles" of the mineral rutile (see page 131). Because the quartz is transparent, the rutile is easy to see. Cat's-eye quartz contains parallel fibers of the mineral asbestos. When rounded and polished smooth, these fibers reflect light in a way that shows a single white line that appears to move as you turn the stone.

Aventurine is a type of quartz that is colored by green mica crystals, giving it a sparkly appearance when polished.

CHALCEDONY

Many of the most familiar varieties of quartz form large, distinct crystals. However, quartz can also occur in a form called "microcrystalline," where the individual crystals are too small to see without a microscope. This gives it a smooth, even appearance. Chalcedony is one of the main forms of microcrystalline quartz. It is white, but trace amounts of other materials can produce other varieties such as green chrysoprase and amber-colored carnelian.

Jasper is a form of chalcedony that is often blood-red. It was used to carve this statue of an Egyptian pharaoh in about 1470 BCE.

AGATE AND ONYX

Some rocks, when split open, reveal a rainbow of colors inside that form concentric bands. This is agate, a form of chalcedony. Agate forms in cavities left when lava cools. Over time, mineral-rich water seeps in and lays down quartz in layers. The layers follow the shape of the original cavity. Onyx is a variety of agate with alternating bands of black and white. Its different colored layers made it popular for carving into brooches or pendants that had a raised portrait or other image, where the background could be black and the raised image white (below).

USING QUARTZ

Although the most famous uses of quartz are as gemstones, it has many practical uses too. Quartz sand is the main ingredient in most glass, and it's also used as a filler in rubber and paint (to make them stronger or thicker). Because quartz is hard and durable, with a high melting temperature, it's used to make molds for foundries where metals are melted. You'll also find quartz sand in playgrounds and on golf courses.

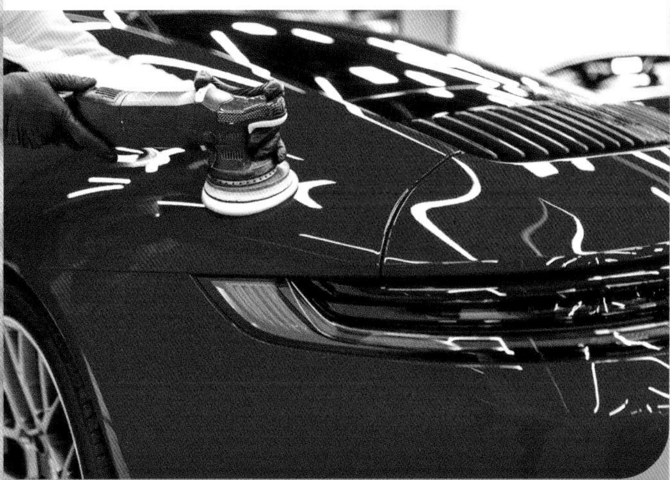

When ground extremely finely, quartz makes a mild abrasive wax that can be used to polish cars without scratching them.

DIAMOND

Coming in at 10 on the Mohs scale (see page 90), diamond is the hardest mineral on Earth. Diamonds are made of pure carbon, but they are considered a mineral rather than an element. Carbon can take different forms, and diamond is just one of them. Its ordered internal structure qualifies it as a mineral.

FACT FILE

- **Name:** from the Greek *adamas*, meaning "I subdue," because of its hardness
- **Color:** yellow, brown, colorless, blue, pink, or brown
- **Cleavage:** perfect
- **Streak:** colorless (harder than the streak plate)
- **Hardness:** 10
- **Specific gravity:** 3.4–3.5
- **Luster:** adamantine

FINDING DIAMONDS

Most diamonds formed billions of years ago, deep down in the mantle where temperatures and pressure are extremely high. They come to the surface during deep-rooted volcanic eruptions, which tear out pieces of mantle rock and bring them to the surface. These eruptions form vertical "pipes" that diamond miners look for. Once they find a pipe, they dig out ore and crush it, then sort through it to find any diamonds.

This old water-filled mine is in Kimberley, South Africa, where the diamond-rich kimberlite rock gets its name.

From this selection of uncut diamonds, only the stones with the clearest crystals and prettiest colors will be cut and polished into gemstones.

BRILLIANT GEMS

We think of diamonds as clear and colorless, but in fact most raw diamonds are brown or yellow. After mining, clear diamonds, or those with a pretty color, are separated out to use as gems, while the less attractive brown ones (left) are used in industry for cutting, drilling, or grinding. A skilled diamond cutter can cut dozens of tiny flat faces into a diamond (right). The way these faces reflect light gives a diamond its brilliant sparkle.

THE HOPE DIAMOND

Diamonds in bright colors, such as pink or blue, are rare and valuable. The Hope Diamond is famous because of its vivid blue color as well as its impressive size—about the size of a walnut. It was mined in India sometime in the 17th century and was sold to King Louis XIV of France. After the French Revolution in the late 18th century, the stone ended up in Britain and then the United States, where it is now on display in a museum.

The Hope Diamond has gone by many names over its history. It gets its current name from once being owned by a London banker named Thomas Hope.

OPAL

Although it is a very popular gemstone, opal doesn't have a distinct crystal structure, so it is classed as a "mineraloid" rather than as a mineral. It has a similar chemical composition to quartz, but the difference is that it also includes water.

FACT FILE

- **Name:** from the Sanskrit *upala*, meaning "precious stone"
- **Color:** often white, yellow, gray, black, or brown with flashes of color
- **Cleavage:** none
- **Streak:** white
- **Hardness:** 5–6
- **Specific gravity:** 1.8–2.2
- **Luster:** vitreous

MANY TYPES

The most common type of opal is called "potch" and is dull-colored. However, other varieties have a pearly appearance and can appear to flash in different colors when you turn them in the light. Fire opal has an intense yellow, orange, or red color, while rare black opal looks dark blue or green, with flashes of color. The most common color of opal used as a gemstone is a pale bluish-green.

This fire opal from Ethiopia reflects rich colors.

The opal in this rock sample from Australia appears to glow under ultraviolet light. Opal miners often use these lights to help them find opal in the surrounding rock.

LAZURITE

The metamorphic rock lapis lazuli is a common gemstone, and the blue mineral lazurite is one of its main components. It is what gives the stone its intense blue color, although lapis lazuli often also contains other blue minerals such as sodalite or haüyne.

FACT FILE

- **Name:** from the Arabic *lazaward*, meaning "blue"
- **Color:** deep blue
- **Cleavage:** indistinct
- **Streak:** bright blue
- **Hardness:** 5–5.5
- **Specific gravity:** 2.4
- **Luster:** dull to vitreous

PRECIOUS BLUE

Lazurite is most commonly found in its massive form (see page 98), meaning that it's a mass of individual crystals that are too small to see without a microscope. Larger crystals have been found, often within a surrounding matrix of calcite, but they are very rare. Because of this, along with its brittleness, lazurite is rarely used on its own as a gemstone. However, the lapis lazuli that it helps to form is widely used.

Afghanistan is the world's leading producer of lazurite and lapis lazuli, which was used to make this necklace.

Lapis lazuli often forms in limestone or marble, where lazurite has replaced parts of the original rock. This sample shows lazurite mixed with white calcite and rusty pyrite.

GARNET

Garnet is best known as a red gemstone, but it's actually a large group of minerals with a similar structure and composition. These minerals can form gems of many different colors, each with their own name—such as green tsavorite or orange spessartine.

FACT FILE

- **Name:** from the Latin *granatus*, meaning "pomegranate" because of the dark-red color
- **Color:** most colors except blue
- **Cleavage:** indistinct
- **Streak:** white
- **Hardness:** 6.5–7.5
- **Specific gravity:** 3.1–4.3
- **Luster:** vitreous to resinous

PLENTIFUL STONE

Garnets often form when aluminum-rich sedimentary rock such as shale goes through metamorphism as a result of high heat and pressure. Garnets can also be found in igneous rocks. They are popular as gemstones, often in place of more expensive rubies. However, because garnet is plentiful and cheap, it's also used as an abrasive in sandpaper, or in sandblasting to wear away metal, stone, or ceramics.

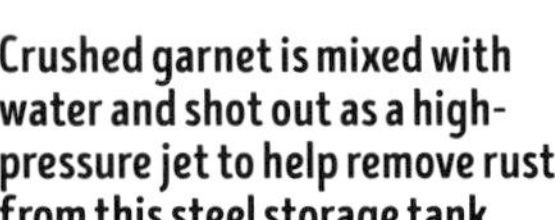

Crushed garnet is mixed with water and shot out as a high-pressure jet to help remove rust from this steel storage tank.

ZIRCON

The mineral zircon is found all over the world in igneous rocks such as granite. However, the grains of zircon are usually so tiny that this important mineral is often overlooked. Zircon is very hard, and its crystals are often revealed when the rest of a rock erodes. Zircon is the oldest mineral to be dated on Earth, because it is so tough and resistant to change.

FACT FILE

- **Name:** from the Arabic *zargun*, meaning "gold color"
- **Color:** yellow, brown, red, colorless, blue, or green
- **Cleavage:** imperfect
- **Streak:** colorless (harder than the streak plate)
- **Hardness:** 7.5
- **Specific gravity:** 4.6–4.7
- **Luster:** vitreous to adamantine

DIAMOND SUBSTITUTE?

Zircon crystals come in a range of colors. When it is cut as a gemstone, colorless zircon sparkles so much like a diamond that it's often used as a substitute. Most natural zircon is yellow, red, or brown, but heating it can often remove its color or change it to blue, green, or another color. Although "zircon" sounds similar to "cubic zirconia," the first is a naturally occurring mineral, while the second is an artificial diamond substitute made in a lab.

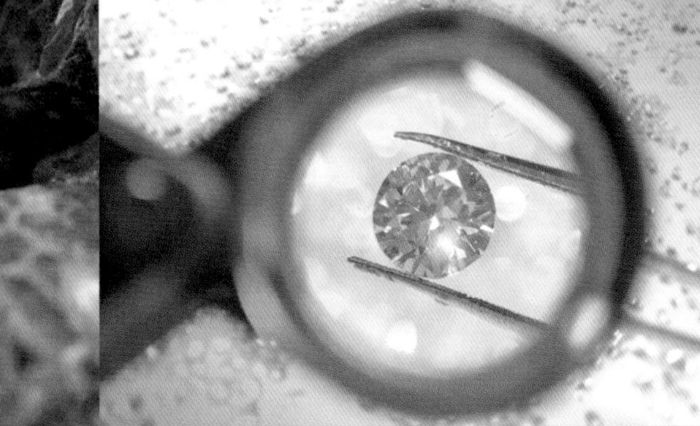

A jeweler looks carefully at the way light refracts through a stone, to distinguish this diamond from zircon.

These are raw uncut zircon crystals. Blue is the most popular color when zircon is used as a gemstone.

JADEITE

For thousands of years, people have been carving a stone called jade into tools, sculptures, and jewelry. The Chinese were masters of carving jade, and it was also used by the Maya and Aztecs of Central America and Mexico. However, in 1863 a French mineralogist discovered that what people called "jade" was actually two separate minerals: jadeite and nephrite (see below).

FACT FILE

- **Name:** from the Spanish *piedra de ijada*, meaning "stone of the side," because it was thought to cure pains in the side
- **Color:** white, green, or other colors
- **Cleavage:** good
- **Streak:** white or colorless
- **Hardness:** 6–7
- **Specific gravity:** 3.2–3.5
- **Luster:** vitreous to greasy

VALUABLE STONE

Jadeite is rarer and more valuable than nephrite. It is a pyroxene mineral (see page 26) that is rich in aluminum. In its pure form, jadeite is white, but it is most commonly found in shades of green, due to impurities. It can also come in a range of different colors. Jadeite is made up of blocky, interlocking crystals, which gives it a granular or "sugary" appearance.

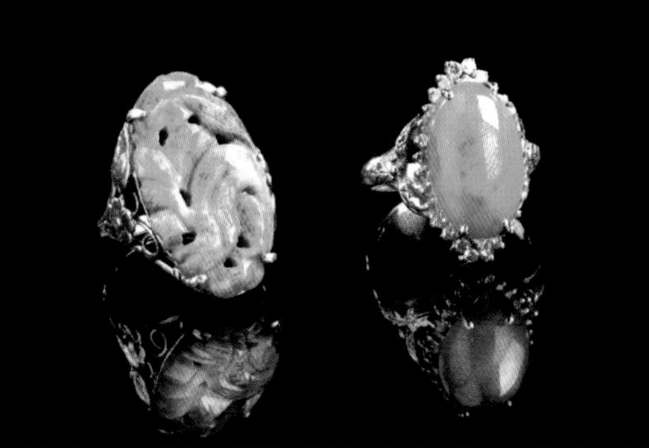

These rings are set with "Imperial Jadeite," which has a vibrant translucent emerald-green color.

This is a mine in Myanmar (Burma), one of the main sources of jadeite. When it was imported to China about 250 years ago, jadeite became more popular than China's native nephrite.

NEPHRITE

Nephrite is the name that scientists give to a tough, dense form of either tremolite or actinolite. These minerals are almost identical, except that tremolite contains magnesium where actinolite contains iron. Nephrite was widely used in ancient China and New Zealand, where its toughness made it ideal for tools and weapons.

FACT FILE

- **Name:** from the Latin *lapis nephriticus*, meaning "kidney stone," because it was thought to cure kidney stones
- **Color:** white, cream, or dark green
- **Cleavage:** perfect
- **Streak:** white or colorless
- **Hardness:** 6–6.5
- **Specific gravity:** 2.6–3.4
- **Luster:** vitreous, dull, or waxy

Nephrite is more common and less valuable than jadeite, but is a popular choice for carvings, beads, and gemstones.

USING NEPHRITE

Like jadeite, nephrite is ideal for carving. It's tough enough to be durable, but still soft enough to carve. When used for jewelry or decorative items, it can be made beautiful by polishing to a glossy sheen. Many ancient people believed that jadeite and nephrite could cure internal complaints.

The Māori of New Zealand believe carved nephrite objects carry a protective force called *mana*.

BERYL

Beryl was once an important ore of the rare metal beryllium, used in spacecraft and scientific tools. However, in 1969 the mineral bertrandite was discovered. It is easier to extract beryllium from this ore, so now beryl is mainly used as a gemstone instead.

FACT FILE

- **Name:** from the Greek *beryllos*, a name for a range of green stones
- **Color:** green, blue, yellow, pink, red, or colorless
- **Cleavage:** imperfect
- **Streak:** colorless (harder than the streak plate)
- **Hardness:** 7.5–8
- **Specific gravity:** 2.6–2.8
- **Luster:** vitreous

ONE MINERAL, MANY GEMS

Trace amounts of different substances can give beryl crystals many different colors. The two most famous are beautiful deep-green emeralds and pale greenish-blue aquamarine. Both are often cut and used in jewelry. However, beryl also comes in other colors, such as pinkish-orange morganite, yellowish heliodor, and colorless goshenite. There are also varieties known as red beryl and green beryl, which is paler in color than emerald.

Emeralds, such as these ones from Colombia, are the most valuable variety of the mineral beryl.

Aquamarine is the sea-blue variety of the mineral beryl. It comes in both transparent and translucent varieties, and is one of the traditional birthstones for people born in March.

MOONSTONE

Moonstone is the name we give to the gem variety of orthoclase (see page 143). The most common colors used in jewelry are whitish and blue, but moonstones can also be found in other colors such as gray or pink. Sri Lanka is the largest producer of moonstone.

FACT FILE

- **Name:** because of its resemblance to the glow of the Moon
- **Color:** white, gray, pink, yellow, or colorless
- **Cleavage:** perfect
- **Streak:** white
- **Hardness:** 6–6.5
- **Specific gravity:** 2.5–2.6
- **Luster:** vitreous to pearly

GENTLY GLOWING

Moonstone has a rare property called adularescence or the schiller effect (see page 143). It makes the stones appear to have a softly glowing light floating just below the surface, and the light seems to move when the angle changes. This effect is caused by the stone's structure, which has thin alternating layers of orthoclase and albite. As light enters the stone and hits the different layers, it bends, reflects, and scatters to create a gentle glowing effect.

The adularescence of a moonstone is named after Mount Adular in Switzerland, where moonstones were mined.

Named for its resemblance to moonlight, moonstones are often believed to bring good luck or used as a calming focus for meditation.

TOURMALINE

Tourmaline is not a single mineral, but a group of related minerals that share similar properties. They come in a range of colors, including blue, green, pink, and colorless. Tourmaline is found around the world, but the biggest producer is Brazil.

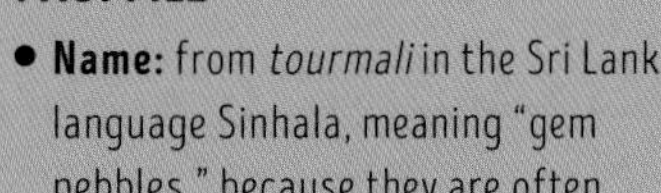

FACT FILE

- **Name:** from *tourmali* in the Sri Lankan language Sinhala, meaning "gem pebbles," because they are often found in gravel deposits
- **Color:** green, brown, black, red, blue, yellow, or pink
- **Cleavage:** indistinct
- **Streak:** white or colorless (when harder than the streak plate)
- **Hardness:** 7–7.5
- **Specific gravity:** 2.8–3.3
- **Luster:** vitreous

THE WATERMELON EFFECT

Tourmaline crystals often show color zoning—this means that there can be different colors in different parts of a single crystal. The most famous pairing is green and pinkish-red. Sometimes a crystal will be pink at one end and green at the other, while others will have a pink center surrounded by green. When cut in cross-section, these crystals look like slices of watermelon.

Watermelon tourmaline is often used in jewelry as the contrasting colors are so striking.

These black tourmaline pebbles have a smooth, tumbled finish. Tourmaline is resistant to weathering, but can be tumbled in flowing river water and often ends up in gravel deposits.

TIGER'S EYE

Tiger's eye is a form of quartz (see page 144) that has a distinct pattern of yellowish-brown stripes. When polished, it has a property known as chatoyancy. This is the same effect as seen in "cat's eye" stones, where a line of light appears to move across the stone.

FACT FILE

- **Name:** because of the amber cat's-eye effect
- **Color:** yellow, amber, and brown
- **Cleavage:** none
- **Streak:** white
- **Hardness:** 7
- **Specific gravity:** 2.7
- **Luster:** vitreous

TRICK OF THE LIGHT

The chatoyancy in tiger's eye is caused by thin fibers of another mineral called crocidolite trapped within the quartz. Over time, these fibers are replaced by silica. The "eye" effect is a band of reflected light moving just beneath the surface. Tiger's eye is often cut to have a rounded shape and then polished to show off its stripes and cat's eye effect. This is a common way of cutting opaque stones.

The brown and amber stripes can make tiger's eye look like polished wood, but it is a mineral.

Tiger's eye is said to resemble the eye of a tiger. People thought that wearing tiger's eye would give them the same power as this majestic animal.

TURQUOISE

Turquoise is a phosphate mineral that includes copper and aluminum, giving it a distinctive bluish-green color. We call this color turquoise, but the name comes from the gemstone and not the other way around. It's one of only a few colors that are named after a mineral.

FACT FILE

- **Name:** from the French *turquois*, meaning "Turkish"
- **Color:** blue or green
- **Cleavage:** good
- **Streak:** white to green
- **Hardness:** 5–6
- **Specific gravity:** 2.6–2.8
- **Luster:** waxy to dull

Robin's-egg blue is the most desirable and valuable color of turquoise, as shown here, while green and yellowish-green are less popular.

BLUE-GREEN GEM

Turquoise is opaque and only very rarely forms distinct crystals. Most turquoise occurs in "massive" forms (see page 98) where the crystals are too small to see. It has been mined and used as a gemstone for thousands of years. Turquoise often contains pieces of the host rock (or "matrix") where the mineral formed. They look like black threads or webbing among the blue or green stone. Turquoise is very porous, so it can absorb liquids that might damage it or change its color.

Native American jewelry from the US Southwest often features turquoise set in silver, as shown in this necklace.

TOPAZ

Topaz is one of the minerals used as a reference on the Mohs scale of hardness (see page 90), coming in at number 8. It's no surprise that gemstones like topaz and diamond appear at the top end of the scale—their hardness and durability are a large part of what makes them so valuable.

FACT FILE

- **Name:** either from the Sanskrit for "fire" or named after an Egyptian island
- **Color:** colorless, yellow, orange, pink, red, or blue
- **Cleavage:** perfect
- **Streak:** colorless (harder than the streak plate)
- **Hardness:** 8
- **Specific gravity:** 3.4–3.6
- **Luster:** vitreous to adamantine

Topaz Lake in Killarney, Canada, is named for its topaz-colored water.

UNCERTAIN HISTORY

No one is quite sure where the name "topaz" comes from. It might refer to Topazios, the old name for an island off the coast of Egypt where stones similar to topaz were once mined. It might also be based on the Sanskrit word *tapaz*, meaning "fire." Whatever its origin, topaz has been highly prized for many centuries. It comes in a range of colors, including yellow, orange, pink, red, and blue.

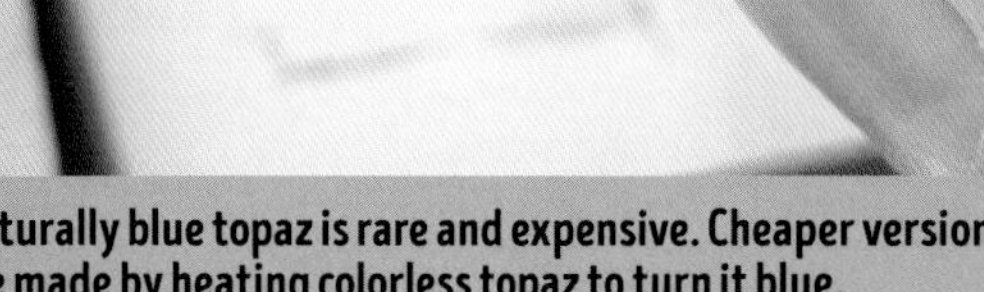

Naturally blue topaz is rare and expensive. Cheaper versions are made by heating colorless topaz to turn it blue.

CORUNDUM

Although both are beautiful, blood-red rubies and deep-blue sapphires look completely different. But these two gemstones are actually variations of the same mineral—corundum. It is only trace amounts of other substances that create the two contrasting colors.

FACT FILE

- **Name:** from the Sanskrit *kuruvinda*, meaning "ruby"
- **Color:** colorless, red, blue, or other colors
- **Cleavage:** none
- **Streak:** colorless (harder than the streak plate)
- **Hardness:** 9
- **Specific gravity:** 3.9–4.1
- **Luster:** adamantine to vitreous

COLORFUL COMBINATIONS

Corundum is aluminum oxide, a simple substance containing just aluminum and oxygen. In its pure form, it is completely colorless and translucent, and is known as "white sapphire." The tiny amounts of other elements that color it create beautiful gems. For example, chromium makes pink, vanadium makes grayish-blue or green, and iron makes pale yellow. All colors of corundum other than red or deep blue are known as "fancy sapphires."

Fancy sapphires are often cheaper than rubies or blue sapphires. Some are heated to improve their color.

RUBY RED

Rubies can range in color from orangey to purplish or brownish, but deep, blood red is the most valuable color. It takes its name from *ruber*, the Latin word for "red." Many rubies come from the southeast Asian countries of Myanmar (Burma), Thailand, Vietnam, and Cambodia, as well as from Afghanistan, Madagascar, and Sri Lanka. When listing gemstone prices by weight, rubies are second only to diamonds.

Corundum features as number 9 on the Mohs Scale (see page 90), just below diamond. Because it is so hard, corundum is often ground and used to make abrasive materials such as sandpaper.

SAPPHIRE BLUE

The name "sapphire" refers only to the deep-blue variety of corundum, where the color is produced by trace amounts of iron and titanium. Sapphires of other colors are often described by their color, such as "pink sapphire" or "yellow sapphire." Sapphires often show pleochroism, meaning that they can appear to be different colors when viewed from different directions. In some countries, sapphires are believed to protect the wearer from evil spirits.

The enormous Logan Sapphire from Sri Lanka is about the size of an egg and may be the world's largest cut sapphire.

AMBER

Amber is not a mineral—it's what's called an organic gemstone. That's because it was made by living things. Amber is tree resin that has fossilized over the course of many years, and it often has a beautiful golden-brown color.

FACT FILE

- **Name:** from the Arabic *anbar*, the name for a similar substance produced by whales
- **Color:** yellow, brown, red, or sometimes green, blue, or black
- **Cleavage:** none
- **Streak:** white
- **Hardness:** 2-2.5
- **Specific gravity:** 1.1
- **Luster:** resinous

THAT'S ELECTRIC!

The ancient Greeks called amber "electrum," and they knew that rubbing amber made it attract lightweight materials—that's where we get the word "electricity" from. Amber has been a popular gemstone for many centuries, and is often carved into beads or small figurines. In Russia's Catherine Palace, 13,000 lb (6,000 tonnes) of decorated amber panels once lined the walls of the Amber Room, before they were lost in World War II.

A reconstruction of the Amber Room which now contains 990 lb (450 kg) of decorated amber panels.

An amber quarry in Yantarny, Russia, near the shores of the Baltic Sea. Most of the world's supply of amber comes from the Baltic Coast.

JET

Most gemstones are known for their brilliant colors, but glossy black jet can be just as beautiful. This organic gemstone is a form of coal, made from the remains of prehistoric plants. Most jet is black, but some is brown or marked with sparkling flecks of pyrite (see page 119).

FACT FILE

- **Name:** from *jaiet*, the French name for it, which refers to an ancient town where it was once found
- **Color:** black or dark brown
- **Cleavage:** none
- **Streak:** black to dark brown
- **Hardness:** 2.5
- **Specific gravity:** 1.3
- **Luster:** velvety to waxy

USING JET

People have carved jet for millennia, dating all the way back to the Stone Age. People turned jet into beads and strung them into necklaces. They also sculpted small figurines from it. During the Middle Ages, people believed that jet had healing powers. They drank from jet bowls or stirred powdered jet into their drinks. Jet became so well-known that it led to the common adjective "jet-black."

This jet pendant found in Britain was carved from around 43-410 CE. The front has faded to a deep brown.

Whitby, on the northeast coast of England, has large deposits of jet. In the 1800s, it became known for the jet jewelry made there.

BLOOD IN THE SEA

The ancient Greeks believed that the first corals grew when Perseus cut off the head of the monster Medusa, and drops of her blood fell into the sea. They wore red coral, which grows in the Mediterranean Sea as well as near Japan and Malaysia, as an amulet (protective jewelry) to ward off evil spirits. A type of black coral grows in the West Indies and around many Pacific islands, and people also use this as a material for jewelry.

Corals are relatively easy to carve and polish. This sculpture was carved from red coral in China.

CORAL

Corals are sea animals that live in colonies and form hard skeletons made of calcium carbonate. Over time, these skeletons can build up to form a coral reef. Most coral that is used as jewelry comes from a particular genus of corals that produce brilliant red or pinkish-orange skeletons.

FACT FILE

- **Name:** from the name of the animal it is made from
- **Color:** red, pink, black, blue, or golden
- **Cleavage:** none
- **Streak:** white
- **Hardness:** 3.5
- **Specific gravity:** 2.6-2.7
- **Luster:** dull to vitreous

Living red coral

The reefs where corals grow are vibrant ecosystems, teeming with a huge diversity of marine plants and animals.

PEARL

Pearls are made by living creatures. They are composed of minerals such as aragonite and calcite, but these minerals are secreted by the animals. Many pearls form inside oysters that live in saltwater, but freshwater molluscs such as mussels can also produce pearls.

FACT FILE

- **Name:** from the Latin *perna*, after the mutton-leg shape of the shellfish
- **Color:** white, cream, yellow, pink, blue, green, or black
- **Cleavage:** none
- **Streak:** white
- **Hardness:** 3
- **Specific gravity:** 2.7
- **Luster:** pearly

Pearls in oyster shell

Pictured at low tide, this oyster bed lies off the coast of South Carolina. Before scuba gear was invented, people held their breath for up to two minutes when diving to find pearls—a very dangerous job.

CULTIVATING PEARLS

Pearls form naturally when a speck of grit gets inside a mollusc's shell. The creature secretes the pearl material to form a layer around the grit that will protect its soft body. Layers build up to form a pearl. People can also farm molluscs and force them to produce pearls by introducing a small shell bead as the irritant. The mollusc is returned to the water until the pearl has grown to the required size.

This pearl necklace dates from the 1890s. Jewelers often look for pearls of the same color and size.

GLOSSARY

ABUNDANT Occurring in large quantities or over a large area.

AGGREGATE A mass of rock particles or mineral grains, or a mixture of both.

ALLOY A metal made by mixing two or more different metals together. The word can also be used for the process of adding one metal to another.

ATOM The basic building block of matter. All matter in the universe is made up of tiny atoms.

CALDERA A large, bowl-shaped depression that forms when a volcano collapses.

CLASTIC Describes rocks that are made up of fragments of minerals, rocks, or other substances that have been broken down and deposited in a new location.

CLEAVAGE The property of some minerals to break apart along flat planes with shapes based on the structure of their crystals. Some rocks also cleave along planes, between the minerals they contain.

COMPOUND A substance made up of two or more elements bonded together.

CORE The innermost layer of many rocky planets or moons. Earth's core is made up mainly of iron and nickel.

CRATON A large and ancient piece of Earth's crust that has largely kept its original form. Cratons make up the core parts of continents.

CRUST The outermost layer of many rocky planets or moons. Earth's crust is a thin layer broken into different plates, which sits on top of the mantle.

CRYSTAL The regular, symmetrical three-dimensional form that a mineral takes, based on the way that its atoms and molecules are put together.

ELEMENT Any of the natural substances that make up all matter in the universe, and which can't be broken down into simpler substances by chemical means.

EROSION The process by which rocks are worn away by weathering and the tiny pieces are then carried away from their original location to a new one.

EXTRUSIVE A term used to describe igneous rocks that formed when lava erupted onto Earth's surface before cooling and hardening.

FOSSIL The remains or imprint of a prehistoric plant or animal that has been preserved and turned into rock.

GEODE A hollow sphere of rock with inner walls that have been coated with layers of mineral crystals.

GLASS A solid substance formed when molten material, such as quartz, cools and hardens too quickly for crystals to form. Most glass is human-made but it can also form naturally in volcanic eruptions or from lightning or meteorite strikes.

HOTSPOT Place where magma rises up through Earth's crust, away from tectonic plate margins. A hotspot often forms a chain of volcanic islands.

HYDROTHERMAL Relating to very hot water deep underground.

IGNEOUS ROCK Rock that forms from the cooling and hardening of molten magma or lava.

INTRUSIVE A term used to describe igneous rocks that formed from magma cooling and hardening underground.

LAVA Molten rock found on Earth's surface that has erupted from a volcano or a fissure in Earth's crust.

LUSTER A way of describing how a mineral absorbs and reflects light, which can be used as a clue to help identify it.

MAGMA Molten rock found below Earth's surface. Some magma is extruded onto the surface in volcanic eruptions, but once this happens it is called lava.

MANTLE The middle layer of many rocky planets or moons. Earth's mantle is a vast area of rock that is mostly solid but behaves like a very, very thick paste over long periods of time.

MASSIVE Describes a rock or mineral where the individual crystalline grains are so small that they can't be seen without a microscope.

METAL A category of substances that are opaque and shiny, often with a high melting point. Metals are usually good conductors of heat and electricity, and can be hammered into shape or pulled into thin wires.

METAMORPHIC ROCK Rock that forms when other types of rock are deformed and changed by high levels of heat and pressure deep underground.

METEORITE A rock from space that travels through Earth's atmosphere without being completely burned up, and lands on the surface. Most meteorites are pieces of asteroids.

MINERAL A naturally occurring substance, not made from living things, with atoms that are arranged in repeating patterns to form crystals.

NON-METAL An element or other substance that doesn't have the same properties as metals, such as being hard and shiny or conducting heat and electricity well.

OPAQUE Describes a substance that does not allow light to pass through it.

ORE A rock that contains useful amounts of valuable metals or minerals that can be extracted from it.

ORGANIC Being made up of carbon compounds that are found in living things.

OXIDE A compound made up of oxygen bonded to another element. For example, rust is iron oxide.

PETRIFIED FOREST An area rich in the remains of prehistoric trees, which have turned to stone by having their organic matter replaced by minerals.

PIGMENT A powder made of a ground-up natural substance that is used to make paint or added to other materials to change their color.

PLASTERBOARD A wall panel used in building and construction, made up of the mineral gypsum layered between thick sheets of paper.

PRECIPITATE When a dissolved substance comes out of a solution to form a solid. This sometimes happens when a solution is over-saturated and cannot hold any more of the dissolved substance. It can also be caused by a chemical reaction.

PRISM A three-dimensional shape with a flat top and bottom connected by flat faces in the shape of parallelograms.

QUARRY A type of open-pit mine where people dig stone out of the ground.

SATURATED Containing so much of a dissolved substance that it is impossible to dissolve any more into it.

SEAM A distinct layer of a rock or mineral.

SEDIMENTARY ROCK Rock that forms from small particles of other rocks or minerals that are deposited in layers, then covered and squeezed until they turn into rock.

SEMI-METAL A substance that shares some, but not all, of its properties with metals.

SILICATE A mineral containing a compound of silicon and oxygen.

SILT A material made up of tiny particles, usually pieces of quartz, that are smaller than the particles in sand but bigger than the particles in clay. Mud is made up largely of silt.

SMELT To heat an ore and use chemical reactions to extract the valuable metals that it contains.

STREAK The colored line left by a mineral when it is scraped on a white ceramic plate; the color of a sample's streak can help to identify which mineral it is.

SUBDUCTION A process in which one edge of a tectonic plate is forced below the edge of another plate. The denser of the two plates subducts (sinks).

TARNISH A thin film that forms on the surface of some metals when exposed to air, usually caused by a chemical reaction with oxygen in the air.

TECTONIC PLATE One of several large, strong regions of Earth's crust and uppermost mantle. Tectonic plates move very slowly, pushing up against some neighboring plates and pulling away from others.

TRANSLUCENT Describes a substance that allows some light to pass through it, but not enough to see shapes clearly through it.

TWINNED Describes crystals that grow together in a particularly symmetrical way in which they share the same side or point.

VEIN Mineral deposit that forms when a fracture in a rock is filled with new mineral material.

VOLCANO A vent in Earth's surface through which magma and lava can erupt. Some volcanoes form tall, cone-shaped mountains, while others are little more than a crack in the ground.

WEATHERING The process by which rocks are changed or broken down by the action of wind, water, temperature, chemical reactions, or living things.

INDEX

PICTURE CREDITS

PHOTOGRAPHY CREDITS

Key l=left, r=right, t=top, b=bottom, c=center, bg=background.

The attributions listed under Photography Credits are for informational purposes only and do not constitute the photographers' endorsement of this publication or Lonely Planet. All related copyrights and trademarks are the property of their respective owners.

Front Cover: Shutterstock.
Alamy: p38 (bl) The Natural History Museum p77 (tl) GRANGER - Historical Picture Archive p122 (br) Dorling Kindersley ltd p126 (cl) IanDagnall Computing p131 (br) The Print Collector p138 (bl) Susan E. Degginger. **Shutterstock:** p1 (bg) Ashish_wassup6730 p2-3 (bg) NAEPHOTO p4-5 (bg) Zhukova Valentyna p6-7 (bg) Antony McAulay p6 (c) Stefano Francini p7 (tl) Pornpimon Ainkaew p7 (tr) Chokniti-Studio p8-9 (bg) Alexey Repka p8 (cl) Artsiom P p8 (br) Mopic p10-11 (bg) biletskiyevgeniy.com p10 (c) FoxGrafy p10 (bl) ian woolcock p11 (c) BlueRingMedia p12-13 (bg) Daniel Prudek p12 (cr) BlueRingMedia p12 (bl) GraphicsRF.com p13 (tr) Rainer Lesniewski p13 (cr) tinkivinki p14-15 (bg) Yvonne Baur p14 (cr) spline_x p14 (bl) Puslatronik p15 (tr) Marco Ritzki p15 (bl) Dima Moroz p16-17 (bg) Chris Curtis p16 (cr) BlueRingMedia p16 (br) sonsart p17 (tl) Diana Will p17 (bl) Mark Brandon p17 (br) Nicola Pulham p18-19 (bg) Vladislav Gajic p18 (tr) Ko Zatu p19 (tl) Alexlukin p19 (tr) Yes058 Montree Nanta p21 (t) finepic p21 (c) Tristan3D p22-23 (bg) Biswaphotography93 p22 (cl) Captain's Art p22 (btl) J. Palys p22 (btr) and (bl) AKaiser p22 (br) TCSO p23 (tl) Cagla Acikgoz p23 (tr) Nordroden p23 (br) Francesco Cantone p24-25 (bg) Virrage Images p24 (cl) Tim photo-video p24 (cc) Love Silhouette p24 (cr) Danilo Ezpino p24 (b) WINDCOLORS p25 (tr) wavebreakmedia p25 (cl) marekuliasz p25 (cr) IngeBlessas p25 (br) Nicholas J Klein p26-27 (bg) BINKONTAN p26 (cl) Tanya_Terekhina p26 (cr) Branko Jovanovic p26 (br) Jirik V p28-29 (bg) Stephen Jingel p28 (cl) StudioMolekuul p28 (bl) Irina Starikova1811 p29 (tr) olpo p29 (br) VladKK p30-31 (bg) OMG_Studio p30 (cl) photo-world p30 (cr) Nyura p30 (bl) ebonyeg p31 (tl) photo-world p31 (tc) RHJPhtotos p31 (tr) fivespots p31 (br) PeopleImages.com - Yuri A p32-33 (bg) PatrickBieniek Germany p32 (cl) J-B-C p32 (cr) Sean Pavone p32 (br) proslgn p33 (tr) Danita Delimont p33 (bl) Jukka Palm 34-35 (bg) Triff p34 (cl) Nikta_Nikta p35 (tl) abriendomundo p35 (tr) Gioele Mottarlini p36-37 (bg) Rtimages p36 (bl) Bjoern Wylezich p37 (tr) Eduardo Cabanas p37 (bl) KPixMining p37 (br) SNeG17 p38-39 (bg) Mrjindukle p38 (cl) Andrii Zastrozhnov p39 (tl) netsuthep p39 (bl) Joe Belanger p40-41 (bg) servickuz p40 (cr) Catmando p40 (bl) Amanita Silvicora p41 (tl) PRILL p41 (bl) Mikhail Nesytykh p41 (cr) Ru Smith p42-43 (bg) Wead p42 (cl) Adwo p43 (tr) WBMUL p43 (br) Evgeny Haritonov p44-45 (bg) Massimo Santi p44 (cl) Samarabbas101 p44 (br) ironwas p45 (tl) Alexey Seafarer p45 (cr) DedMityay p45 (br) rook76 p46-47 (bg) Aqib Yasin p46 (cl) atiger p46 (br) Anusorn Abthaisong p47 (tr) feedbackstudio p47 (cr) Ekaterina Pokrovsky p47 (bl) Jacob Lund p48-49 (bg) Daniil Toxic p48 (c) Rainer Lesniewski p49 (t) Peter Hermes Furian p49 (br) Josemaria Toscano p50-51 (bg) EB Adventure Photography p50 (c) Yusiki p51 (tl) meunierd p51 (tr) Guoqiang Xue p51 (bl) Wollertz p51 (br) Mary Buermann p52-53 (bg) Elena_Suvorova p52 (tl) corlaffra p52 (cl) Amanda Mohler p52 (bl) Lost_in_the_Midwest p53 (tl) Aleksandar Todorovic p53 (tr) Nido Huebl p53 (bl) Wirestock Creators p54-55 (bg) Mark Green p54 (c) Nasi_lemak p54 (bl) Luis Inacio P Prado p55 (tl) Alexandree p55 (tr) Bjoern Wylezich p55 (bl) alejojimenezyt p55 (br) SAHATS IGOA LOPEZ p56-57 (bg) Galyna Andrushko p56 (tl) SCStock p56 (tr) Marco A. Huanca p56 (bl) pauloalberto82 p56 (br) Adwo p57 (tl) sunsinger p57 (tr) Julio Ricco p57 (bl) Rodrigo Garrido p57 (br) R.M. Nunes p58-59 (bg) Dmitry Pichugin p58 (c) Meda01 p58 (bl) Jen Watson p59 (tl) Seqoya p59 (tr) Torsten Pursche p59 (bl) Radek Borovka p59 (br) TR_Studio p60-61 (bg) NAEPHOTO p60 (tl) Salparadis p60 (tr) Travel Stock p60 (bl) COLOMBO NICOLA p60 (br) Jiri Balek p61 (tl) kavram p61 (tr) Hiromi Ito Ame p61 (bl) Simone Crespiatico p61 (br) Jean van der Meulen p62-63 (bg) Marcin Krzyzak p62 (c) okili77 p63 (tl) Puripat Lertpunyaroj p63 (tr) saiko3p p63 (cl) Chris Button p63 (bl) MIR MASROOR AHMAD p63 (br) MarcelClemens p64-65 (bg) Yevhenii Chulovskyi p64 (tl) Wirestock Creators p64 (cl) mehdi33300 p64 (cr) Stanislav Simonyan p64 (b) Jakl Lubos p65 (tl) vidoc Olga p65 (tr) BBA Photography p65 (bl) Alfiya Safuanova p65 (br) Martin Mecnarowski 66-67 (bg) mr. wijannarongk kunchit p66 (c) Nasi_lemak p66 (bl) cnyy p66 (tl) John Wreford p66 (tr) In Green p66 (bl) Andrey Kuzmichev p66 (br) Irina Wilhauk p68-69 (bg) Sven Hansche p68 (tr) GENNADY TEPLITSKIY p68 (cl) corlaffra p68 (bl) MudaCom p69 (tl) Vixit p69 (tr) MOAimage p69 (bl) Nguyen Quang Ngoc Tonkin p69 (br) m7 p70-71 (bg) Photos BrianScantlebury p70 (c) Porcupen p70 (br) Spotmatik Ltd p71 (tl) Lee Risar p71 (tr) aleskramer p71 (bl) Stanislav Fosenbauer p71 (br) Martin Helgemeir p72-73 (bg) Taras Vyshnya p72 (tl) Greg Brave p72 (bl) Tomas Lesa p72 (br) donvictorio p73 (tl) Will Dale p73 (tr) Charles Bergman p73 (bl) Damsea p73 (br) Islamic Footage p74-75 (bg) Gaearon Tolon p74 (c) Aleksandr_Lysenko p74 (bl) Wirestock Creators p75 (tl) Eleanor Scriven p75 (bl) polarman p75 (br) Dale Lorna Jacobsen p76-77 (bg) B.Forenius p76 (c) Peter Hermes Furian p77 (tr) Jacques Dayan p77 (bl) Globe Guide Media Inc p77 (br) JC Photo p78-79 (bg) Inna Reznik p78 (c) nadia_if p78 (b) Ja Het p79 (tr) Evgeny Atamanenko p80-81 (bg) Olga Migacheva p80 (cl) Claudio Lucca p80 (cr) AnnaStills p81 (tl) popicon p81 (tr) Nikolai V Titov p81 (bl) MUNGKHOOD STUDIO p82-83 (bg) Cooldyx p82 (cl) 10110010101101 p82 (bl) Rachel Hoyt p82 (br) ESstock p83 (tr) mikeledray p83 (bl) Greens and Blues p84-85 (bg) avtk p84 (tr) Standret p84 (bl) RP designs p85 (tr) Svetlana123 p86-87 (bg) Andres Sonne p86 (cl) Yes058 Montree Nanta p86 (bl) michal812 p86 (br) Hanna Valui p87 (tr) Alexandru Nika p87 (br) Vladislav Gajic p88-89 (bg) Goldsithney p88 (tr) Shy Radar p89 (cl) and (cr) Yes058 Montree Nanta p89 (br) Albert Russ p90-91 (bg) Pornpimon Ainkaew p90 (l1) lamTK p90 (l2) Yes058 Montree Nanta p90 (l3) olpo p90 (l4) Collective Arcana p90 (l5) Yes058 Montree Nanta p90 (l6) Bjoern Wylezich p90 (l7) and (l8) vvoe p90 (l9) Minakryn Ruslan p90 (l10) MXW Stock p91 (tr) Michael LaMonica p91 (cl) Alex_NB p91 (cr) Michael LaMonica p92-93 (bg) Chokniti-Studio p92 (cl) ggw p92 (bl) urfin p93 (tl) A.Sych p93 (bl) Yes058 Montree Nanta p94-95 (bg) Phakawan N p94 (cl) Marianna_ Zh p94 (cr) PhotographyByMK p95 (tr) Lost_in_the_Midwest p95 (bc) pixelman p96-97 (bg) Arcady p96 (cr) Bjoern Wylezich p96 (br) Kat Om p97 (c bg) Bill Florence p97 (cl) Alejandro Lafuente Lopez p97 (cr) SewCreamStudio p98-99 (bg) Evgeny Haritonov p98 (cr) Pond Saksit p98 (br) olpo p100 (t bg) Sergii Figurnyi p100 (tl) Yes058 Montree Nanta p100 (b bg) Nicola Pulham p100 (bl) Breck P. Kent p101 (bg) vallefrias p101 (tr) Yes058 Montree Nanta p101 (tl) KrimKate p101 (cr) Andrew Bassett p101 (b) Jess Kraft p101 (bg) Jarous p102 (tl) TR_Studio p102 (tr) Claudio Rossol p102 (cl and cr) vvoe p103 (t bg) kamatari p103 (tr) volkann p103 (tl) Bjoern Wylezich p103 (b bg) Kovalchuk Oleksandr p103 (bl) ARSbright p103 (br) New Africa p104 (t bg) EWY Media p104 (tl) Yes058 Montree Nanta p104 (tc) oksmit p104 (tr) www.sandatlas.org p104 (b bg) Eduardo Cabanas p104 (bl) Yes058 Montree Nanta p104 (br) Carlos Aranguiz p105 (t bg) Global Marble Collection p105 (tl) Tyler Boyes p105 (b bg) lialina p105 (bl) Yes058 Montree Nanta p105 (br) Bennian p106 (t bg) CMPMLD p106 (tl) domnitsky p106 (tr) Morphart Creation p106 (b bg) rweisswald p106 (bl) Yes058 Montree Nanta p107 (bg) Sophiaiws p107 (tr) Aleksandr Pobedimskiy p107 (tl) p107 (cr) Breck P. Kent p107 (br) A G Baxter p108 (t bg) ON-Photography Germany p108 (tl) Alexlukin p108 (tr) tenkl p108 (b bg) Ievgen Kryshen p108 (bl) Yes058 Montree Nanta p108 (br) Ra17 p109 (t bg) EB Adventure Photography p109 (tr) WH_Pics p109 (tl) CactusPilot p109 (b bg) Thomas Holt p109 (bl) michal812 p109 (br) Mr SW Photo p110 (bg) Walter Bilotta p110 (tl) vvoe p110 (tr) saiko3p p110 (bl) Tyler Boyes p110 (bc) Ganna Zelinska p110 (br) kaitong.yepoon p111 (t bg) Adwo p111 (tr) Tyler Boyes p111 (tl) hadot 760 p111 (b bg) PBouman p111(bl) Yes058 Montree Nanta p111 (br) N. Rotteveel p112 (t bg) Munimara p112 (tl) vvoe p112 (tr) ALEKHIN ELDAR p112 (b bg) Beekeepx p112 (bl) www.sandatlas.org p112 (br) LesPalenik p113 (t bg) Nuno Barradas p113 (tl) www.sandatlas.org p113 (b bg) Dr. Norbert Lange p113 (bl) Diego Ioppolo p114 (b) and (tl) macrowildlife p114 (br) Tomas Pavelka p115 (t bg) Arkadiusz Komski p115 (tr) Bjoern Wylezich p115 (tl) Sergey Goryachev p115 (b bg) Luet p115 (bl) RHJPhtotos p115 (br) demarcomedia p116 (t bg) Nataliya Hora p116 (tl) Bjoern Wylezich p116 (tr) Oleg_Yakovlev p116 (b bg) mineral vision p116 (bl) Bjoern Wylezich p116 (br) Sebastian Janicki p117 (t bg) dindumphoto p117 (tr) Bjoern Wylezich p117 (tl) Peter Hermes Furian p117 (b bg) Lost_in_the_Midwest p117 (bl) Cagla Acikgoz p117 (br) PNSJ88 p118 (t bg) MIGUEL G. SAAVEDRA p118 (tl) Albert Russ p118 (tr) KrimKate p118 (b bg) mineral vision p118 (bl) Miriam Doerr Martin Frommherz p118 (br) Albert Russ p119 (t bg) frank_peters p119 (bl) ABCDstock p119 (b bg) Dr. Norbert Lange p119 (bl) Marco Fine p119 (br) Gemstones By Boat p120 (t bg) Damian Pawlos p120 (tl) Omagana p120 (tr) Dan Olsen p120 (b bg) JavierLJ p120 (bl) Mineralogist p121 (t bg) OHishiapply p121 (tr) Yes058 Montree Nanta p121 (tl) Albert Russ p121 (b bg) Henner Damke p121 (bl) vvoe p121 (br) Dan Olsen p122 (t bg) Image134 p122 (tr) Vasyl Rohan p122 (b bg) Elisa Locci p123 (t bg) Jim and Lynne Weber p123 (tr) Minakryn Ruslan p123 (tl) vvoe p123 (b bg) Albert Russ p123 (bl) Cagla Acikgoz p123 (br) Cavan-Images p124 (bg) Nil Kulp p124 (tl) KrimKate p124 (tr) muratart p124 (c) Tutor Comunicazione p124 (bl) sergey Kolesnikov p125 (t bg) canadastock p125 (tr) Alejandro Lafuente Lopez p125 (tl) COULANGES p125 (b bg) vladimir salman p125 (bl) Fokin Oleg p125 (br) Yavdat p126-127 (bg) Alizada Studios p126 (tl) Minakryn Ruslan p126 (tr) Cagla Acikgoz p126 (br) ElyaPhoto p127 (t bg) Mario Deambrogio p127 (tr) leksandr Pobedimskiy p127 (tl) Albert Russ p127 (bl) Ibe van Oort p127 (br) jimena terraza p128 (t bg) Bill Florence p128 (tl) Alejandro Lafuente Lopez p128 (tr) SewCreamStudio p128 (bg) lembi p128 (bl) Minakryn Ruslan p128 (br) losmandarinas p129 (t bg) ronstik p129 (b bg) Misne p129 (br) Ono Bawono p130 (t bg) mineral vision p130 (tl) Nikki Zalewski p130 (tr) Michael LaMonica p130 (b bg) komkrit Preechachanwate p130 (bg c) LightField Studios p130 (bl) losmandarinas p130 (br) Michael LaMonica p131 (tr) vvoe p131 (tl) Skshoot p131 (b bg) Daniel Prudek p131 (bl) Yes058 Montree Nanta p132 (t bg) Nigel Jarvis p132 (tl) P. Leveille p132 (tr) New Africa p132 (b bg) mineral vision p132 (bl) Yes058 Montree Nanta p132 (br) Dan Olsen p133 (t bg) Thiago B Trevisan p133 (tr) Cagla Acikgoz p133 (tl) Roman Belogorodov p133 (b bg) alexvav p133 (bl) Andriy Kananovych p133 (br) losmandarinas p134 (bg) Galyna Andrushko p134 (tl) Sever180 p134 (tr) Oreena p134 (bl) Studio Romantic p135 (t bg) William Cushman p134 (tr) KrimKate p135 (tl) TipxJi p135 (bl) Nyura p135 (br) Angel House Studio p136 (t bg) Ivan Boryshchak p136 (tl) Tyler Boyes p136 (tr) Kunertus p136 (b bg) Jason Benz Bennee p136 (bl) Christopher PB p136 (brt) COULANGES p136 (brl) Albert Russ p136 (brr) Paulrommer SL p137 (t bg) Gunnar Rathbun p137 (tr) COULANGES p137 (tl) Dan Olsen p137 (b bg) Love all this photography p137 (bl) Bjoern Wylezich p137 (br) Myriam B p2138 (t bg) Sej Saraiya p138 (tl) Tyler Boyes p138 (tr) orook p138 (b bg) vandycan p138 (bc) losmandarinas p138 (br) spline_x p138 (t bg) MelaMari p139 (tr) Zbynek Burival p139 (b bg) SewCreamStudio p139 (bl) Sun_fl0wer p139 (br) Nicole Kwiatkowski p140 (t bg) Robert Harding Video p140 (tl) Minakryn Ruslan p140 (tr) Hyperborean_treasures p140 (b bg) mineral vision p140 (bl) Moha El-Jaw p140 (br) vvoe p141 (t bg) mineral vision p141 (tr) Bjoern Wylezich p141 (tl) Marykor p141 (b bg) Nyura p141 (bl) Exler p141 (br) zebra0209 p142 (t bg) olpo p142 (tl) vvoe p142 (tr) MarcelClemens p142 (b bg) Kavic.C p142 (bl) Yes058 Montree Nanta p143 (t bg) HelenField p143 (tr) Alejandro Lafuente Lopez p143 (tl) photoBeard p143 (bl) Breck P. Kent p143 (br) popgallery p144-145 (bg) Arctic ice p144 (tl) Nadezhda Bolotina p144 (tr) FiledIMAGE p144 (bl) Sebastian Janicki p144 (br) mineral vision p145 (tl) vvoe p145 (bl) Scott Rothstein p145 (br) hedgehog94 p146 (bg) Nordroden p146 (tl) Retouch man p146 (tr) Jennifer Sophie p146 (cl) MarcelClemens p146 (cr) CeltStudio p146 (br) p147 (t bg) Adwo p147 (tr) Cagla Acikgoz p147 (tl) Abdul Matloob p147 (b bg) olpo p147 (bl) Sebastian Janicki p147 (br) Milla77 p148 (t bg) Funtay p148 (tl) S_E p148 (b bg) Yut chanthaburi p148 (bl) Imfoto p148 (br) Nut Korpsrisawat p149 (tr) Nyura p149 (tl) W. Scott McGill p149 (b bg) Napoleonka p149 (bl) Minakryn Ruslan p149 (br) CreativeFireStock p150 (t bg) Arzakae p150 (tl) KaterinaSB p150 (tr) photo-world p150 (b bg) altanakin p150 (bl) Minakryn Ruslan p150 (br) p151 (t bg) Aleksandr Nedviga p151 (tr) KaterinaSB p151 (tl) Jota_Visual p151 (b bg) Pajaska p151 (bl) J. T. Davis p151 (br) Reload Design p152 (t bg) AkulininaOlga p152 (tl) Sebastian Janicki p152 (tr) Warren Price Photography p152 (b bg) Chiyacat p152 (bl) vvoe p152 (br) LanKS p153 (bg) PhotoSGH p153 (tr) Bjoern Wylezich p153 (tl) Finesell p153 (cr) photo33mm p154 (t bg) Birute Vijeikiene p154 (tl) Ansis Klucis p154 (tr) Sergey_Bogomyako p154 (b bg) andYLand p154 (bl) Moha El-Jaw p155 (t bg) sylvae p155 (tr) Cindy Cwaygel p155 (b bg) Kim McGrew p155 (bl) Maxal Tamor p155 (br) James McDowall p156-157 Elena_Suvorova p158-159 Vladislav Gajic p160 Stephen Jingel. **Brooklyn Museum:** p53 (br). **Cardiff University:** p43 (bl) Dr. James Panton. **Courtesy of the Library of Congress:** p52 (cr). **Creative Commons:** p21 (b) p72 (cl) p120 (br) p26 (bl) Pascal Terjan p27 (bl) Medvedev p28 (cr) CSHL p35 (br) Ghoneime p36 (br) DougRM p39 (cr) Anatoly Mikhaltsov p91 (br) James St. John p93 (cr) Ryan Somma p96 (cl) var Leidus p119 (tr) John Chapman (Pyrope) p122 (bl) Robert M. Lavinsky p127 (b) Stowarzyszenie Miłośników Ziemi Tarnogórskiej p129 (tl) kevinzim / Kevin Walsh p134 (cr) Alexander Van Driessche p135 (b bg) Analogue Kid p139 (tl) Strekeisen p143 (b bg) Chaughten p145 (tr) Vassil p149 (tb) Arezarni p153 (bl) Andrew Bossi p155 (tr) Ron Pastorino p155 (tl) David Monniaux. **Emmanuel Douzery:** p9 (cr). **JNCASR:** p68 (cr). **Los Angeles County Museum of Art:** p102 (br). **NASA:** p34 (br) Goddard/University of Arizona p85 (br) p106 (br) JPL-Caltech/MSSS p114 (cl) JPL. **Tim Creyts:** p75 (tc). **UCL:** p27 (tr) Prof. David Dobson p88 (cr) Dr. Frances Cooper p113 (tr) and p122 (tl) Prof. John Brodholt p113 (br) Dr. Andrew Thomson. **York Museums Trust:** p154 (br). **Illustrations by Daniel Limon**.